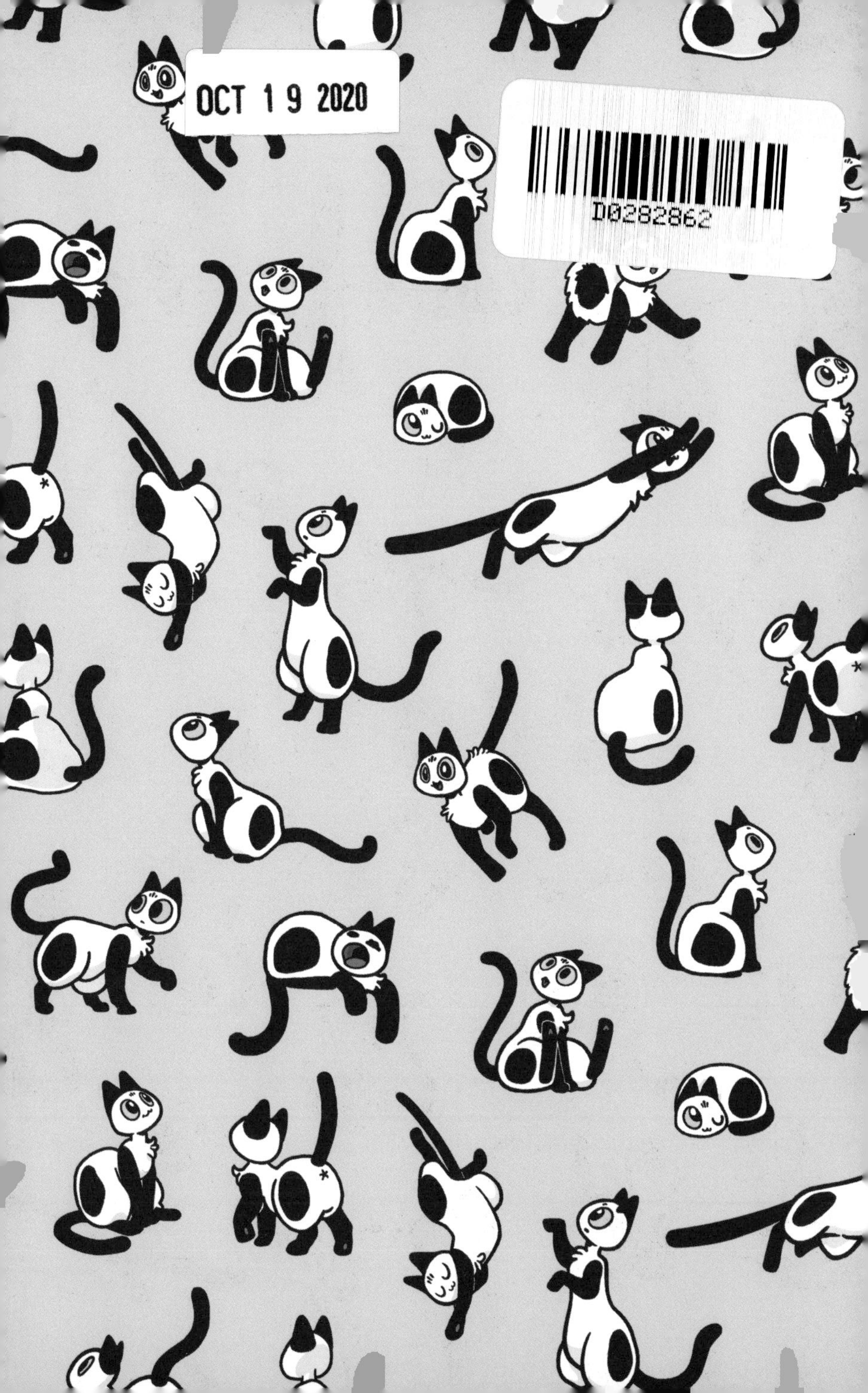

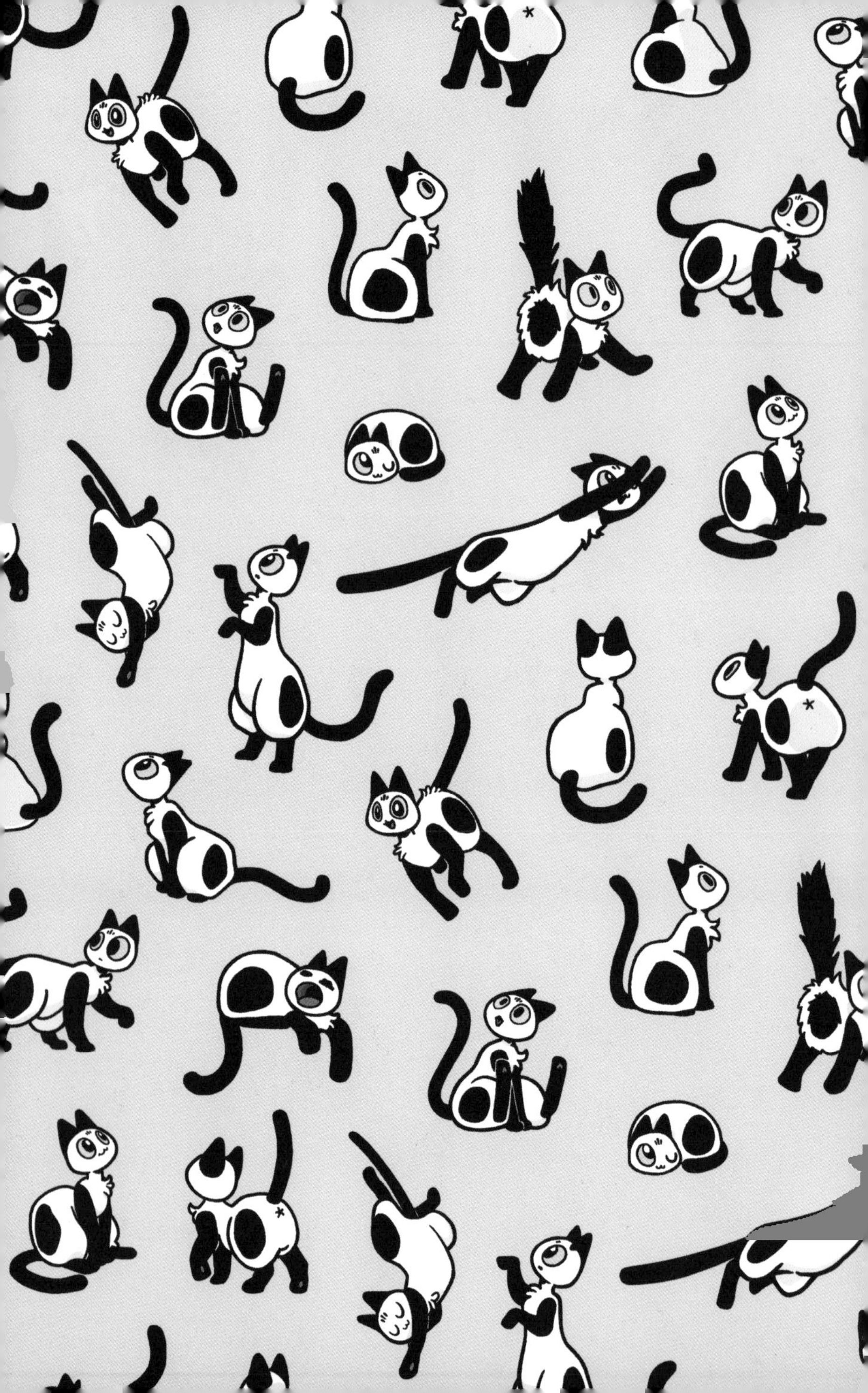

FRANKIE COMICS

EDITED BY AMANDA MEADOWS

DESIGN BY RACHEL DUKES

ONI
PRESS

AN ONI PRESS PUBLICATION

FRANKIE COMICS

BY RACHEL DUKES

Designed by Rachel Dukes
Edited by Amanda Meadows
Additional Design by Sonja Synak

Published by Oni-Lion Forge Publishing Group, LLC

James Lucas Jones, president & publisher • **Sarah Gaydos**, editor in chief
Charlie Chu, e.v.p. of creative & business development • **Brad Rooks**, director
of operations • **Amber O'Neill**, special projects manager • **Harris Fish**, events
manager • **Margot Wood**, director of marketing & sales • **Devin Funches**, sales &
marketing manager • **Katie Sainz**, marketing manager • **Tara Lehmann**, publicist
Troy Look, director of design & production • **Kate Z. Stone**, senior graphic
designer • **Sonja Synak**, graphic designer • **Hilary Thompson**, graphic designer
Sarah Rockwell, junior graphic designer • **Angie Knowles**, digital prepress lead
Vincent Kukua, digital prepress technician • **Shawna Gore**, senior editor • **Amanda
Meadows**, senior editor • **Robert Meyers**, senior editor, licensing • **Jasmine
Amiri**, senior editor • **Grace Bornhoft**, editor • **Zack Soto**, editor • **Chris Cerasi**,
editorial coordinator • **Steve Ellis**, vice president of games • **Ben Eisner**, game
developer • **Michelle Nguyen**, executive assistant • **Jung Lee**, logistics coordinator

Joe Nozemack, publisher emeritus

1319 SE Martin Luther King, Jr. Blvd.
Suite 240
Portland, OR 97214

onipress.com | lionforge.com
facebook.com/onipress | facebook.com/lionforge
twitter.com/onipress | twitter.com/lionforge
instagram.com/onipress | instagram.com/lionforge

mixtapecomics.com
instagram.com/mixtapecomics
twitter.com/mixtapecomics

First Edition: August 2020
ISBN 978-1-5493-0688-4
eISBN 978-1-62010-723-2

1 2 3 4 5 6 7 8 9 10

Library of Congress Control Number 2019945893

Printed in South Korea through Four Colour Print Group, Louisville, KY.

For Mike and Frankie.

Without you, this book
would not be *pawsible*.

"Finding Frankie"

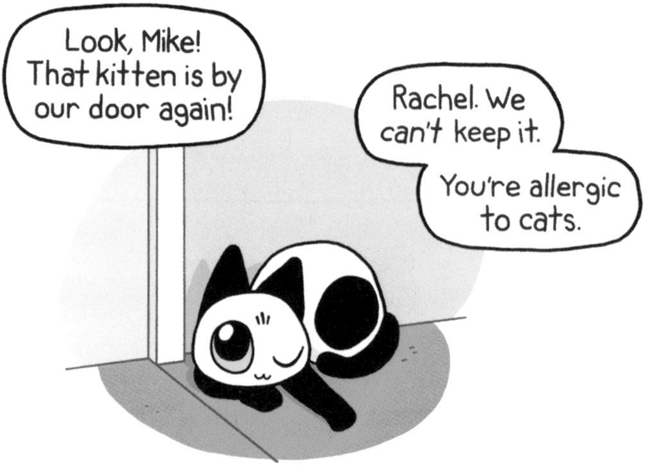
Look, Mike! That kitten is by our door again!
Rachel. We can't keep it.
You're allergic to cats.

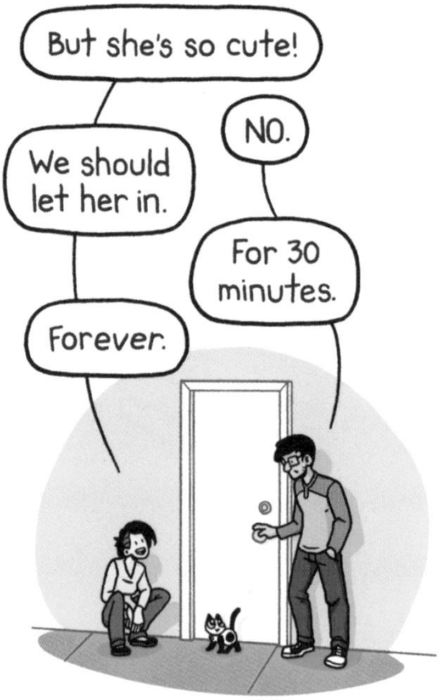
But she's so cute!
We should let her in.
NO.
Forever.
For 30 minutes.

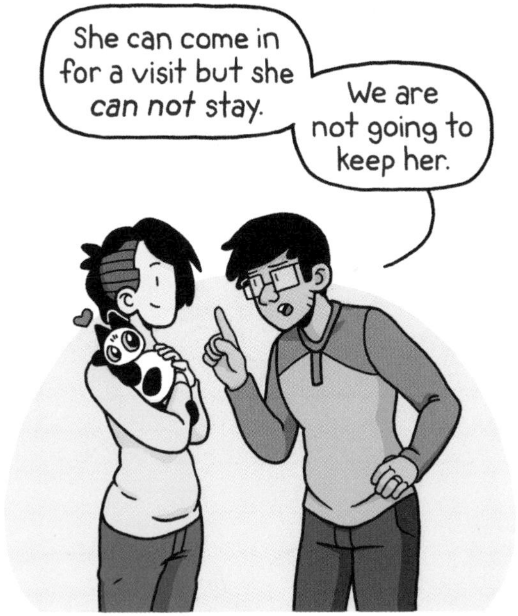
She can come in for a visit but she *can not* stay.
We are not going to keep her.

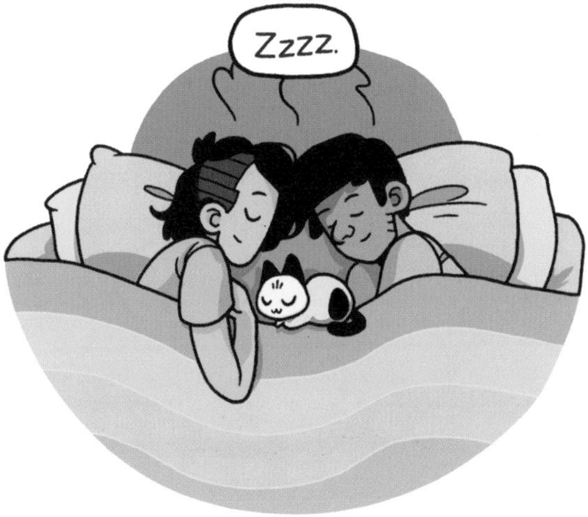
Zzzz.

"Night Song"

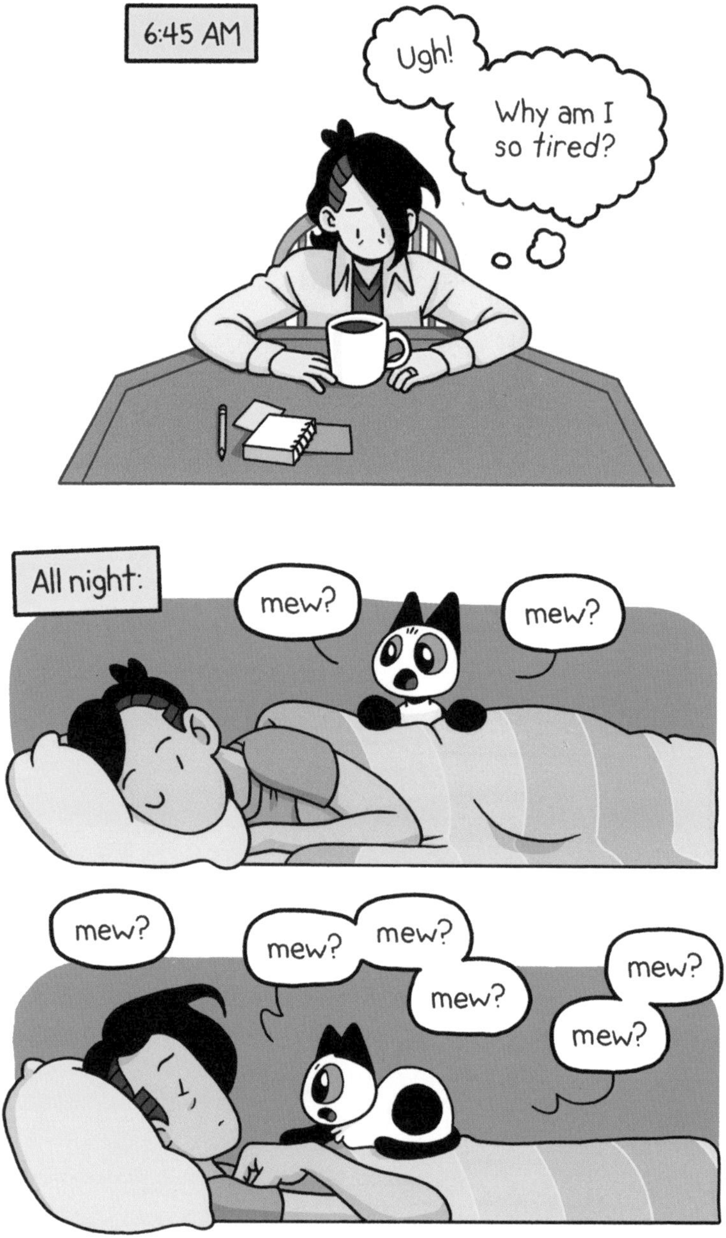
6:45 AM
Ugh!
Why am I so tired?
All night:
mew?
mew?
mew?
mew?
mew?
mew?
mew?
mew?

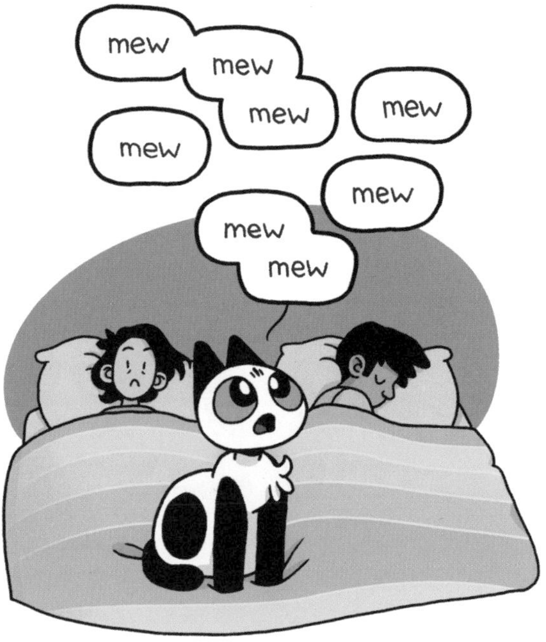
mew
mew
mew
mew
mew
mew
mew
mew

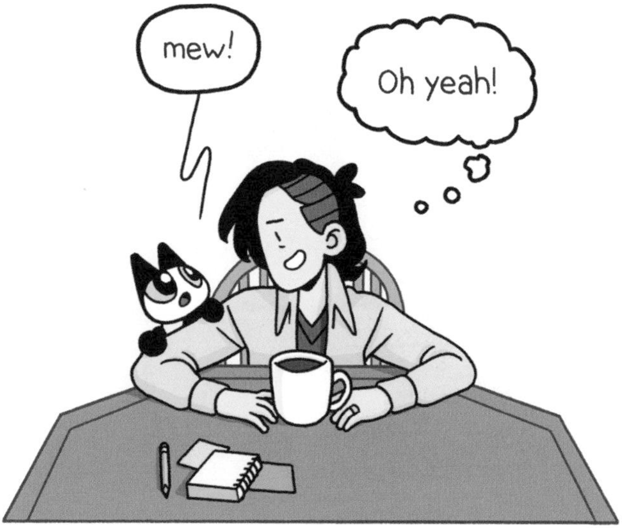
mew!
Oh yeah!

"Comfort"

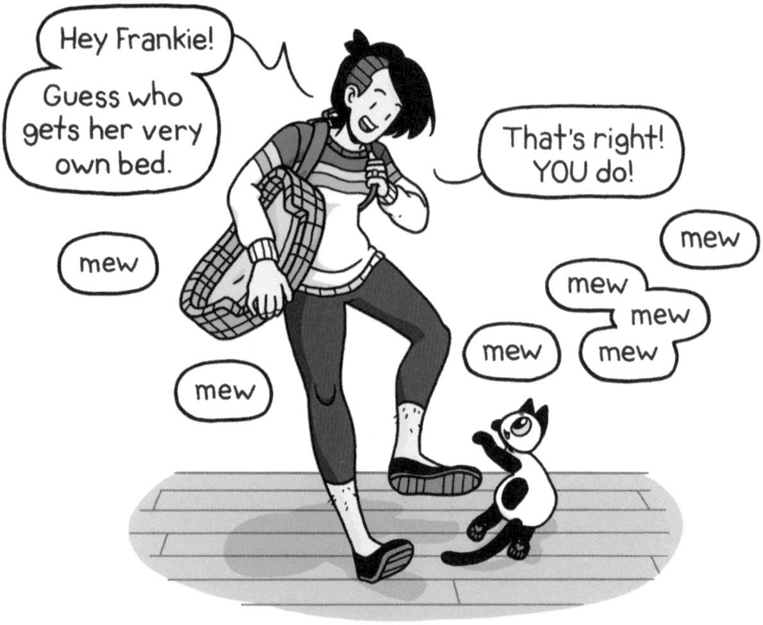
Hey Frankie!
Guess who gets her very own bed.
That's right! YOU do!
mew
mew
mew
mew
mew
mew
mew

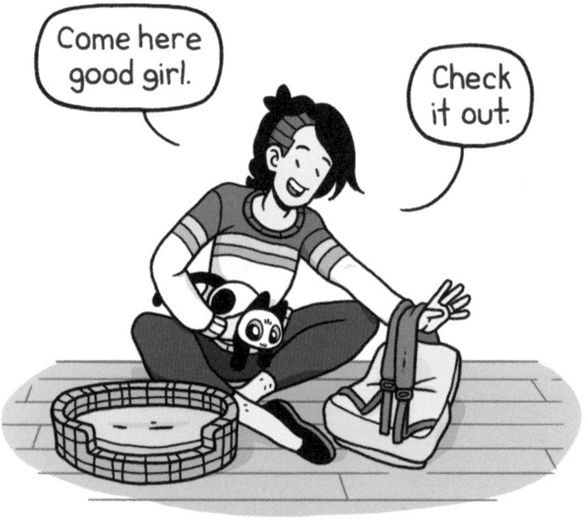
Come here good girl.
Check it out.

"Bedroom Eyes"

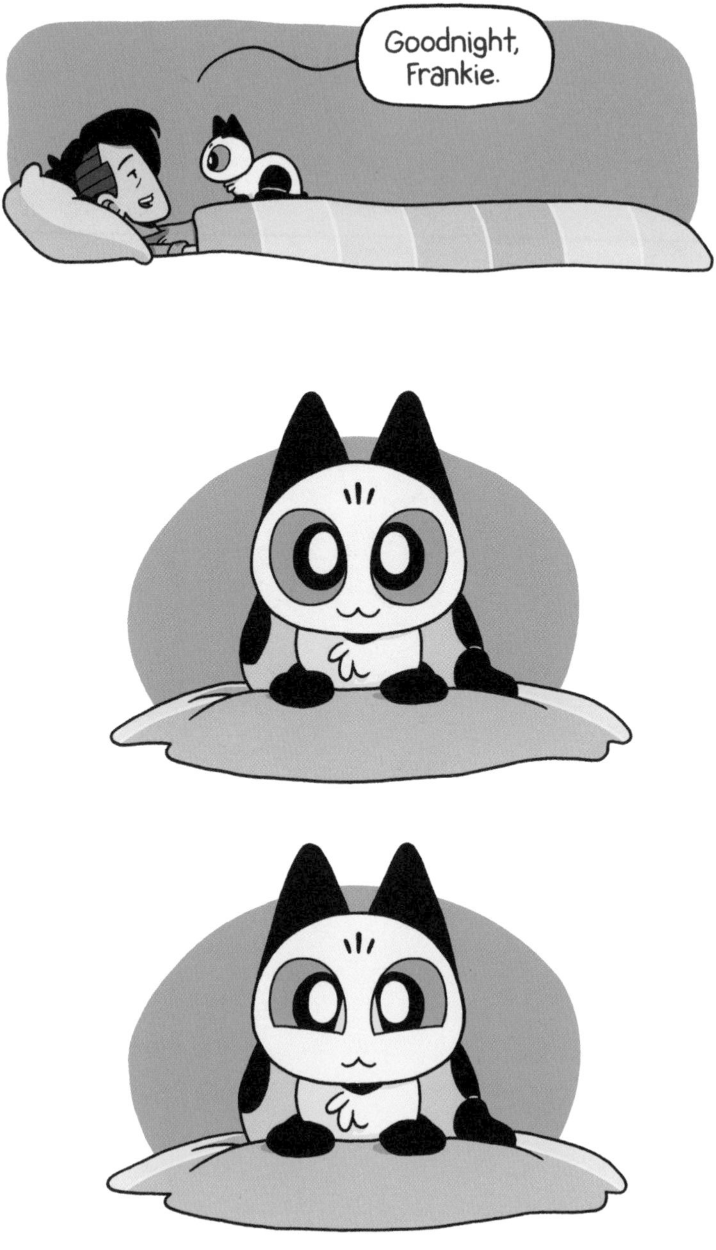
Goodnight, Frankie.

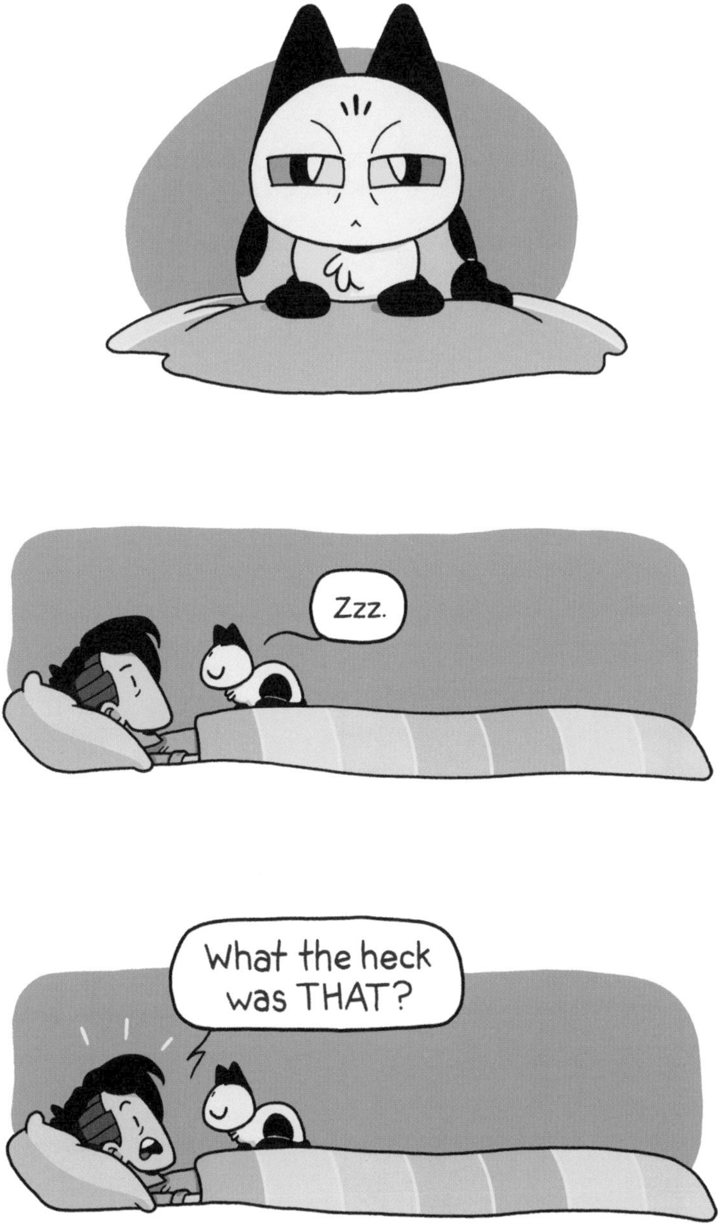
Zzz.
What the heck was THAT?

"Cuddles"

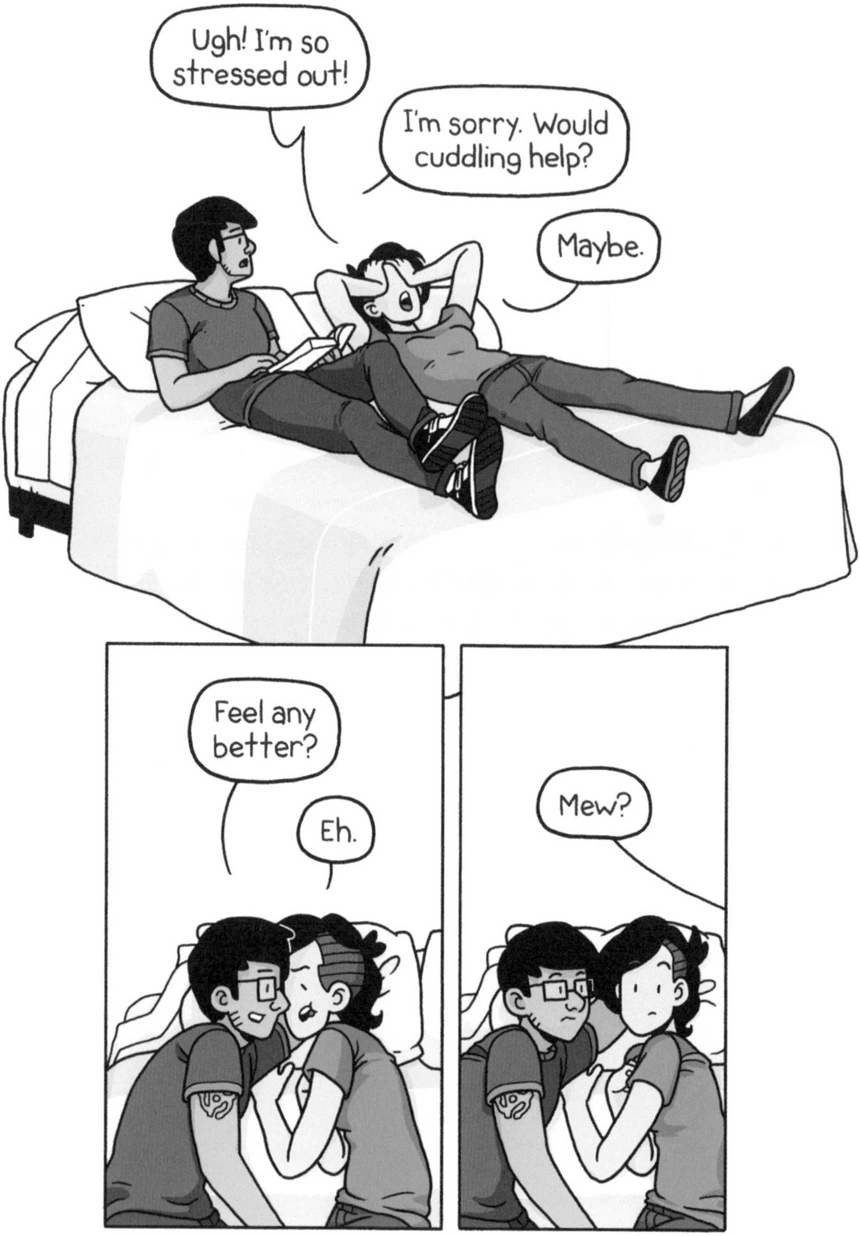
Ugh! I'm so stressed out!
I'm sorry. Would cuddling help?
Maybe.
Feel any better?
Eh.
Mew?

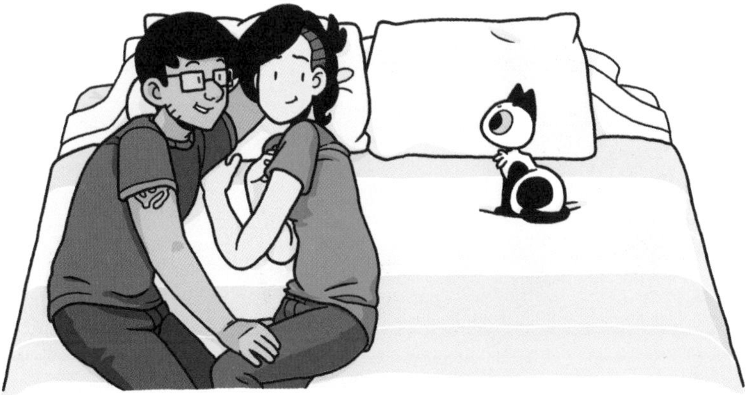

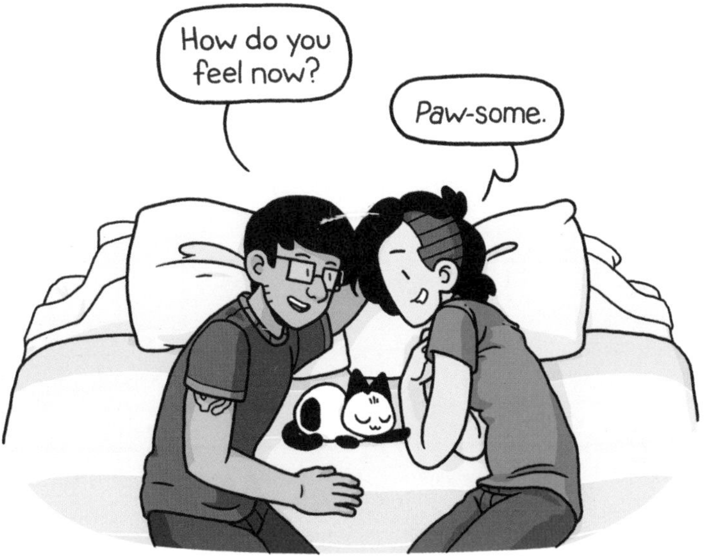
How do you feel now?
Paw-some.

"Sanitation"

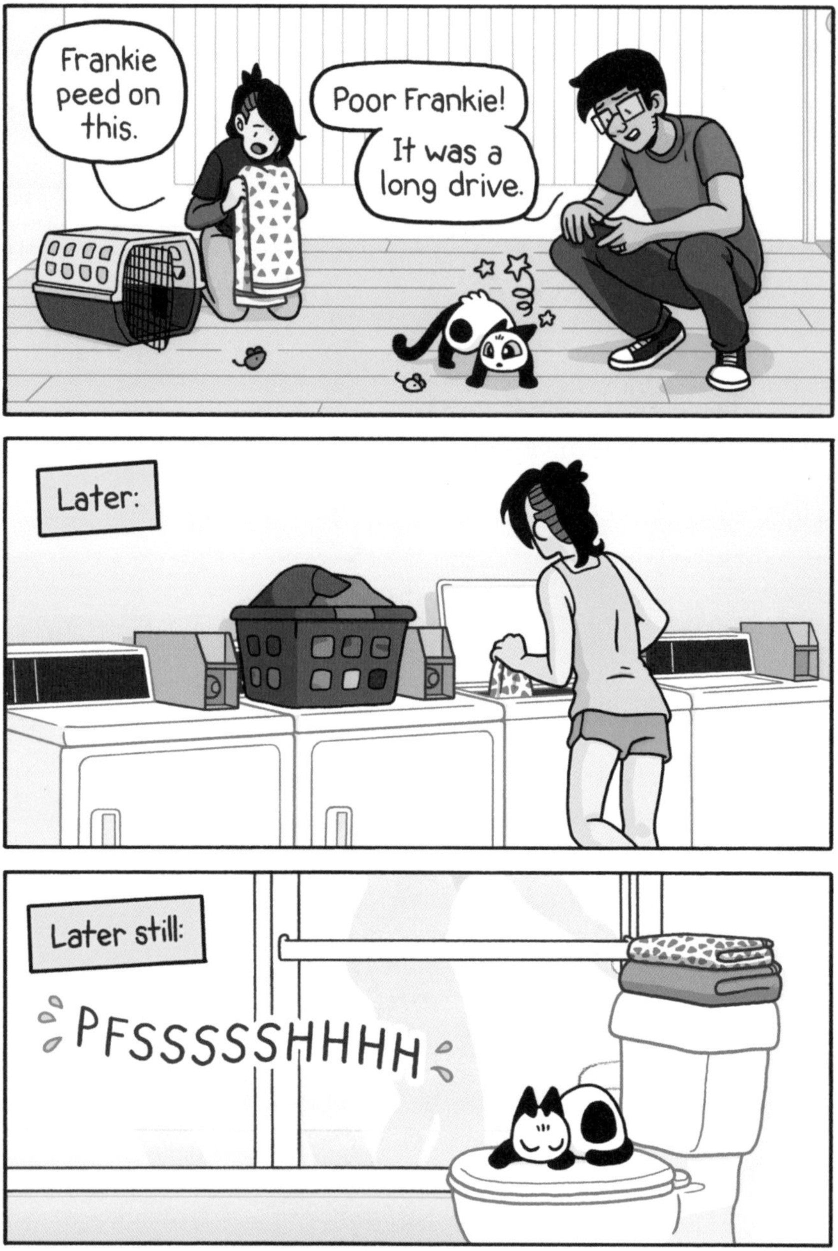
Frankie peed on this.
Poor Frankie!
It was a long drive.
Later:
Later still:
PFSSSSSHHHH

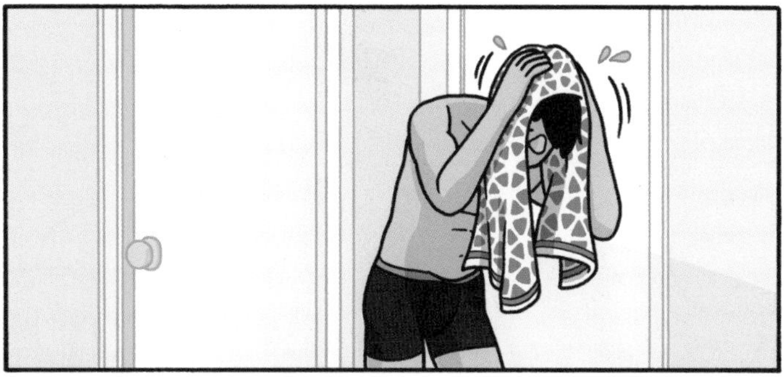

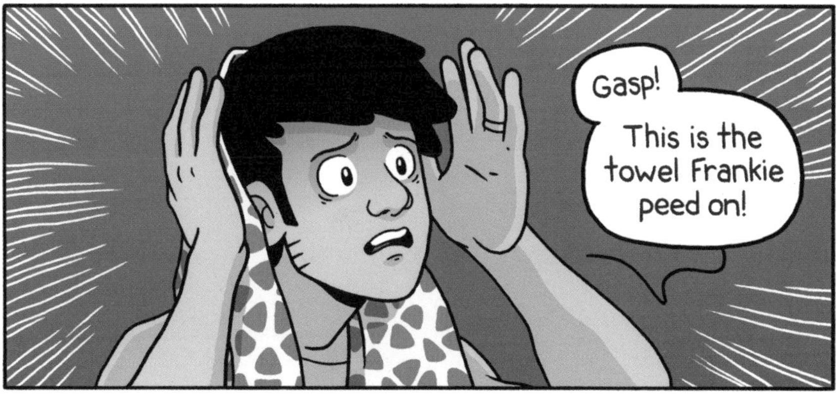
Gasp!
This is the towel Frankie peed on!

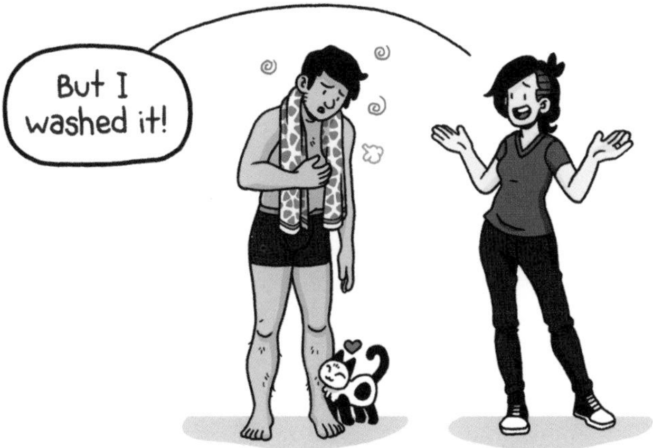
But I washed it!

"Maintenance"

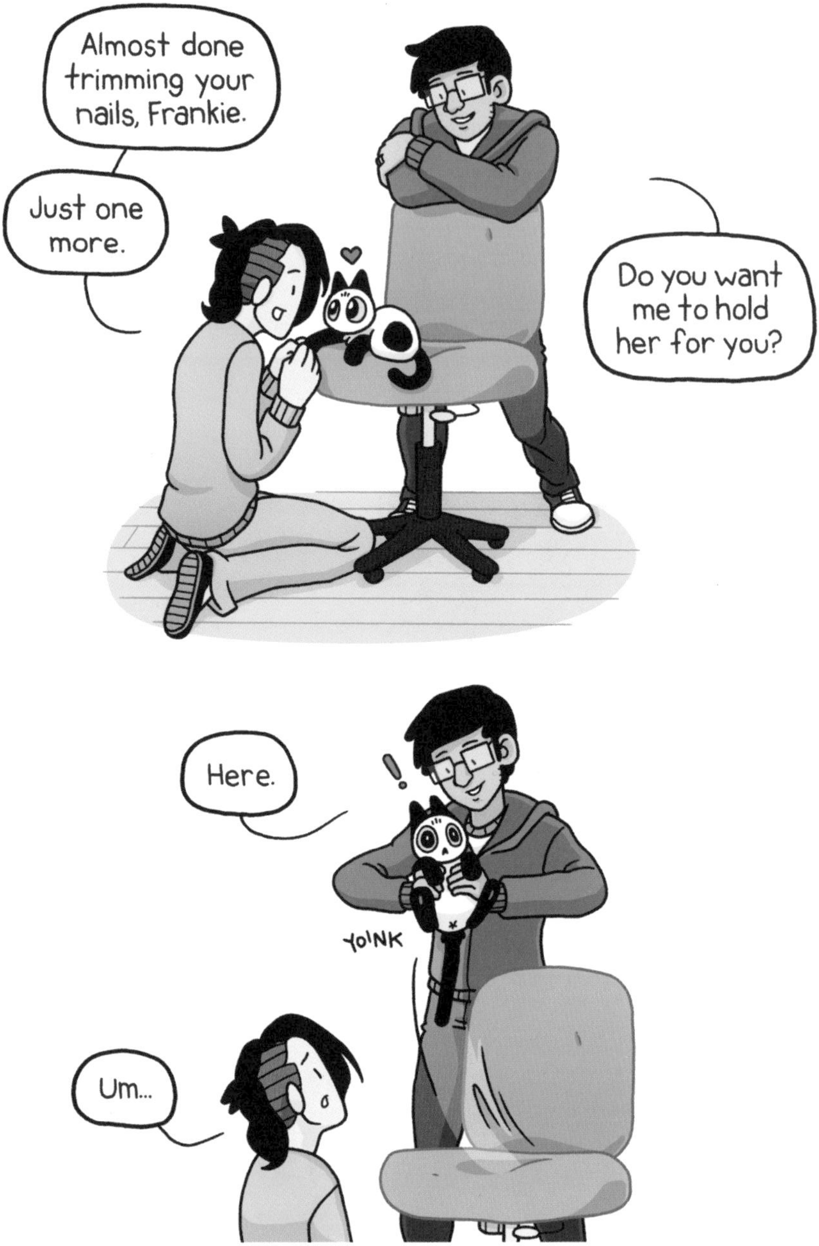
Almost done trimming your nails, Frankie.
Just one more.
Do you want me to hold her for you?
Here.
YOINK
Um...

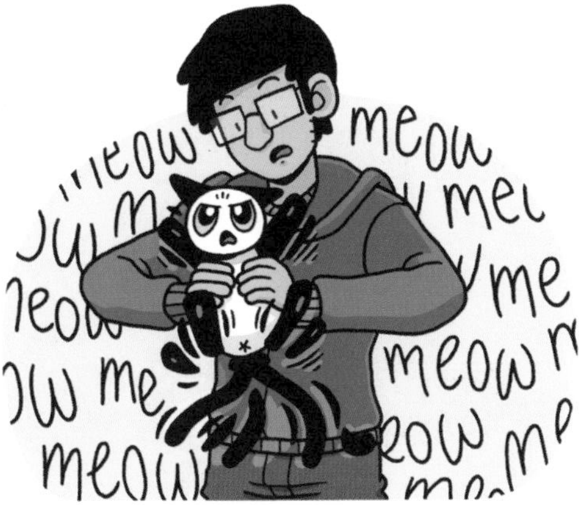
meow
meow
meow

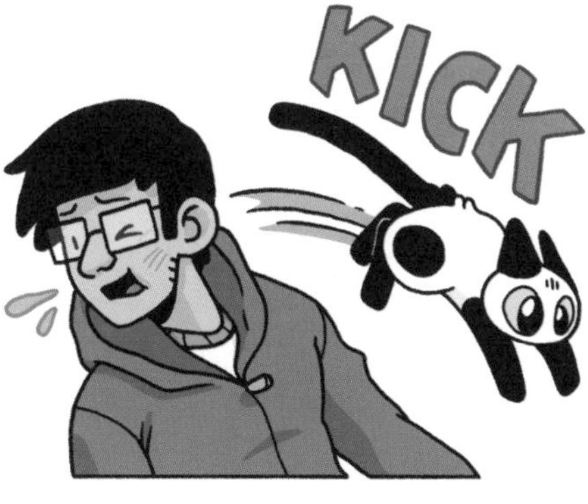
KICK

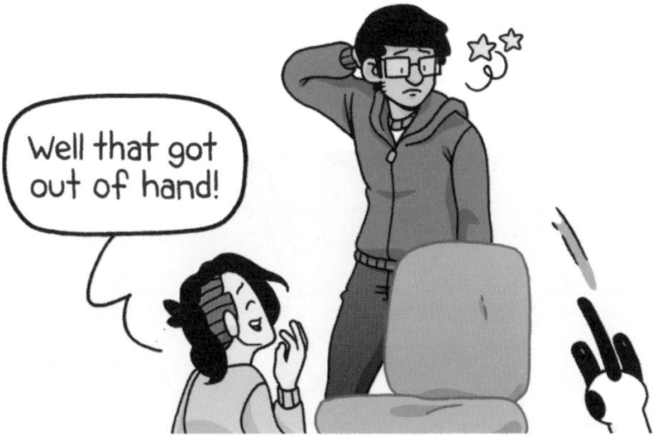
Well that got out of hand!

"Bath Time 1"

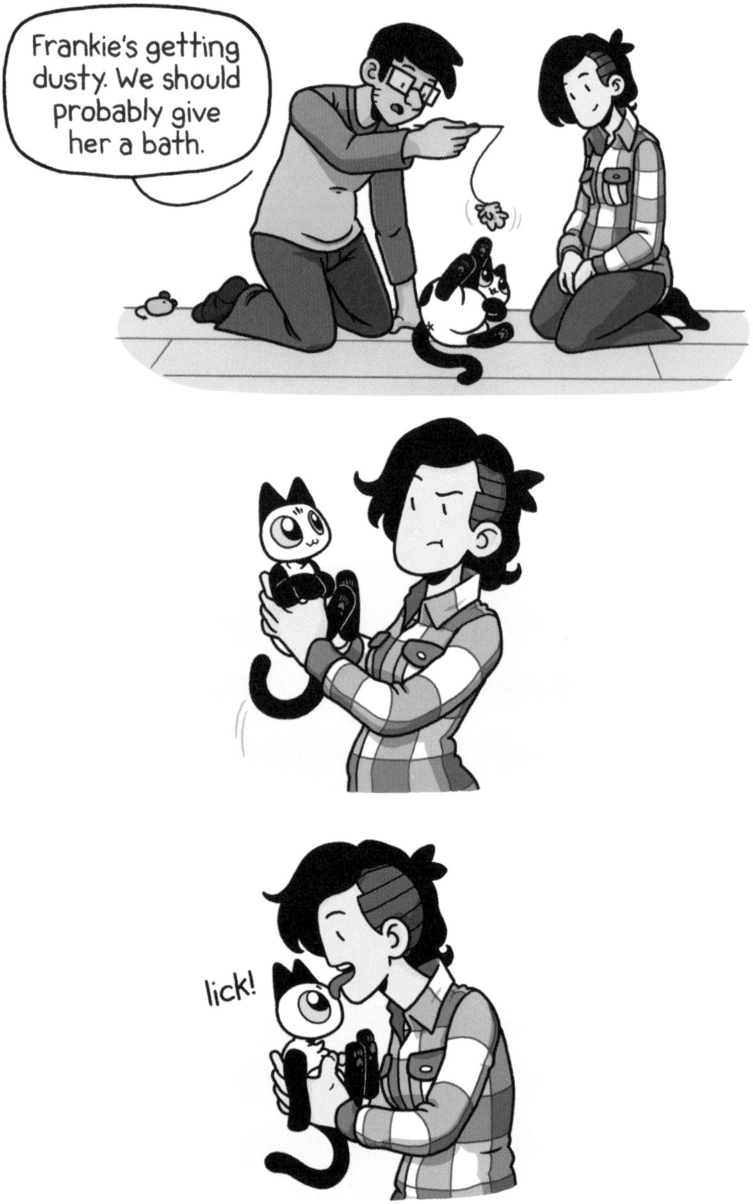
Frankie's getting dusty. We should probably give her a bath.
lick!

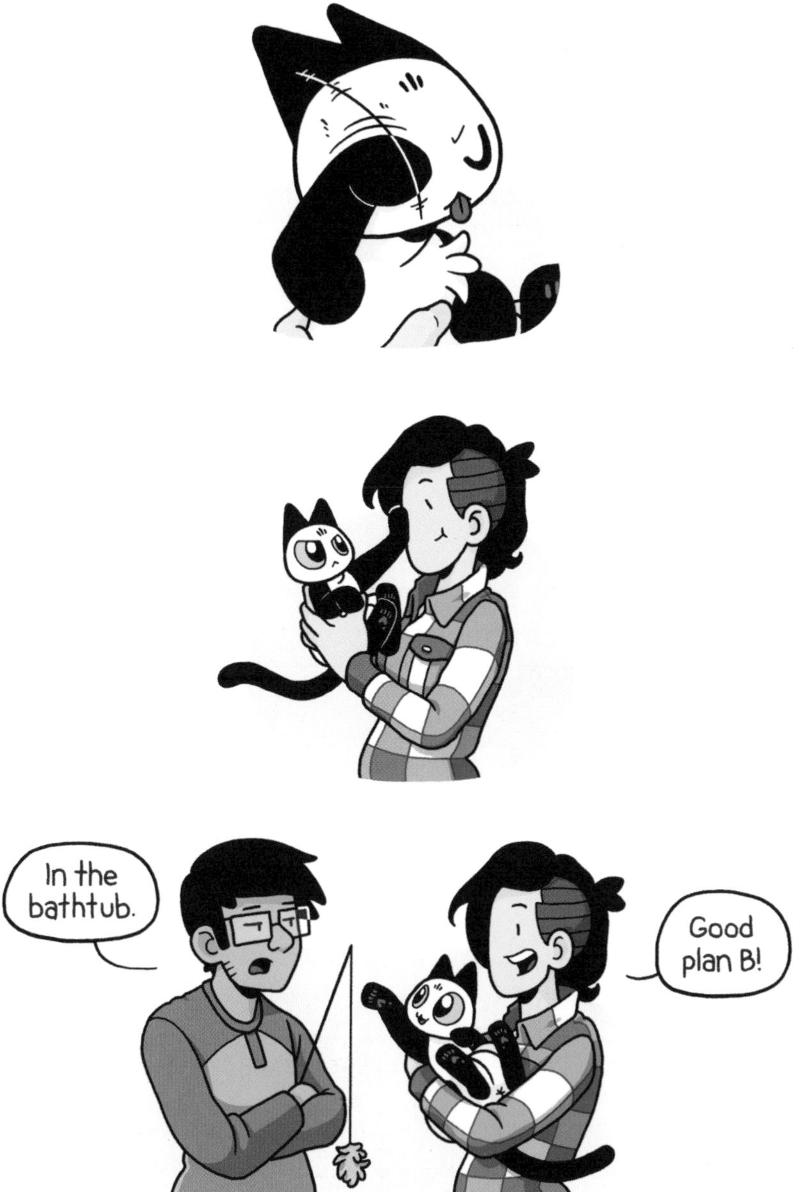
In the bathtub.
Good plan B!

"Bath Time 2"

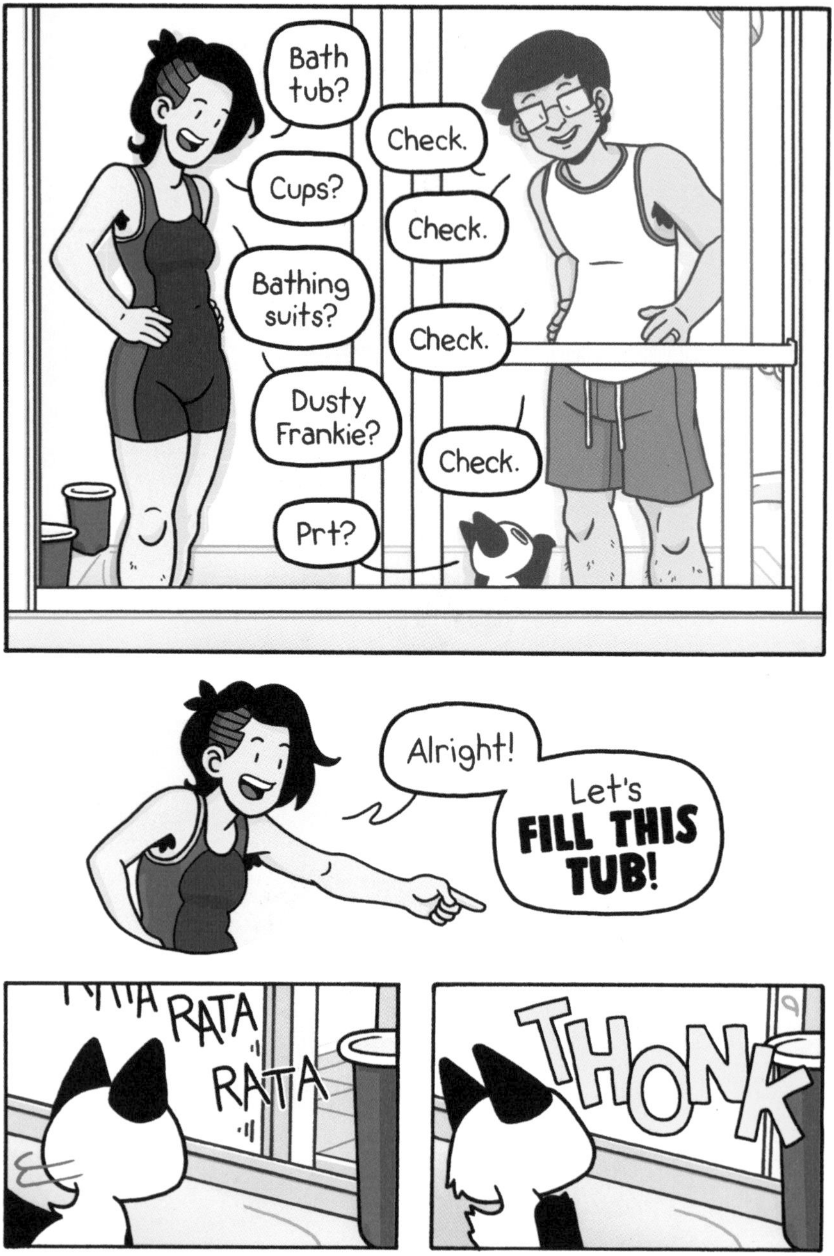
Bath tub?
Check.
Cups?
Check.
Bathing suits?
Check.
Dusty Frankie?
Check.
Prt?
Alright!
Let's FILL THIS TUB!
RATA
RATA
THONK

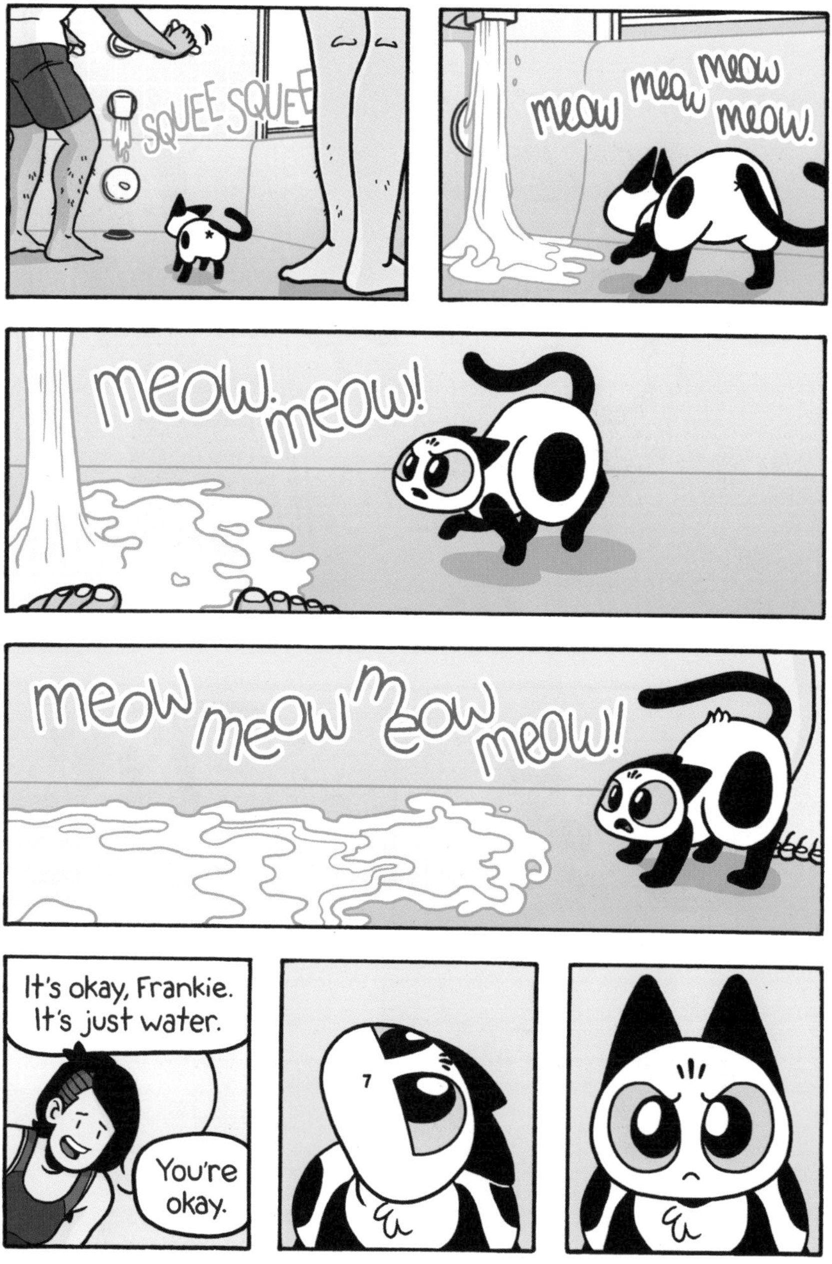
SQUEE SQUEE
meow meow meow meow.
meow. meow!
meow meow meow meow!
It's okay, Frankie. It's just water.
You're okay.

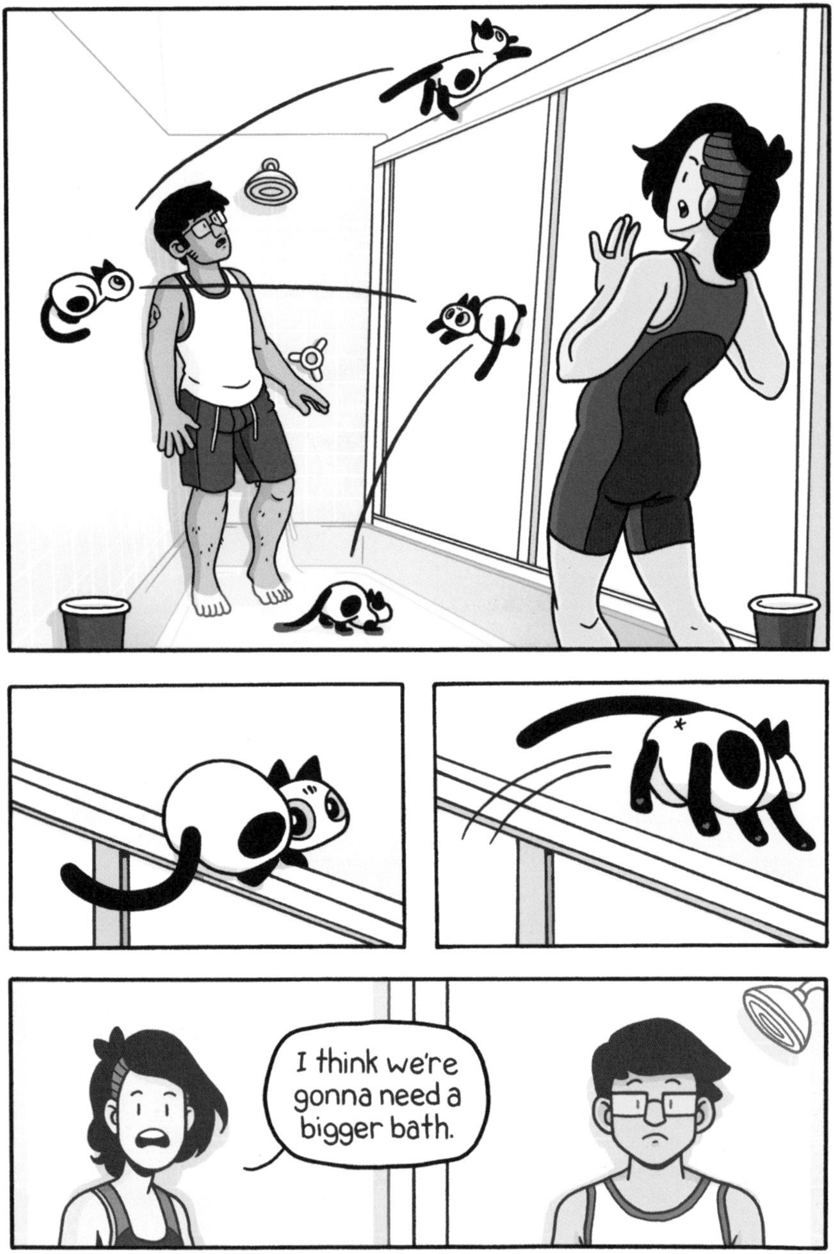
I think we're gonna need a bigger bath.

"Can't Buy Me Love"

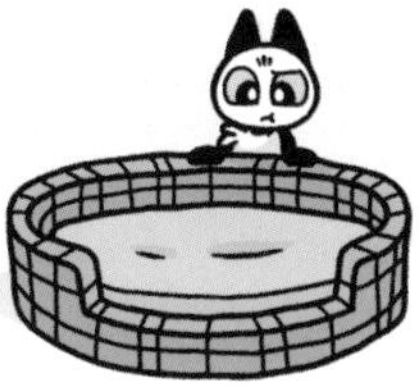

Pet bed: $10

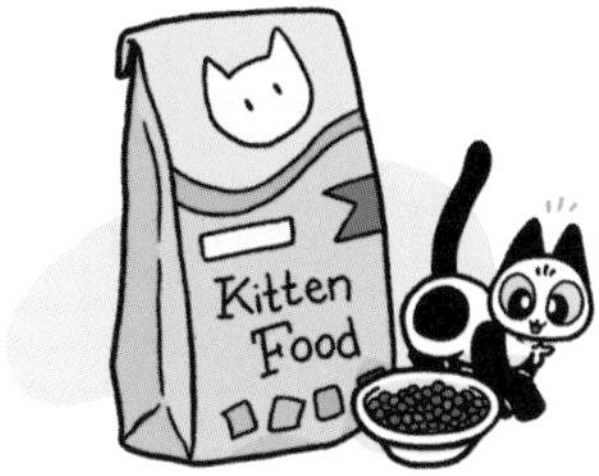
Kitten Food

Dry food: $12

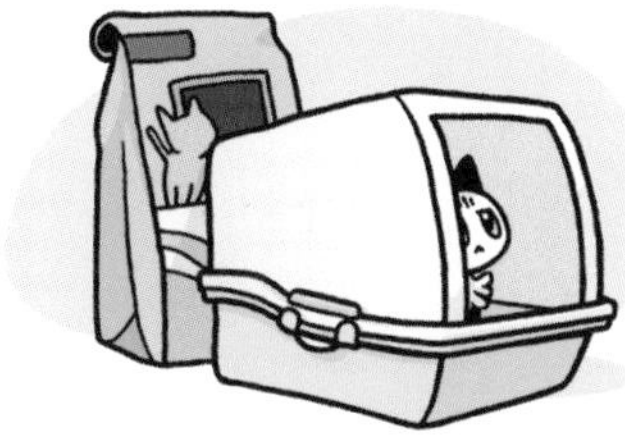

Litter and litterbox: $20

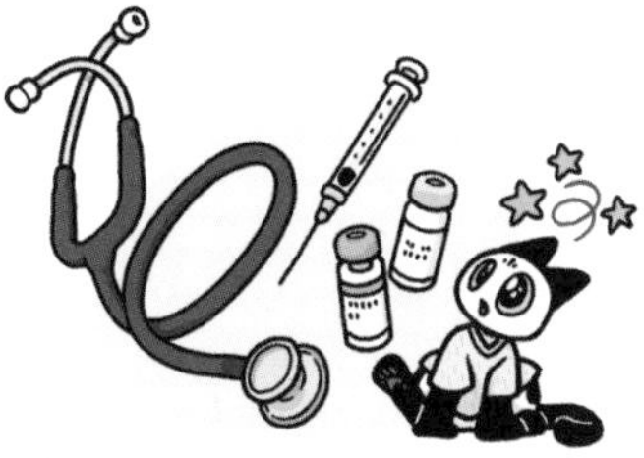

Shots and spay: $100

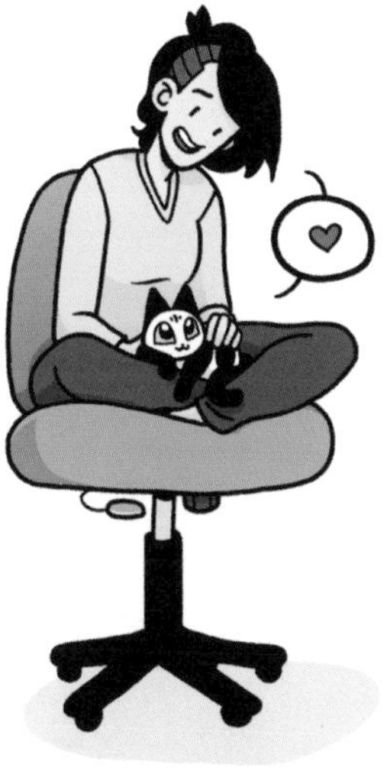

A kitten to share my chair with: ***priceless!***

"Language Barrier"

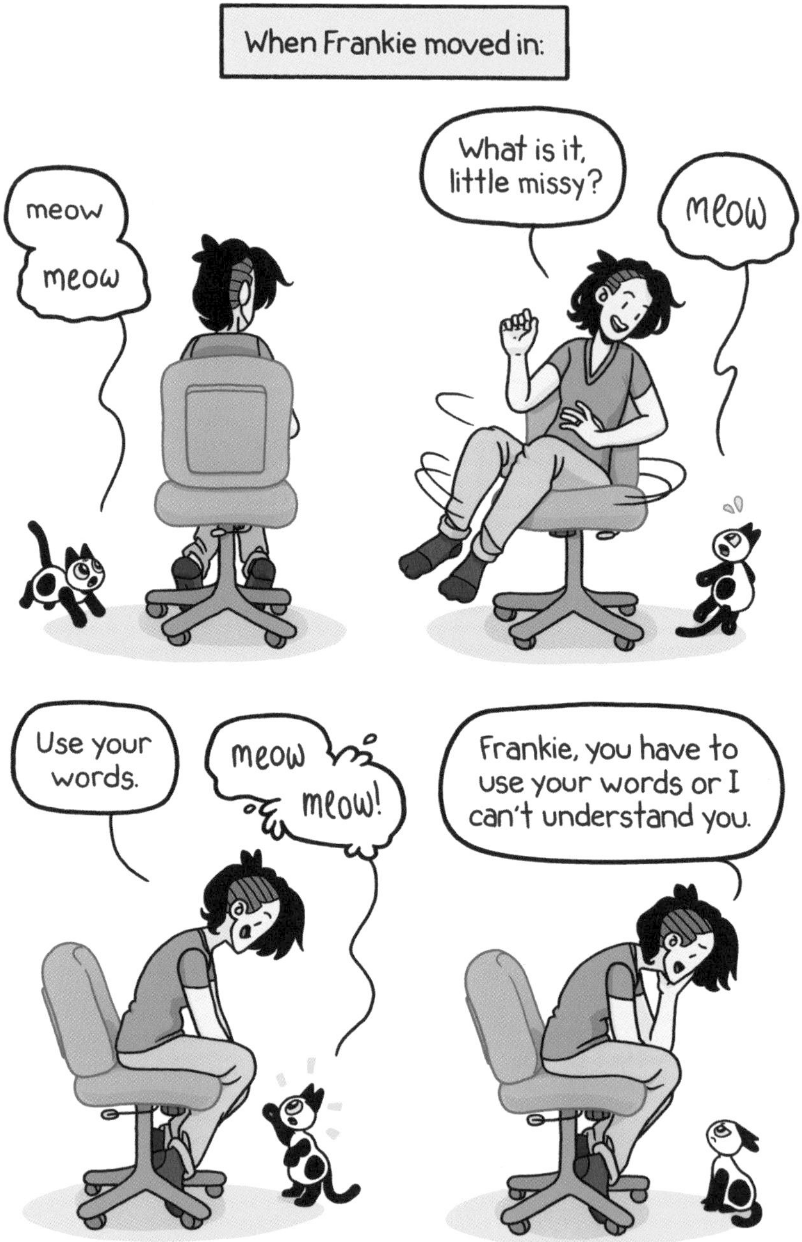
When Frankie moved in:
meow
meow
What is it, little missy?
meow
Use your words.
meow
meow!
Frankie, you have to use your words or I can't understand you.

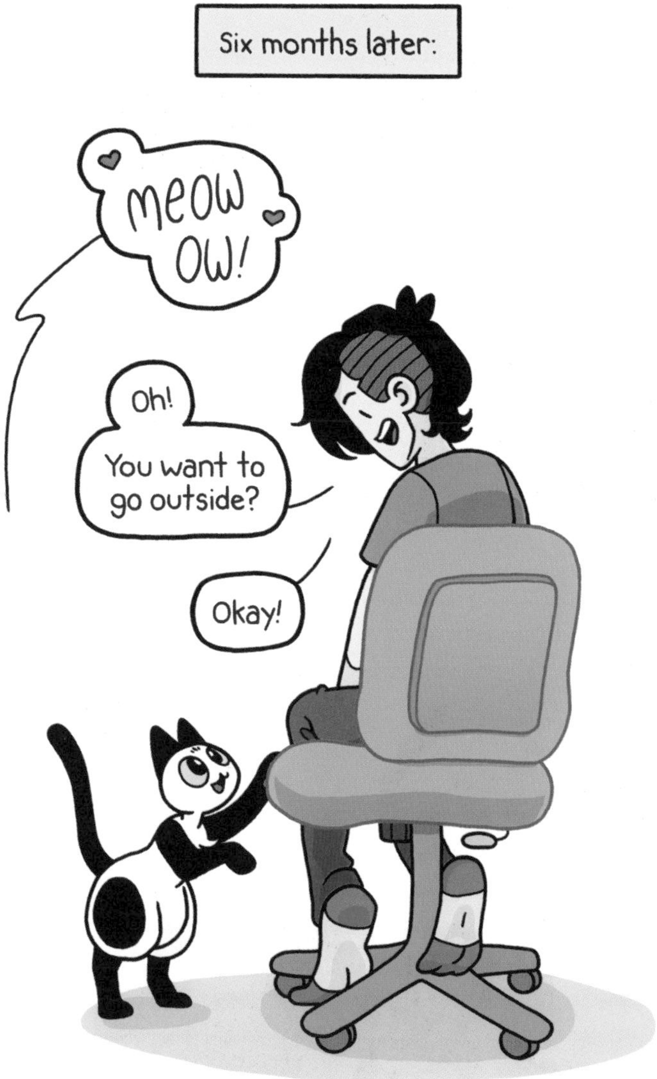
Six months later:
meow ow!
Oh!
You want to go outside?
Okay!

"Nicknames"

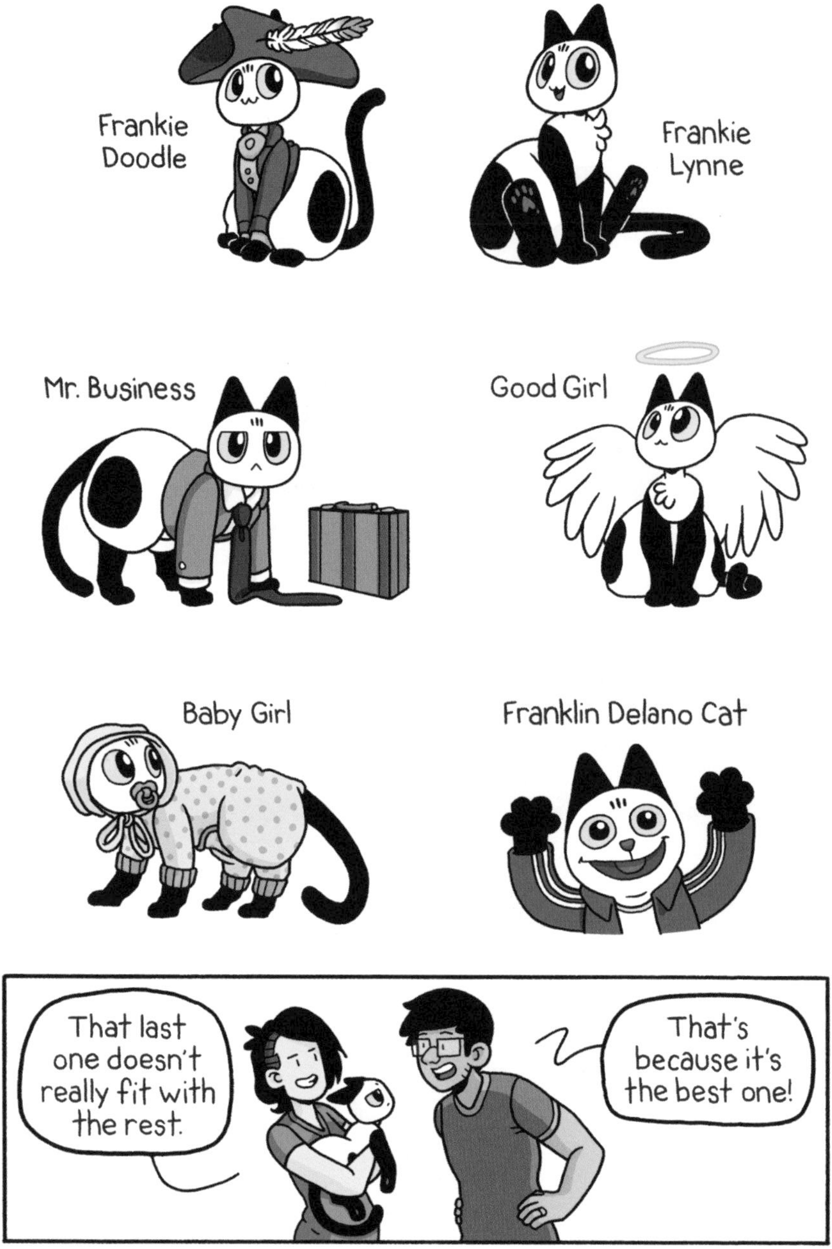

Frankie Doodle
Frankie Lynne
Mr. Business
Good Girl
Baby Girl
Franklin Delano Cat
That last one doesn't really fit with the rest.
That's because it's the best one!

"Affection"

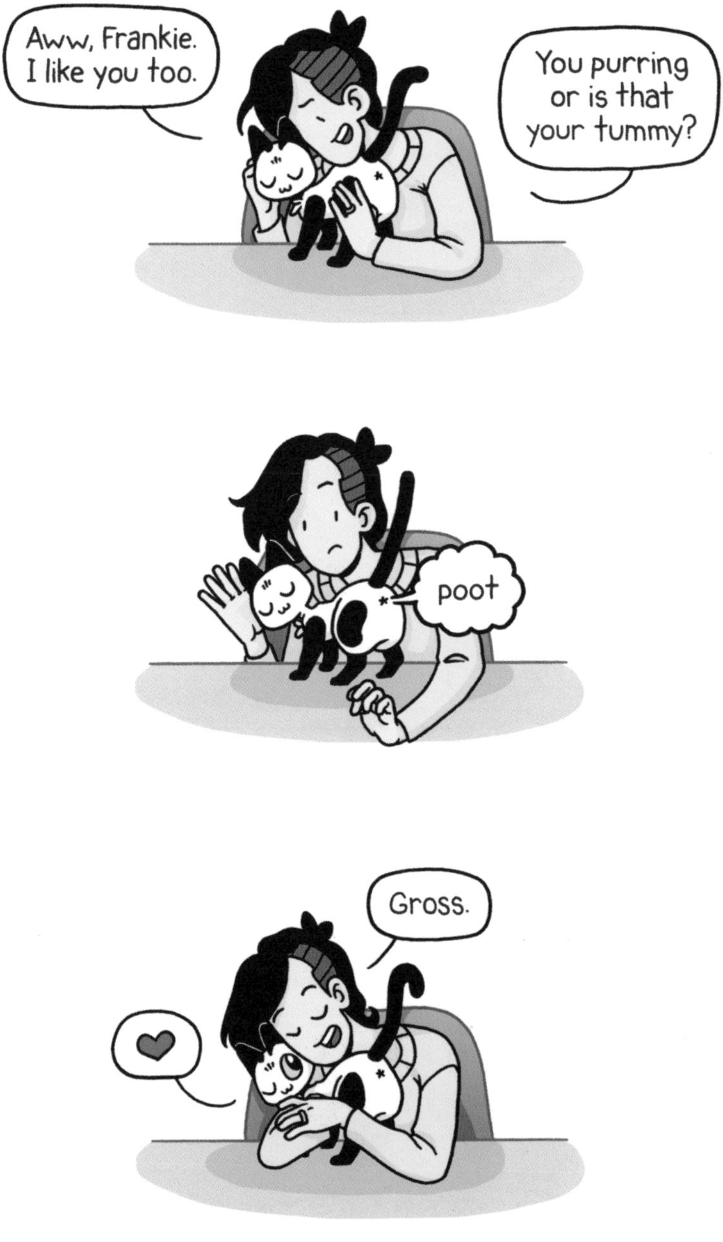
Aww, Frankie. I like you too.
You purring or is that your tummy?
poot
Gross.

"Alarm Cat"

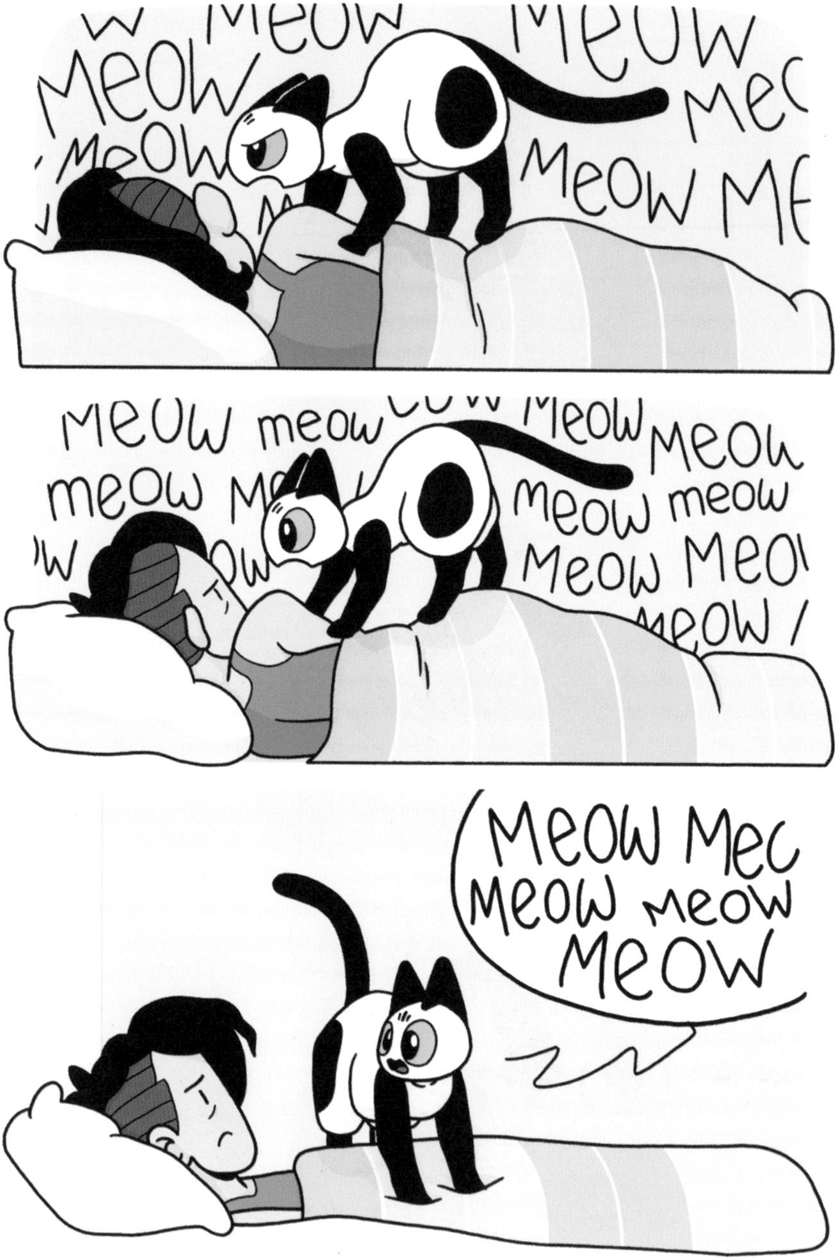
Meow Meow Meow Meow
meow meow Meow Meow
meow meow meow
Meow Meow
Meow
Meow meow
Meow

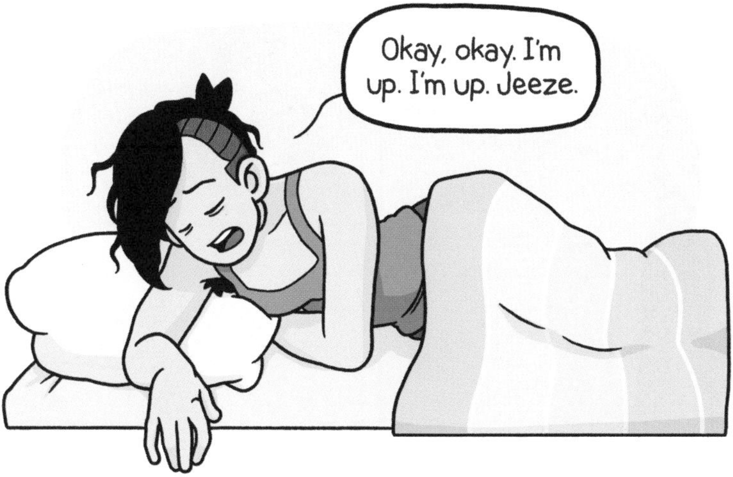
Okay, okay. I'm up. I'm up. Jeeze.

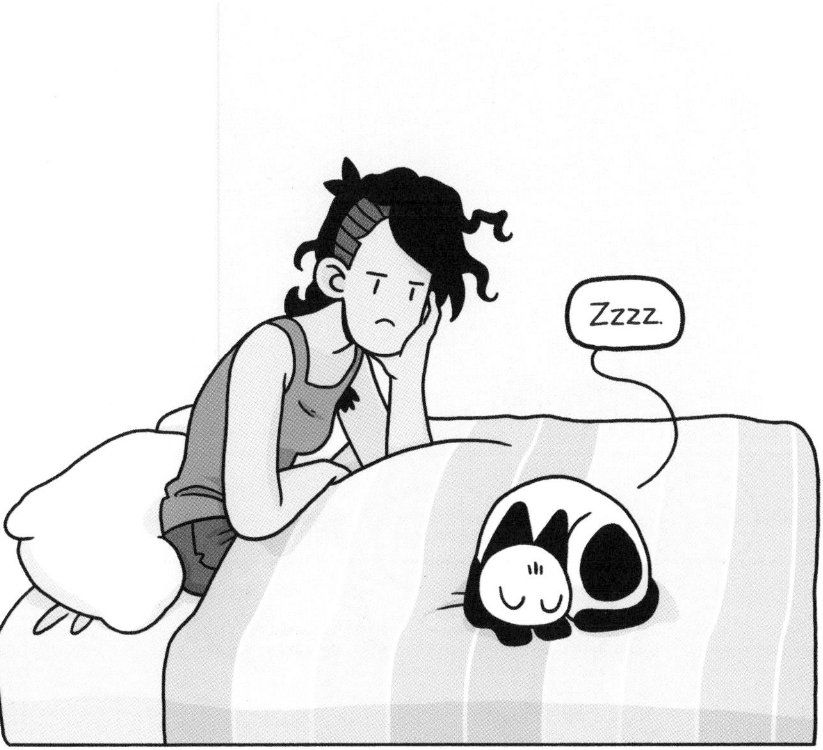
Zzzz.

"Morning Routine"

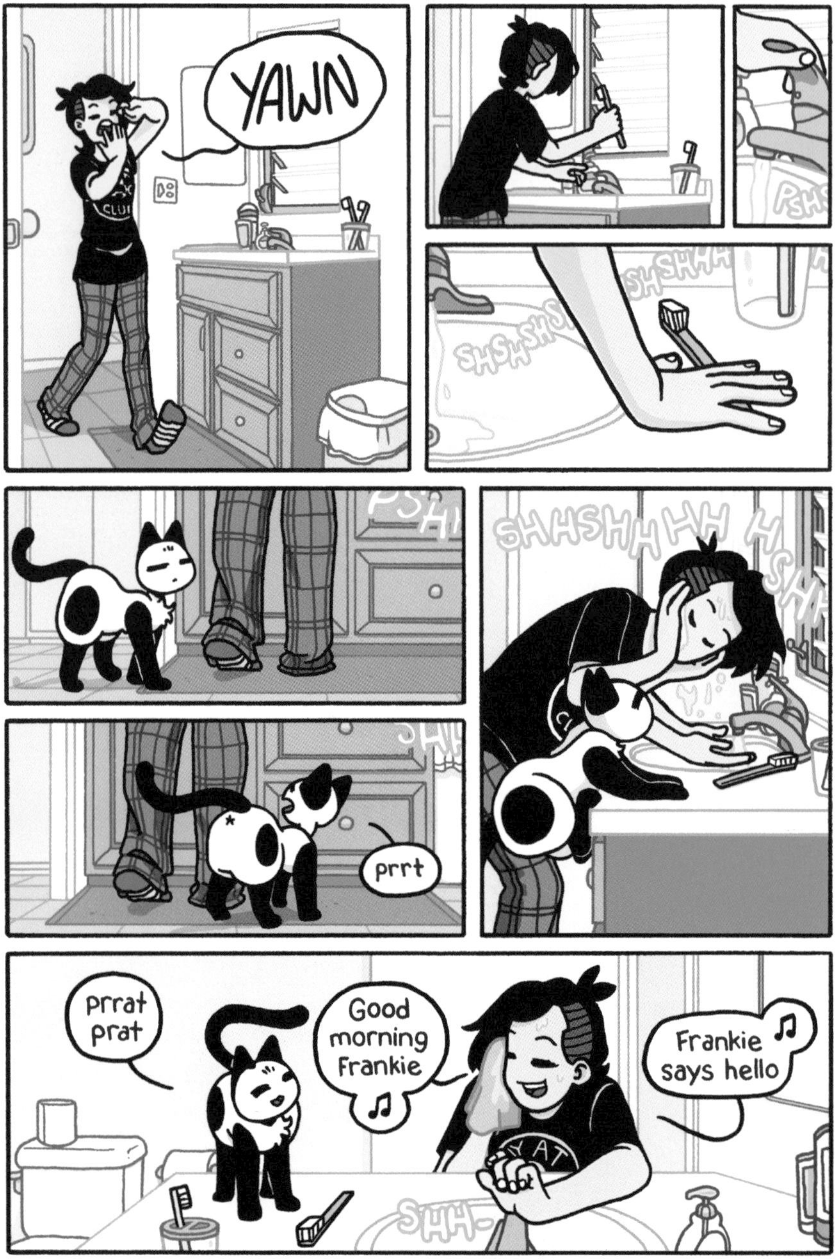
YAWN
prrt
prrat
prat
Good morning Frankie ♫
Frankie says hello ♫
SHH-

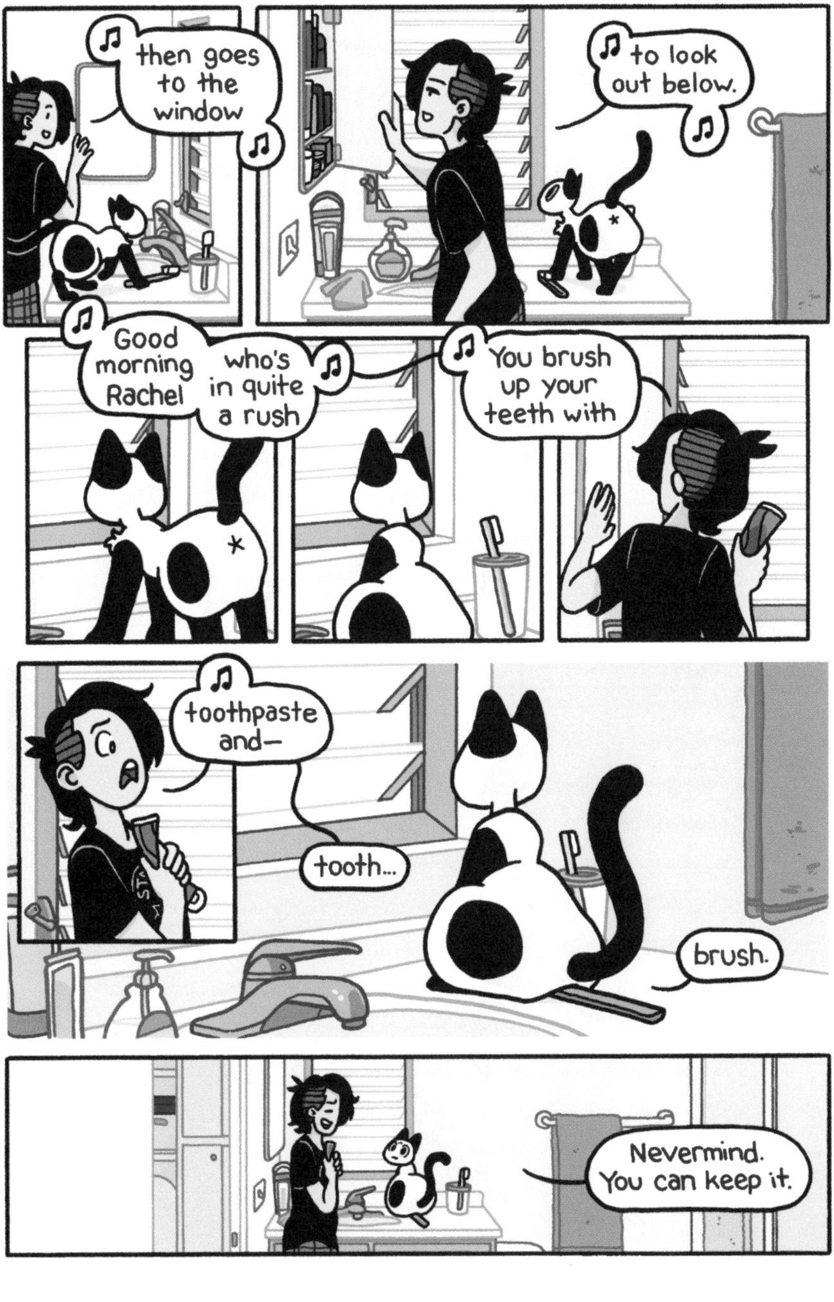

♫ then goes to the window ♫
♫ to look out below. ♫
♫ Good morning Rachel
who's in quite a rush ♫
♫ You brush up your teeth with
♫ toothpaste and—
tooth...
brush.
Nevermind. You can keep it.

"Work Out"

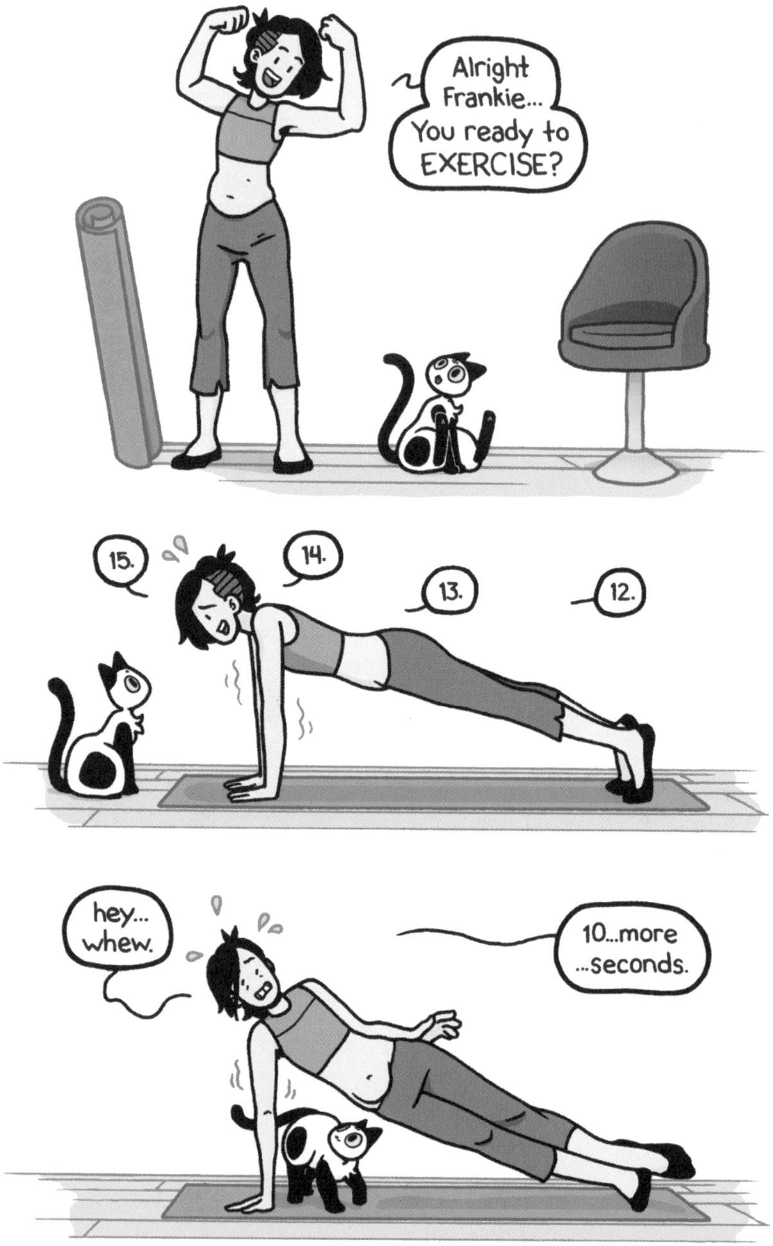
Alright Frankie... You ready to EXERCISE?
15.
14.
13.
12.
hey... whew.
10...more ...seconds.

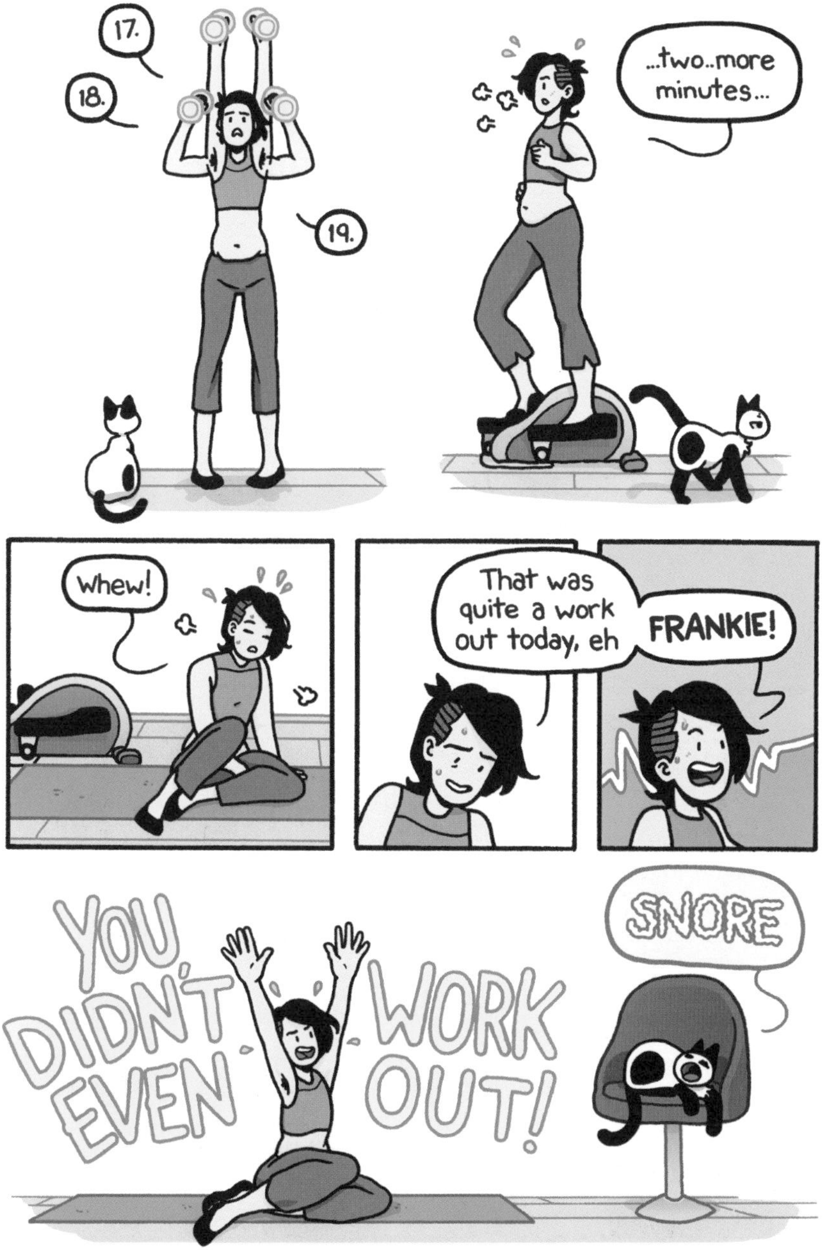
17.
18.
19.
...two..more minutes...
Whew!
That was quite a work out today, eh
FRANKIE!
YOU DIDN'T EVEN WORK OUT!
SNORE

"Facetime"

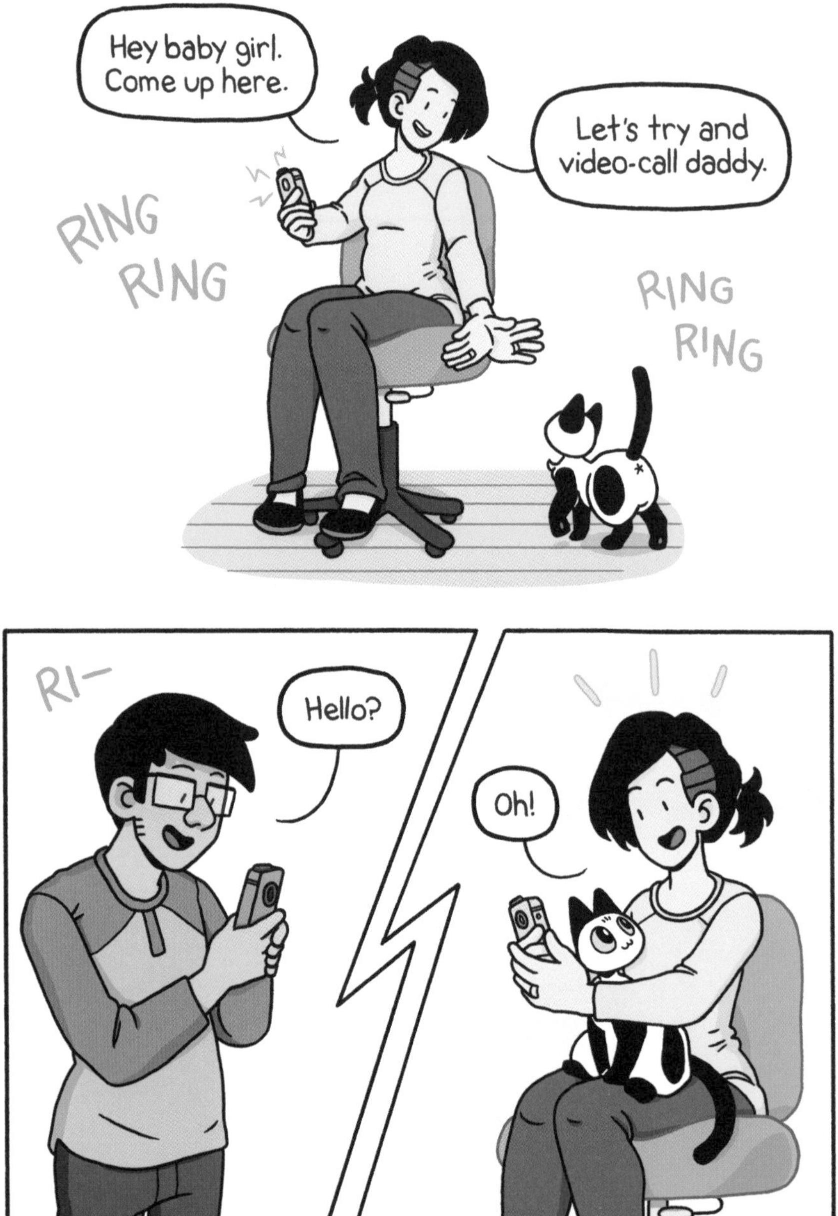

Hey baby girl. Come up here.
Let's try and video-call daddy.
RING RING
RING RING
RI—
Hello?
Oh!

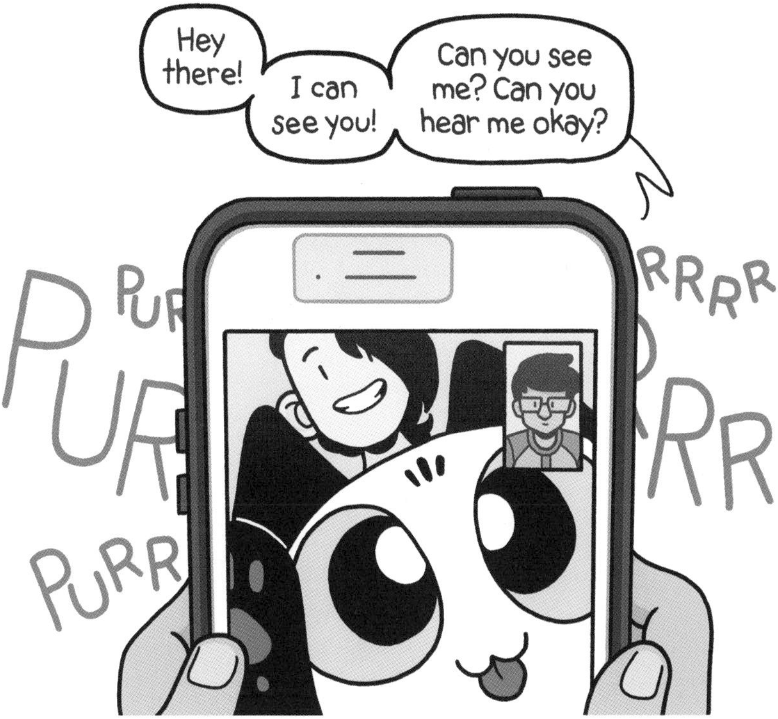
Hey there!
I can see you!
Can you see me? Can you hear me okay?
PURR
PURR
PURRRRRR
PURR

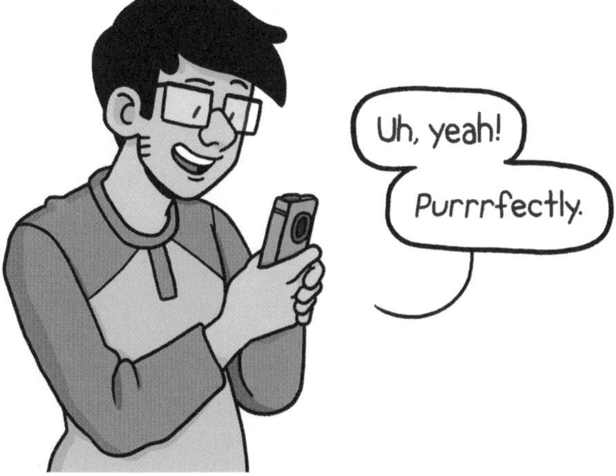
Uh, yeah!
Purrrfectly.

"Asks"

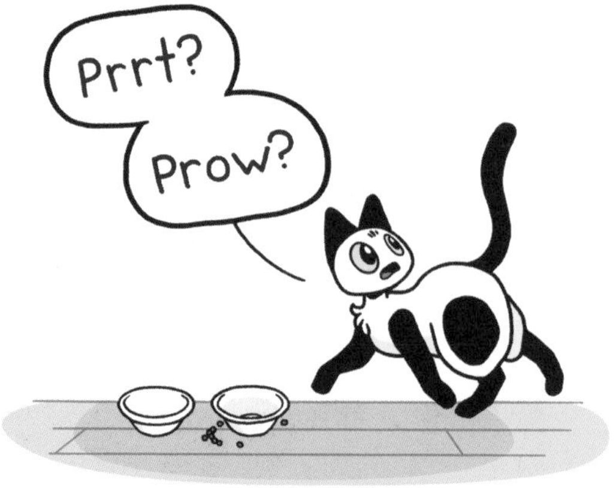
Prrt?
Prow?

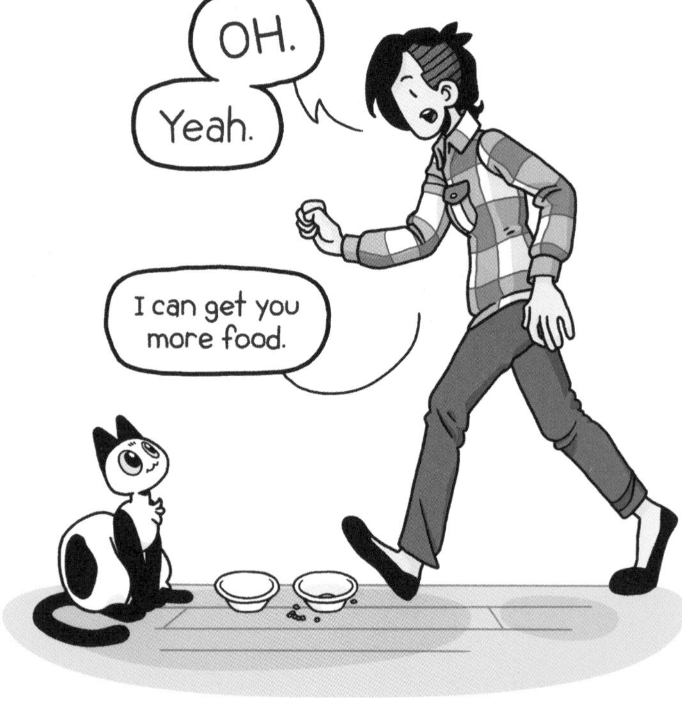
OH.
Yeah.
I can get you more food.

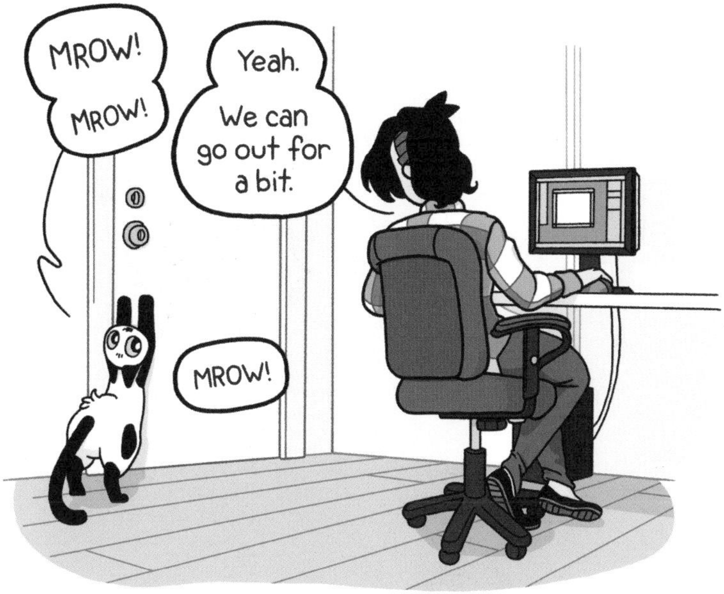
MROW!
MROW!
Yeah.
We can go out for a bit.
MROW!

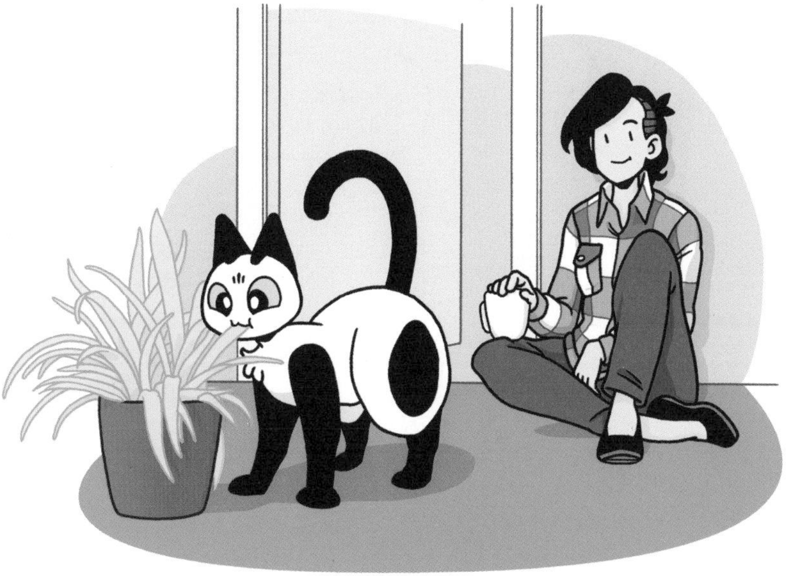

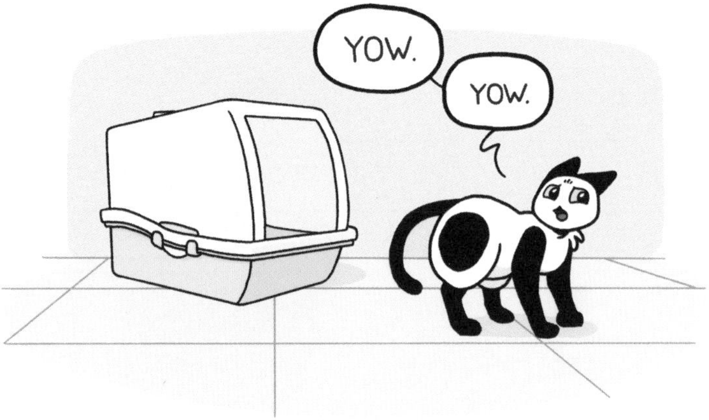
YOW.
YOW.

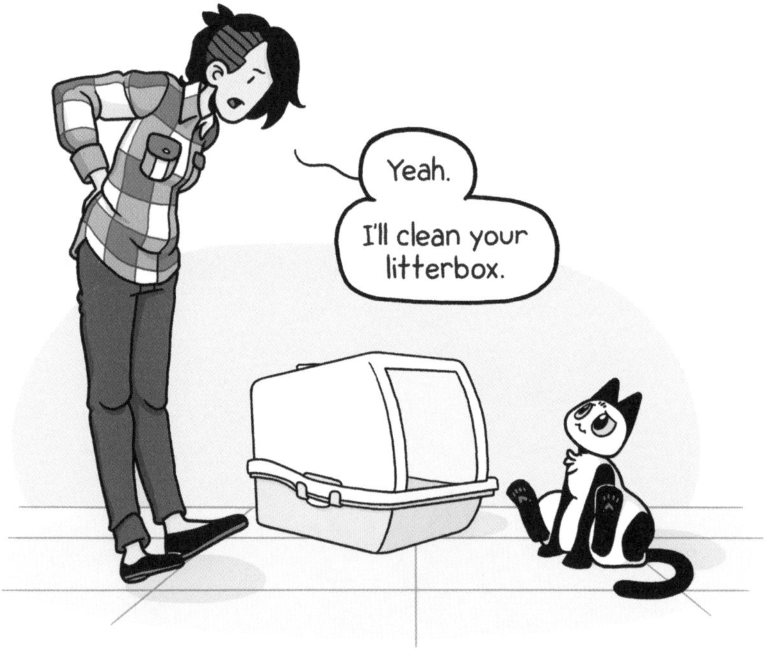
Yeah.
I'll clean your litterbox.

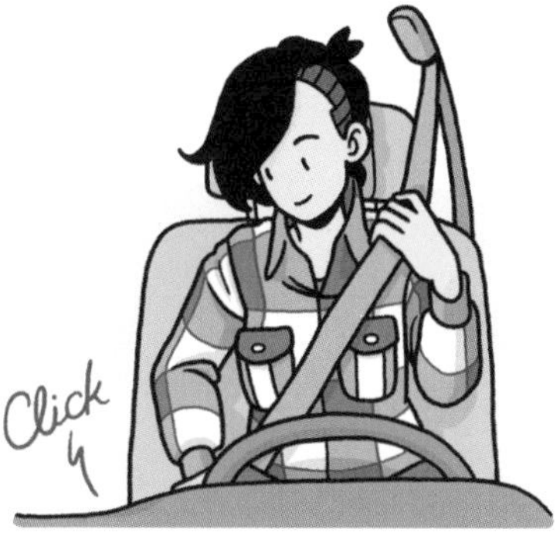
Click

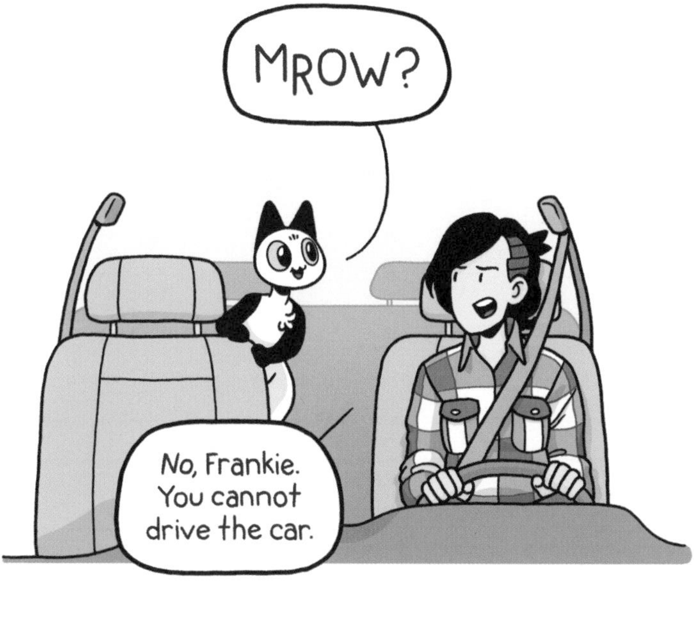
MROW?
No, Frankie. You cannot drive the car.

"Greet The Day"

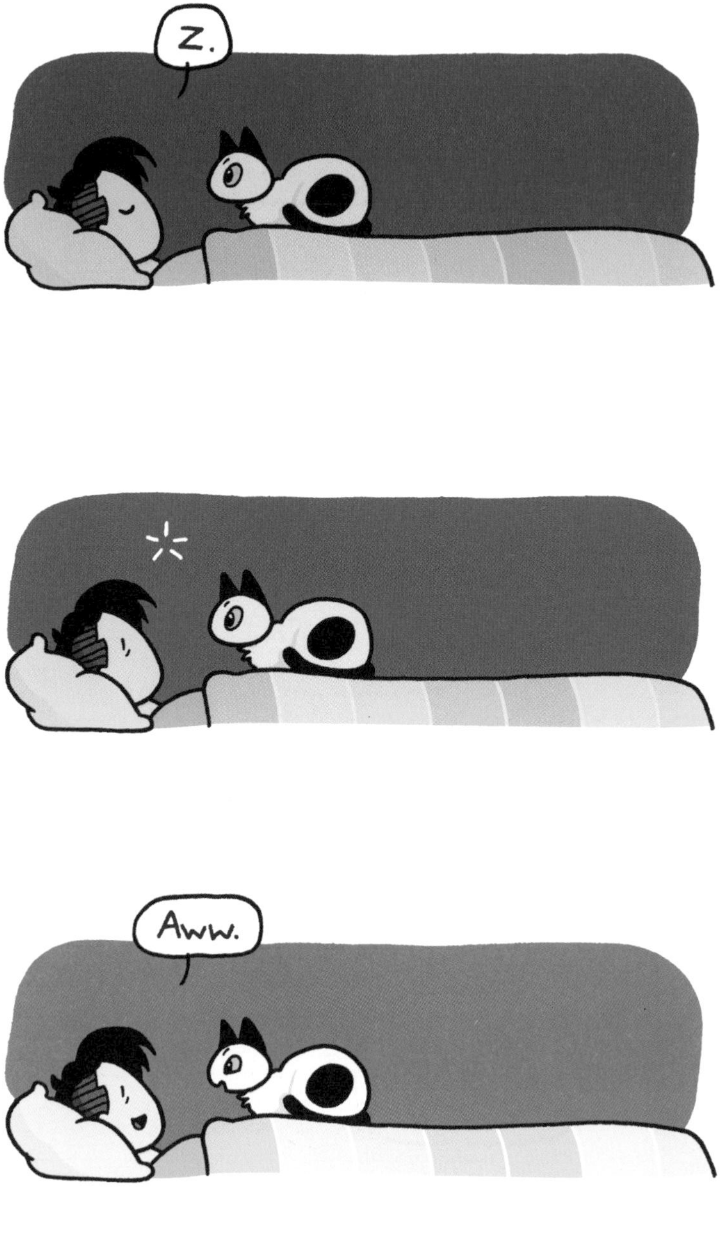
Z.
Aww.

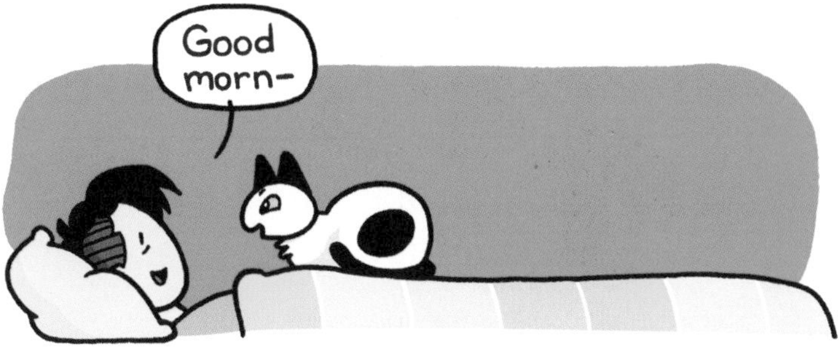
Good morn-

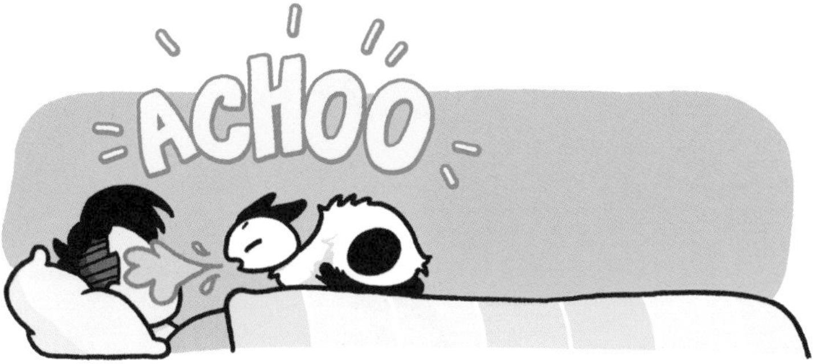
ACHOO

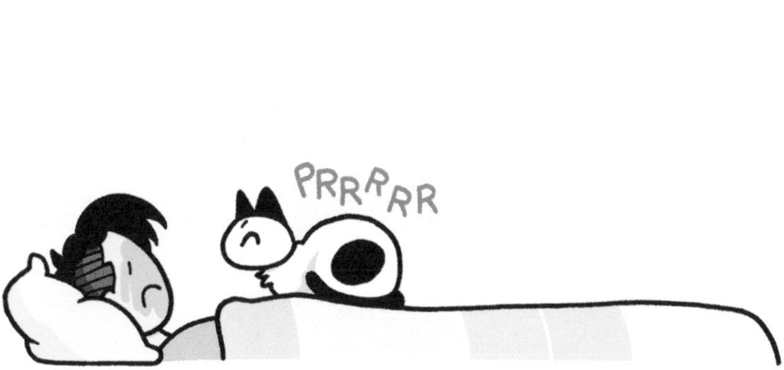
PRRRRR

"Offense And Defense"

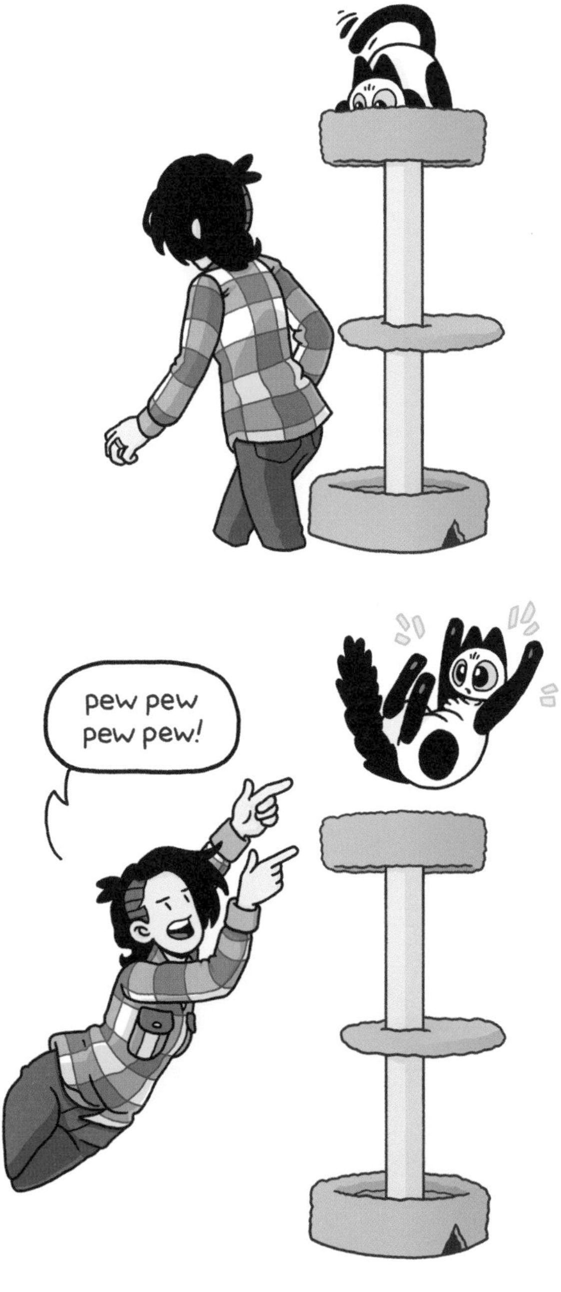
pew pew
pew pew!

"Sound Effects"

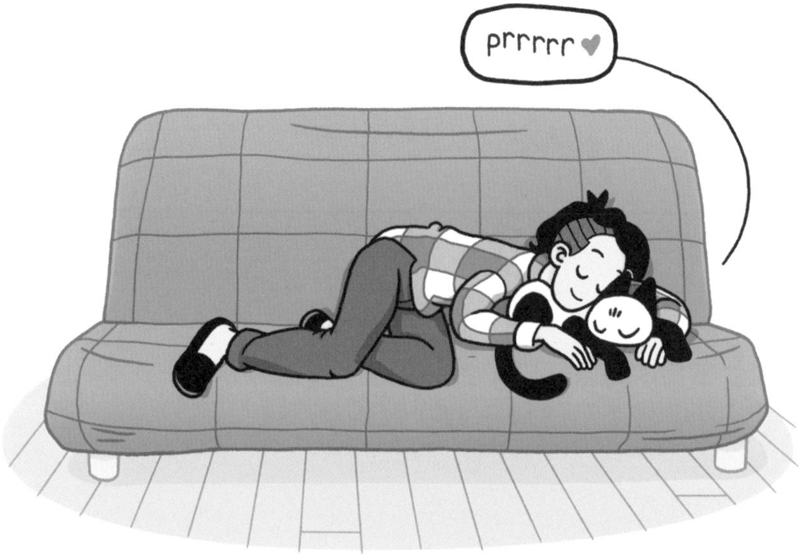
prrrrr ♥

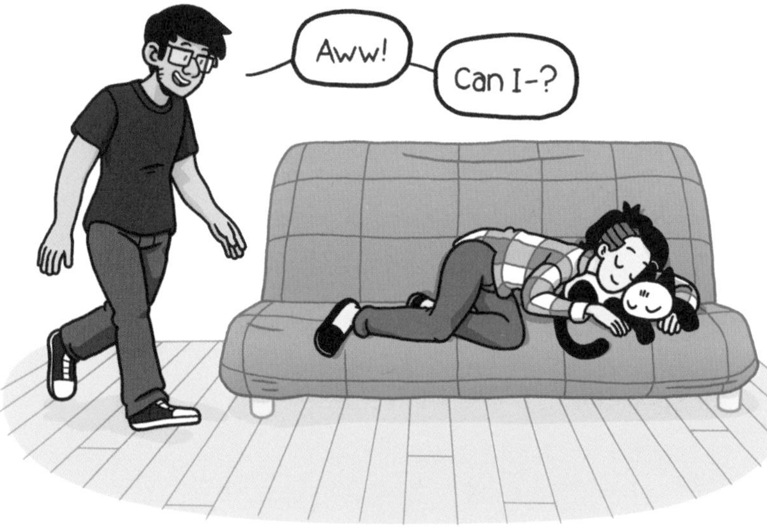
Aww!
Can I-?

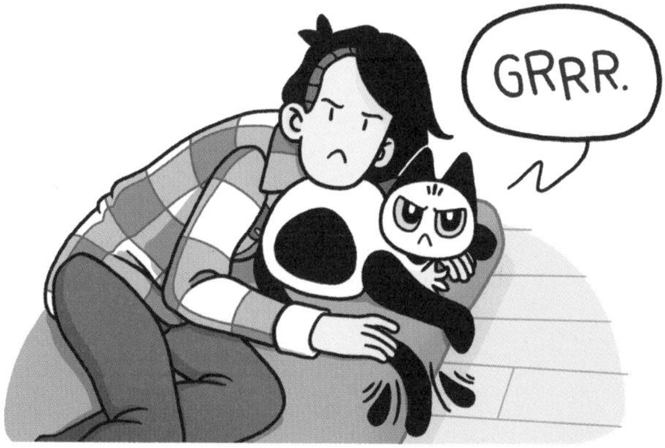
GRRR.

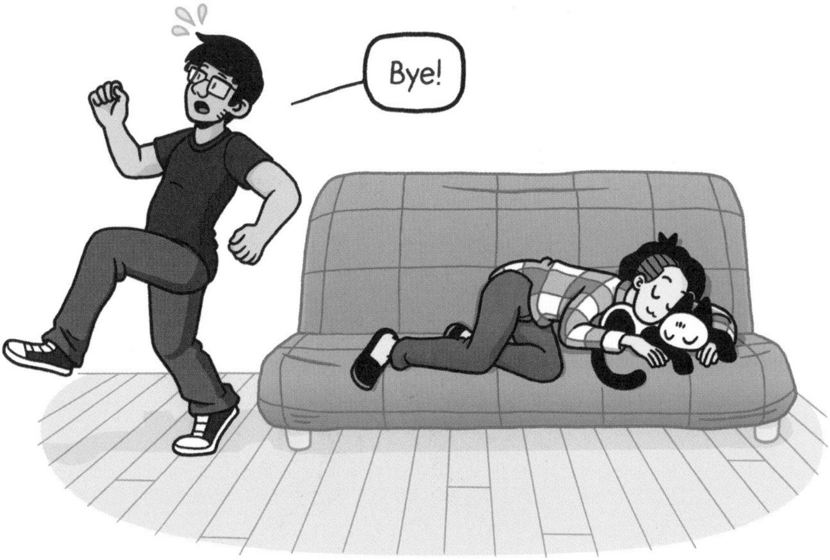
Bye!

"Cheeseburger"

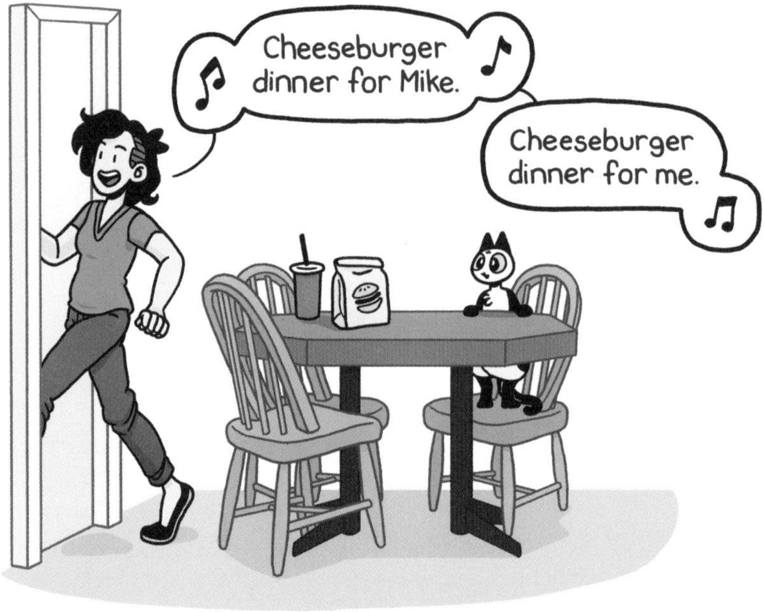

Cheeseburger dinner for Mike.
Cheeseburger dinner for me.

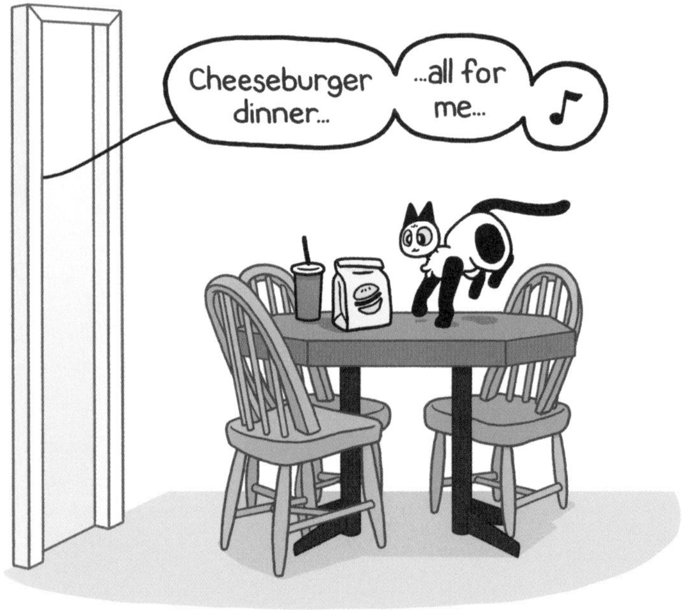

Cheeseburger dinner...
...all for me...

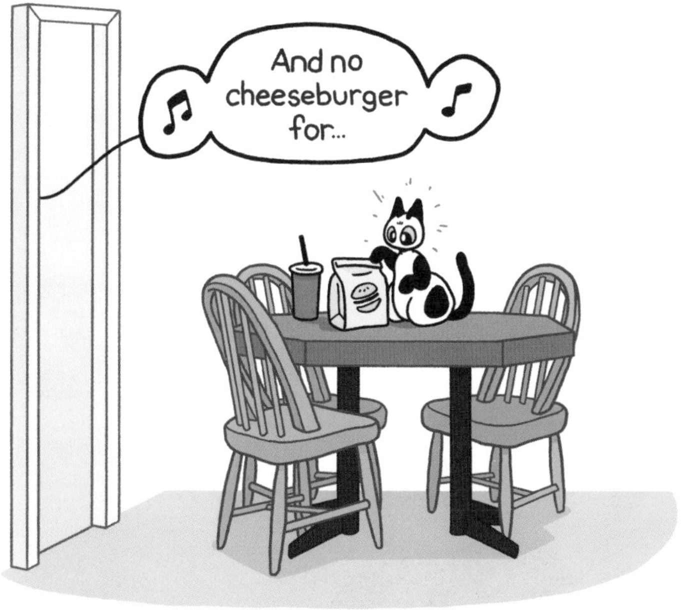
And no cheeseburger for...

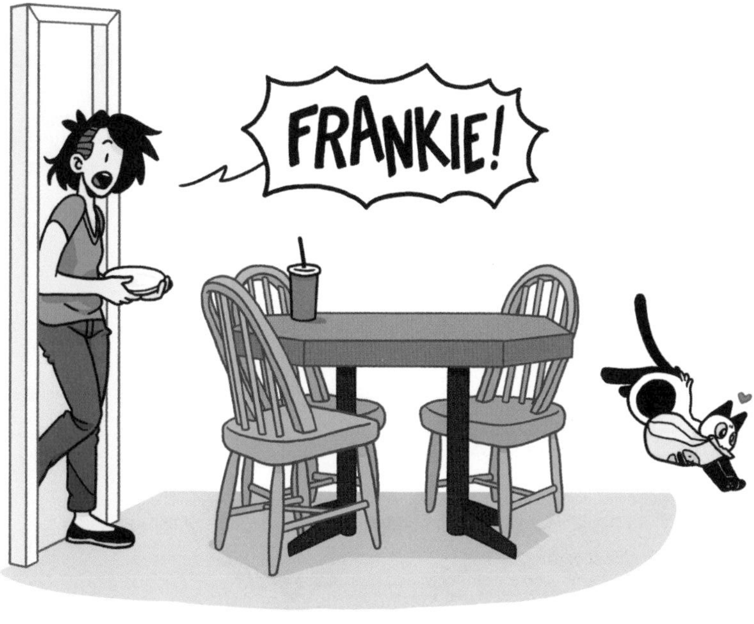
FRANKIE!

"Food Critic"

Food Frankie Likes:

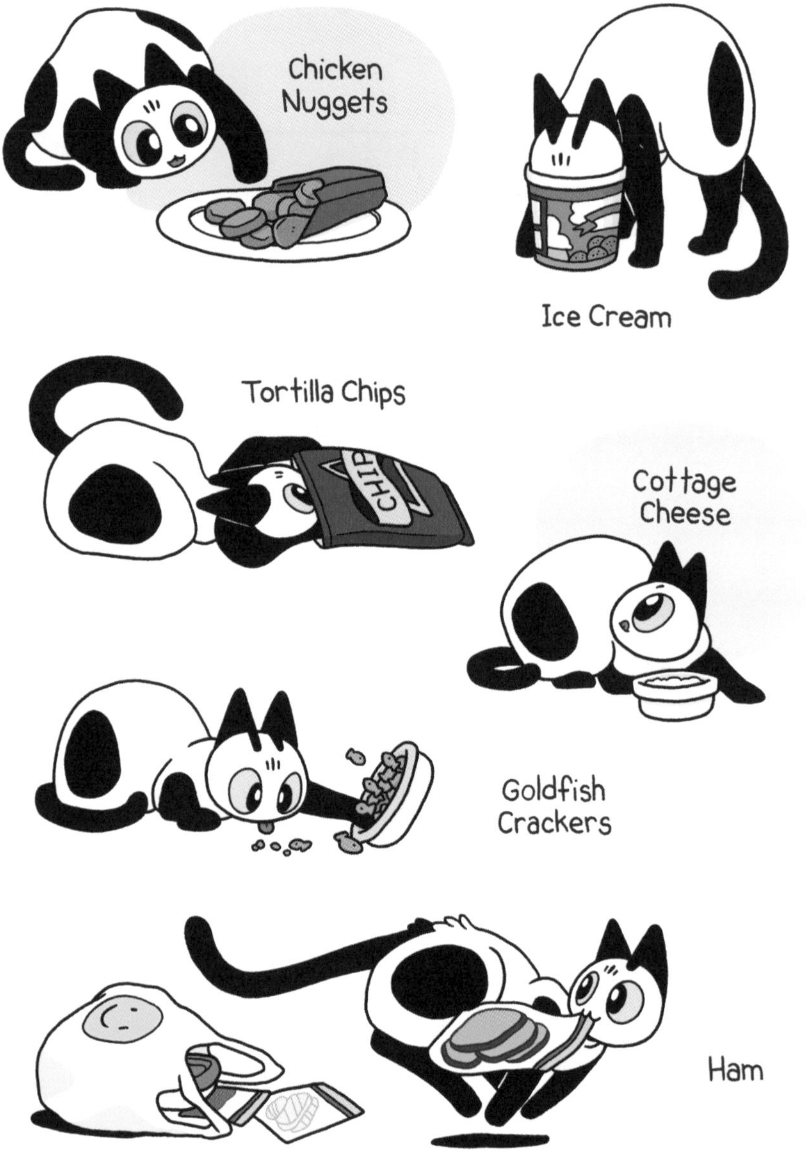
Chicken Nuggets
Ice Cream
Tortilla Chips
CHIPS
Cottage Cheese
Goldfish Crackers
Ham

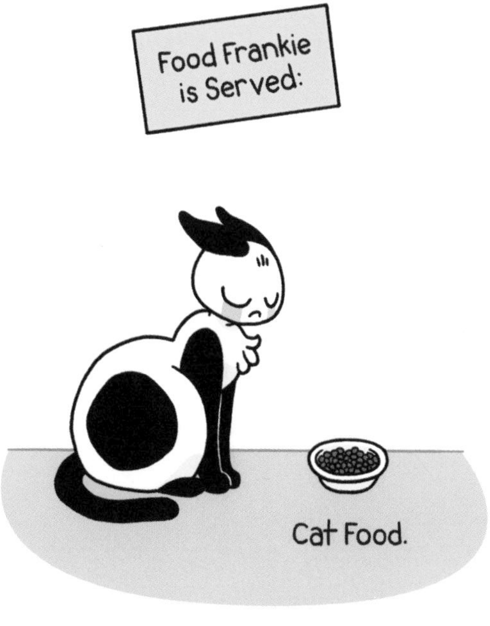
Food Frankie
is Served:
Cat Food.

"Kitty Food"

No, Frankie... Pasta is not for kitties.

Go eat your food.

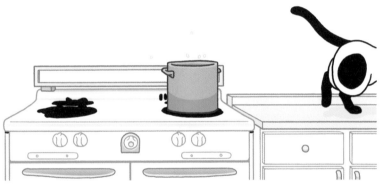

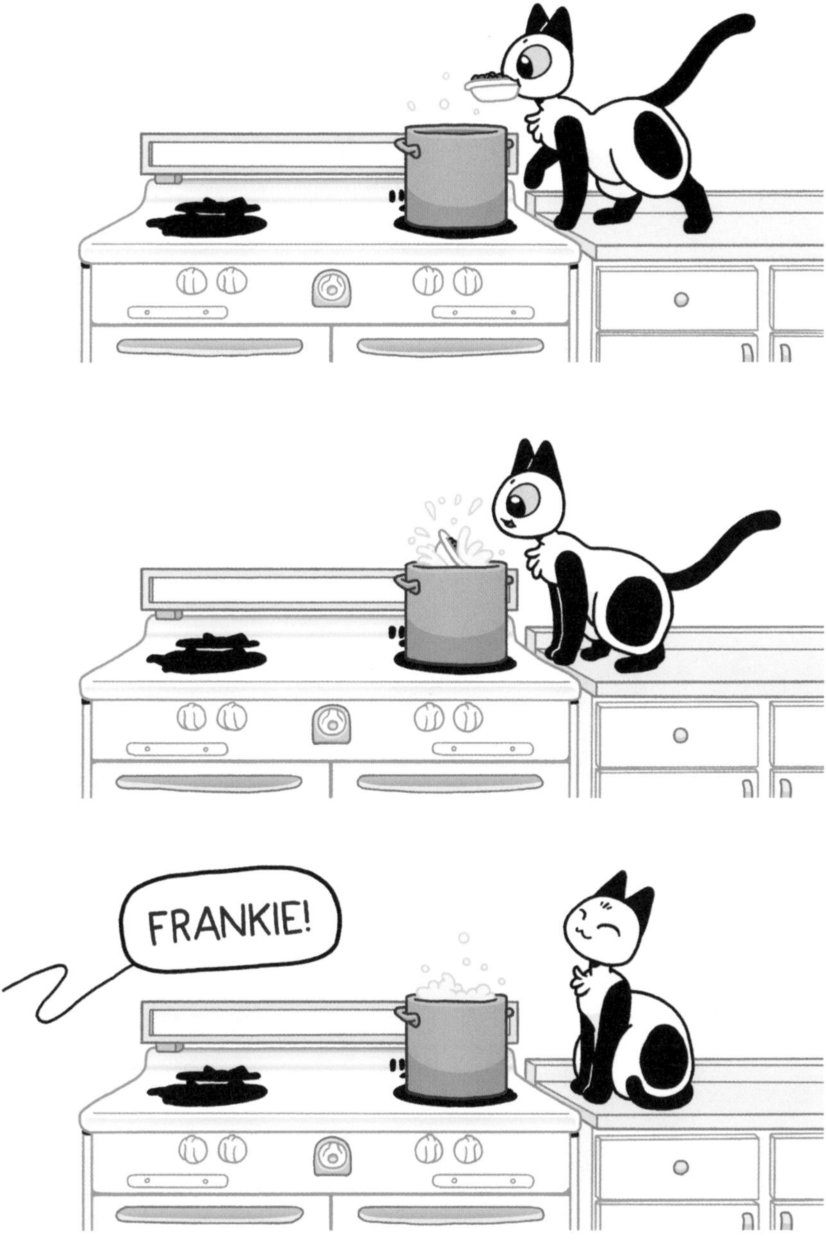
FRANKIE!

"Pizza Saver"

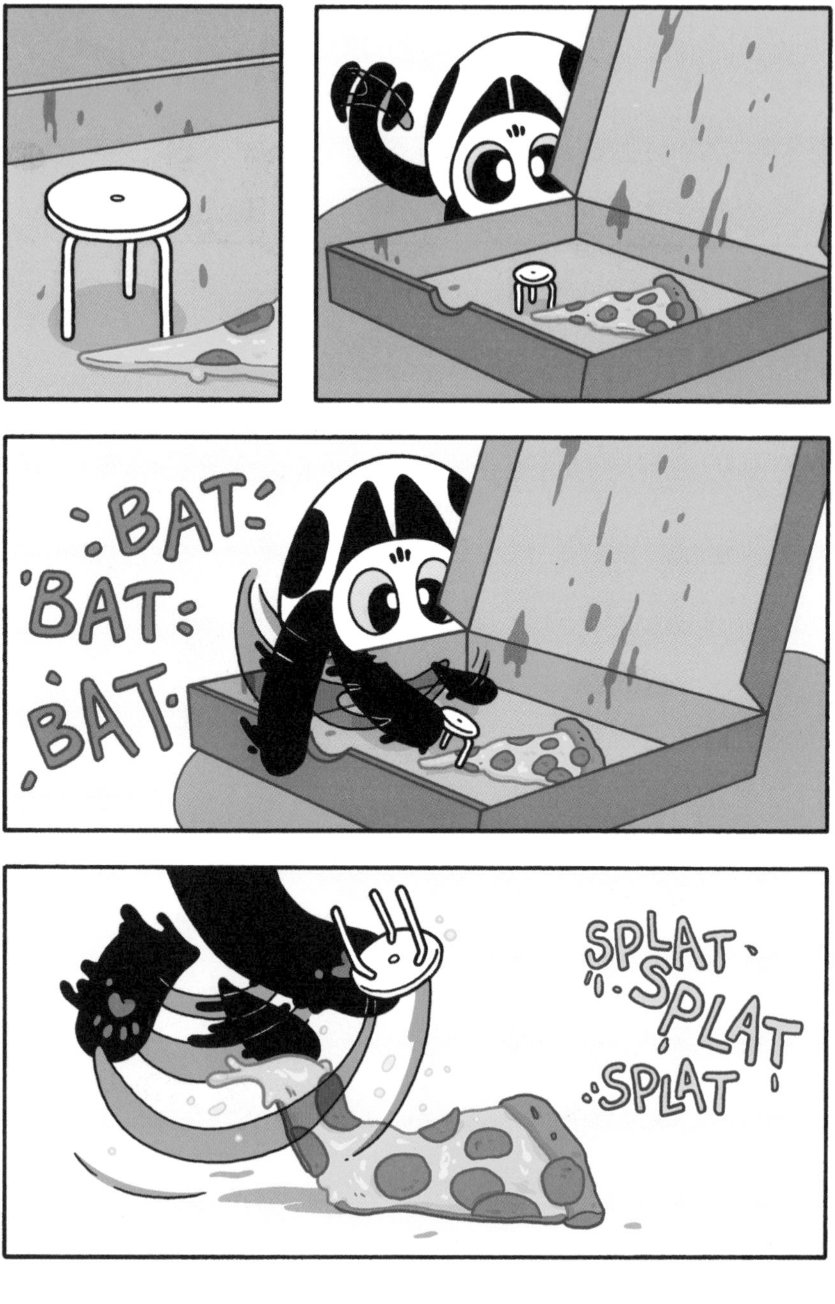
BAT
BAT
BAT
SPLAT
SPLAT
SPLAT

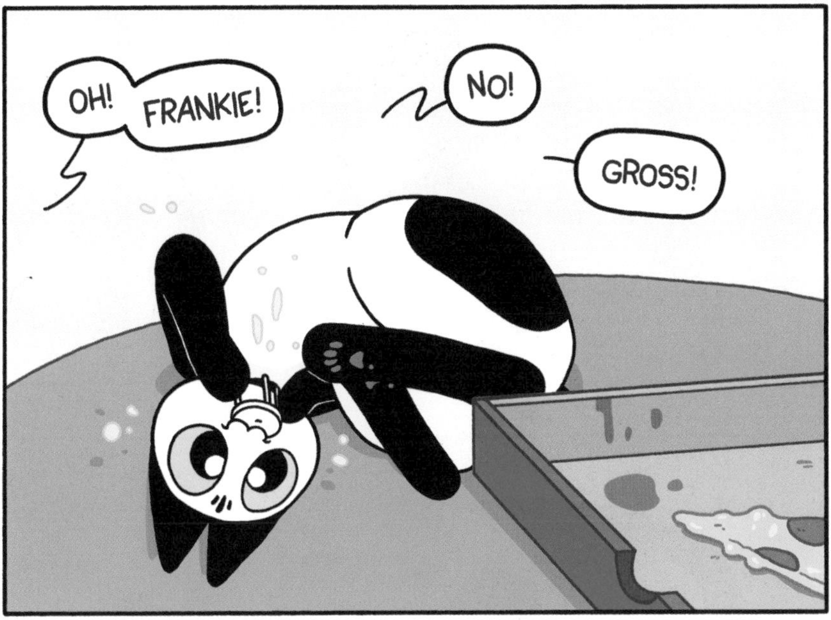
OH! FRANKIE!
NO!
GROSS!

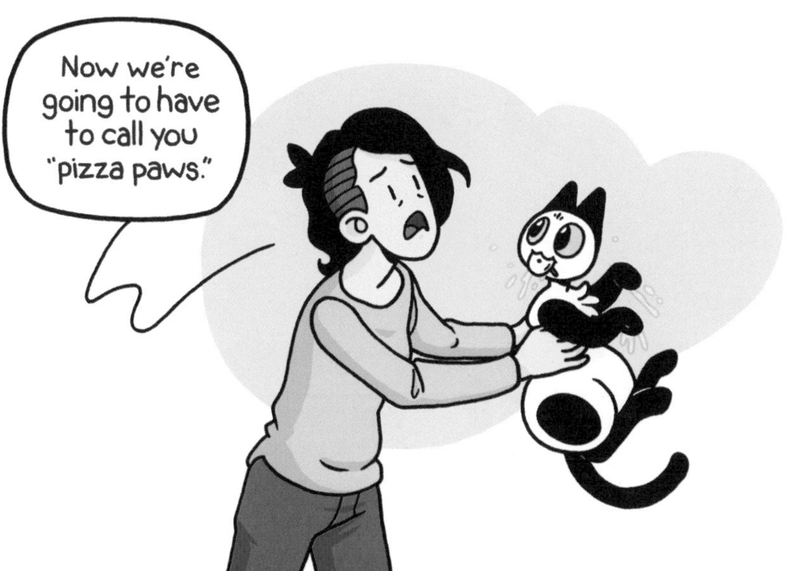
Now we're going to have to call you "pizza paws."

"Hypothetical"

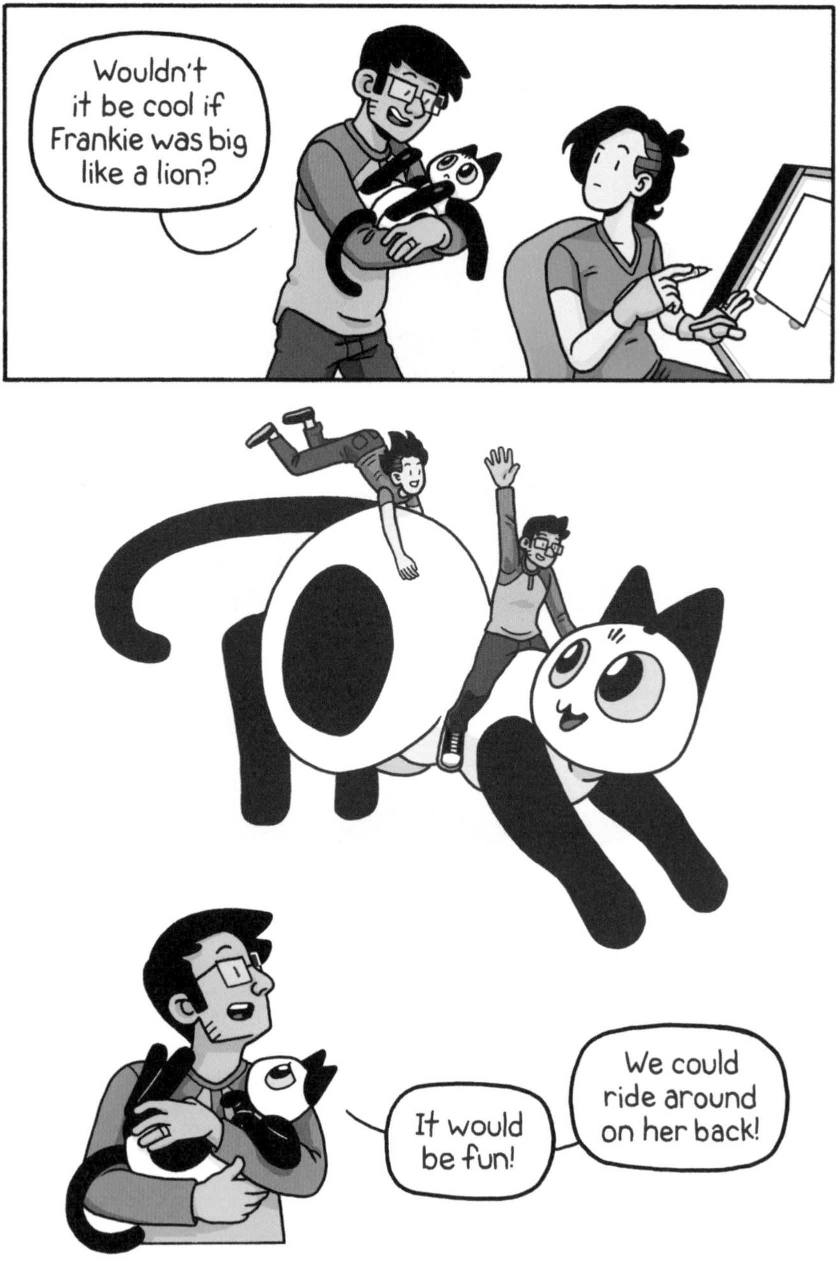
Wouldn't it be cool if Frankie was big like a lion?
It would be fun!
We could ride around on her back!

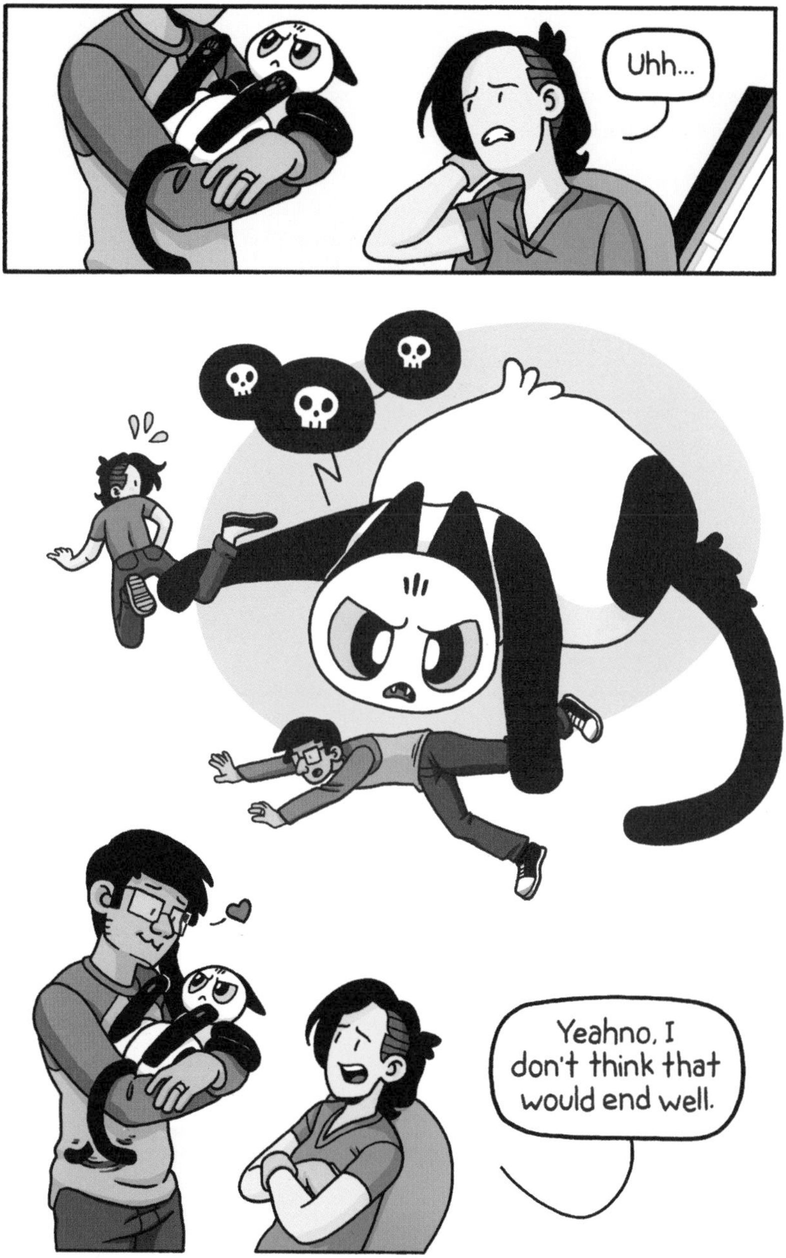
Uhh...
Yeahno, I don't think that would end well.

"Cat Versus Human"

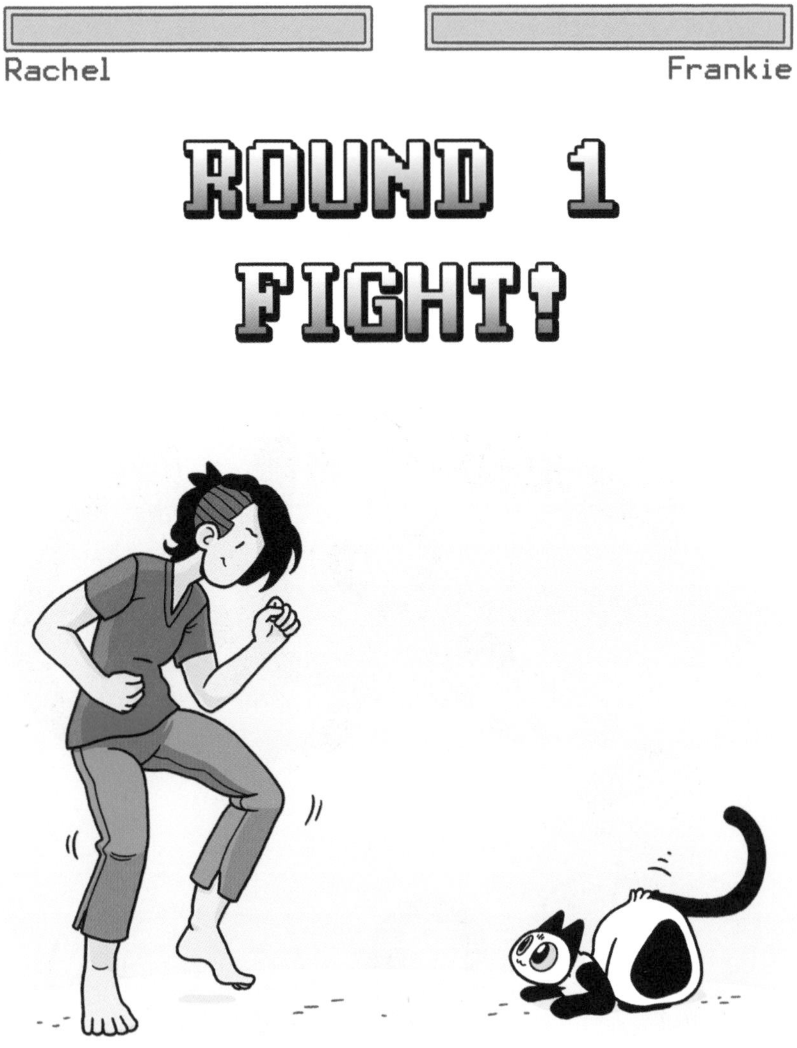
Rachel
Frankie
ROUND 1
FIGHT!

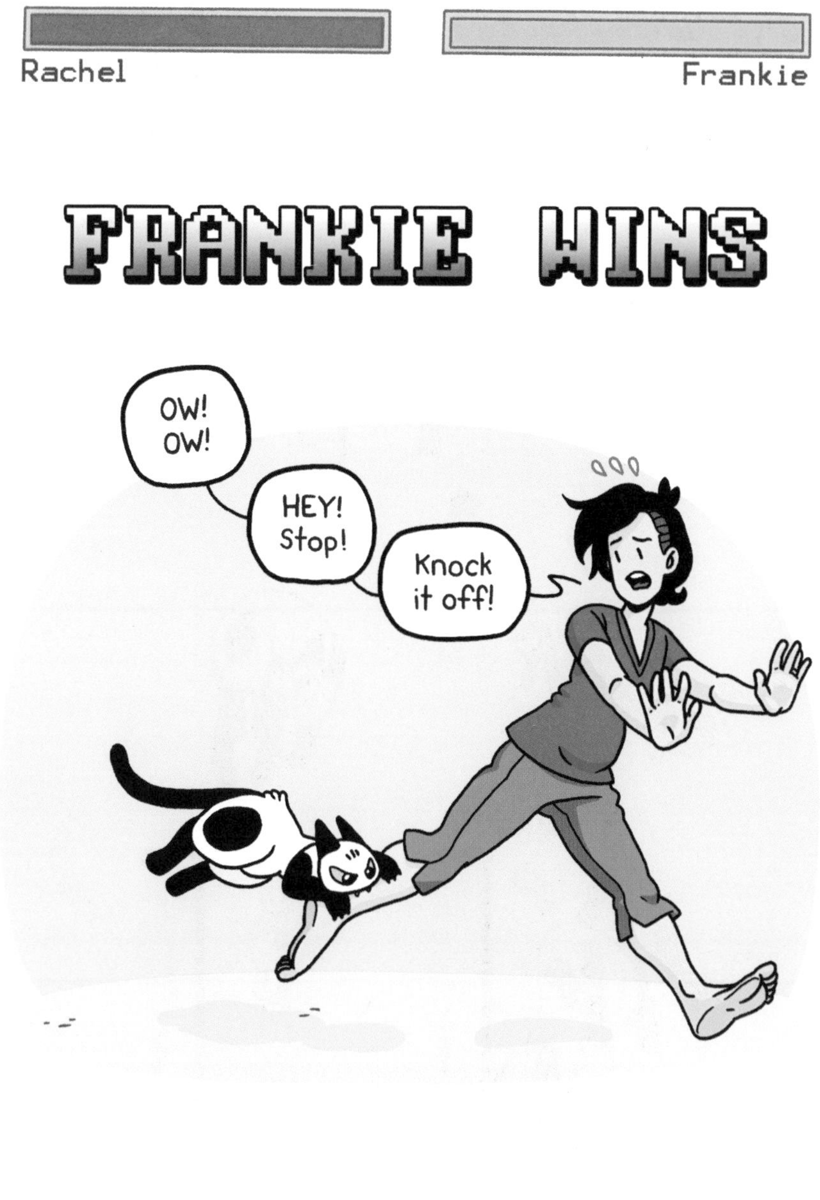
Rachel
Frankie
FRANKIE WINS
OW! OW!
HEY! Stop!
Knock it off!

"Flying Frankie"

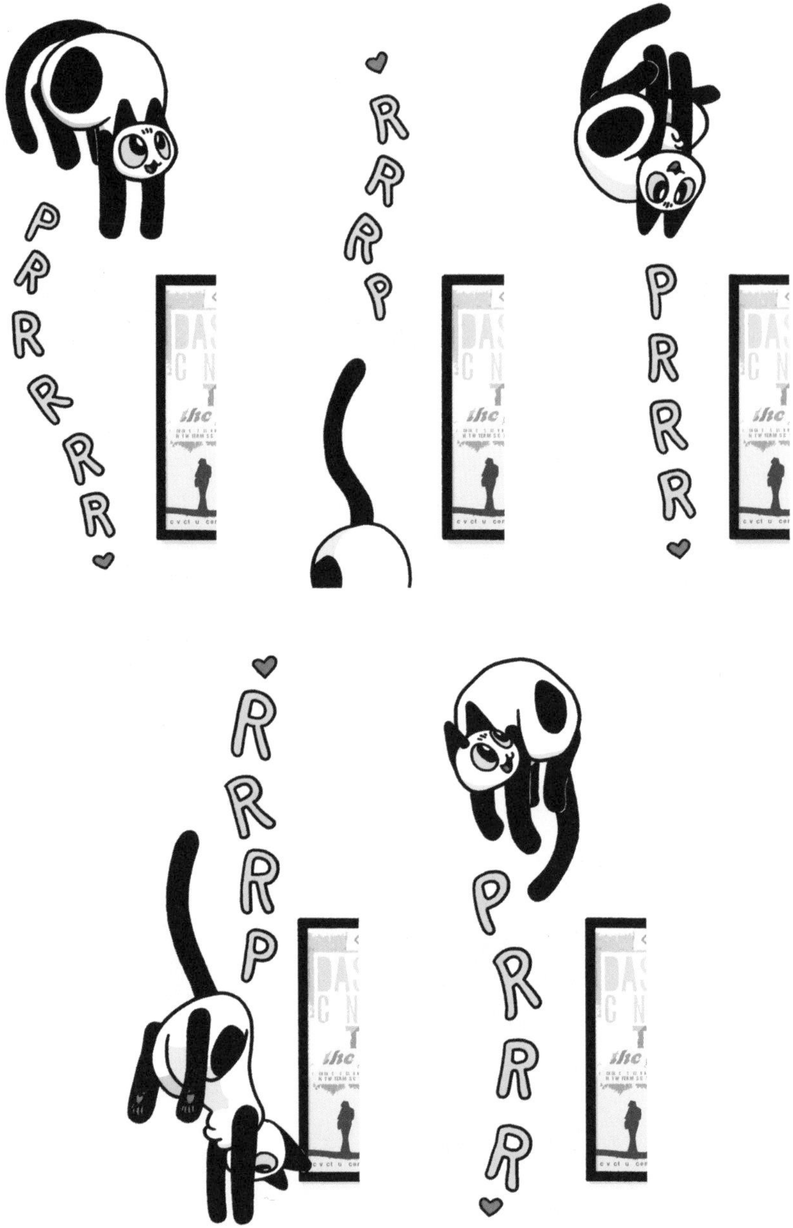
PRRRRR
RRRP
PRRRR
RRRP
PRRRR

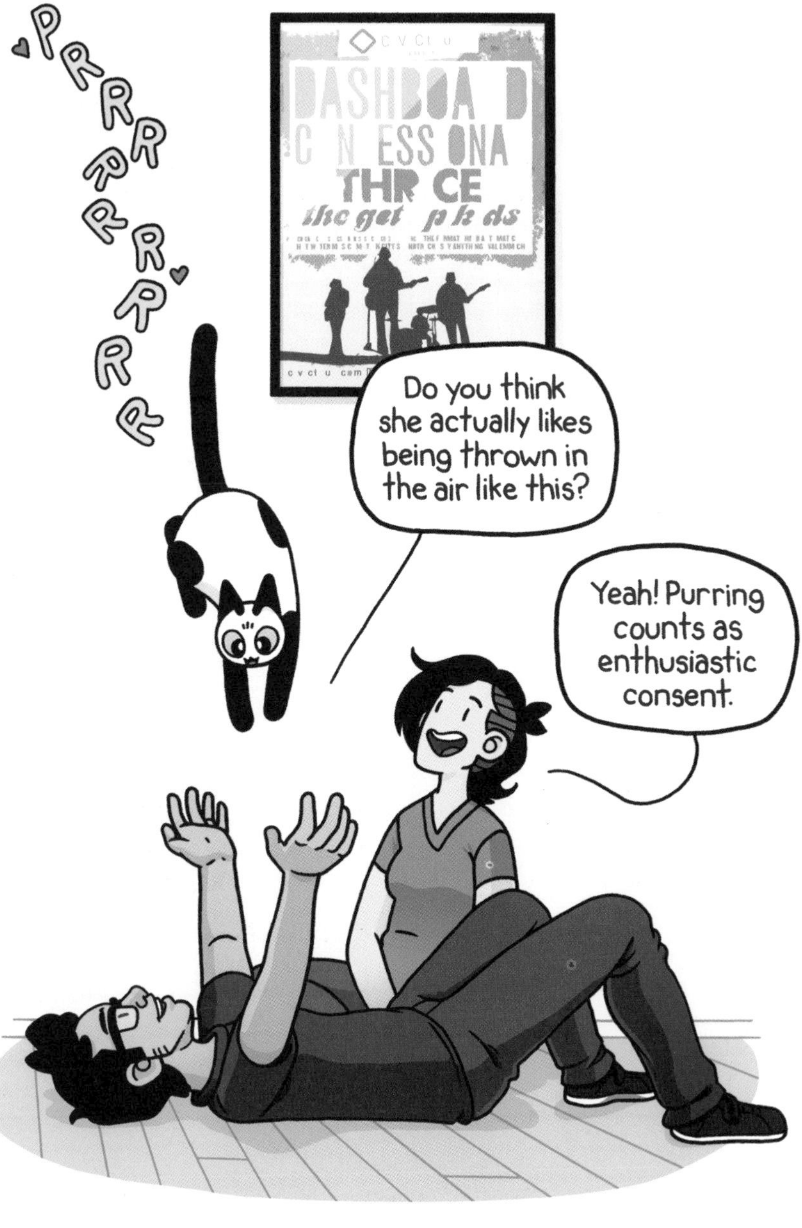
PRRRRRRRRR
Do you think she actually likes being thrown in the air like this?
Yeah! Purring counts as enthusiastic consent.

"Life With / Out A Cat"

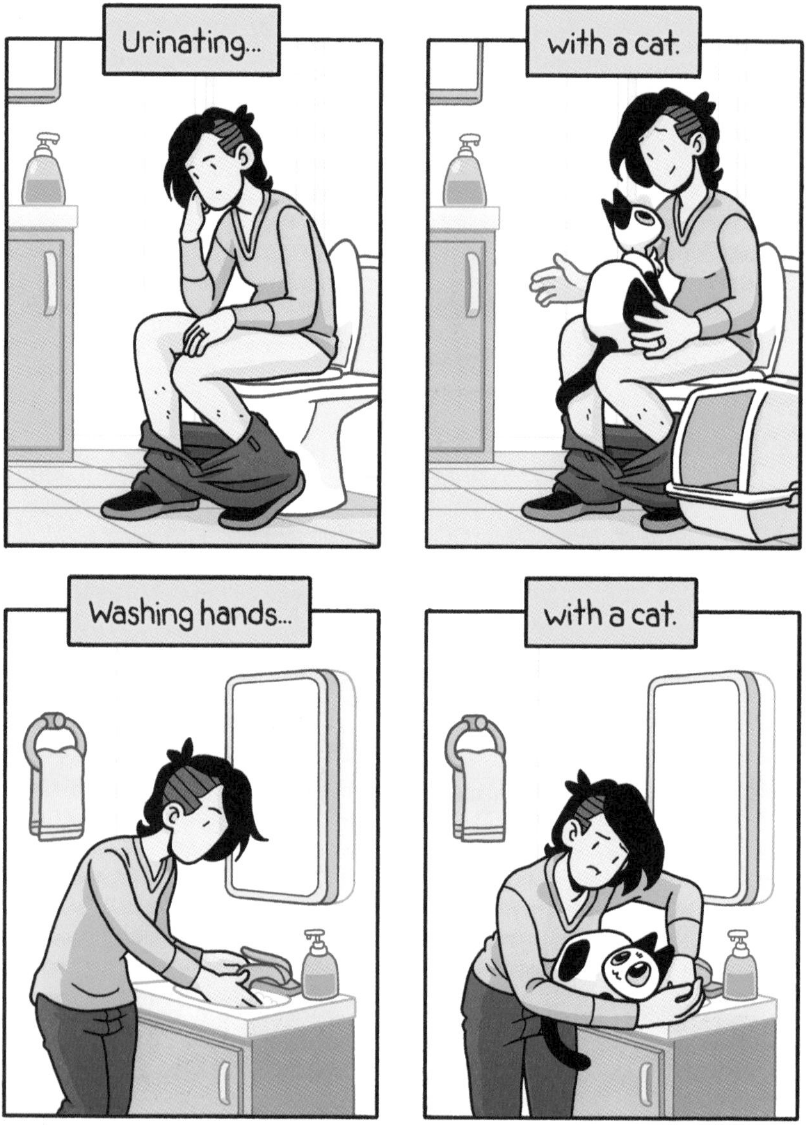
Urinating...
with a cat.
Washing hands...
with a cat.

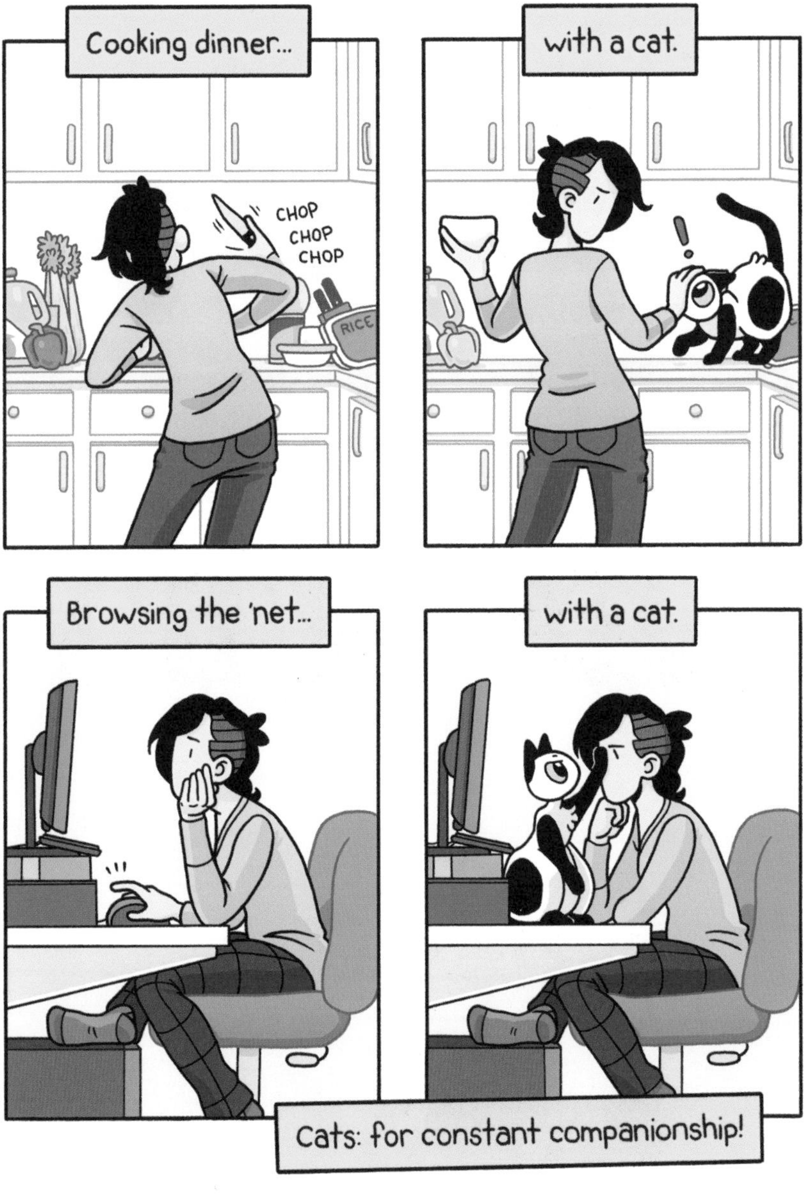
Cooking dinner...
CHOP
CHOP
CHOP
RICE
with a cat.
!
Browsing the 'net...
with a cat.
Cats: for constant companionship!

"Alternate Uses For Your Cat"

Scarf: versatile!

Pillow: fluffy!

Foot warmer: warm!

Vacuum: convenient!

Squeegee:
maybe not!

"Wake Up Call"

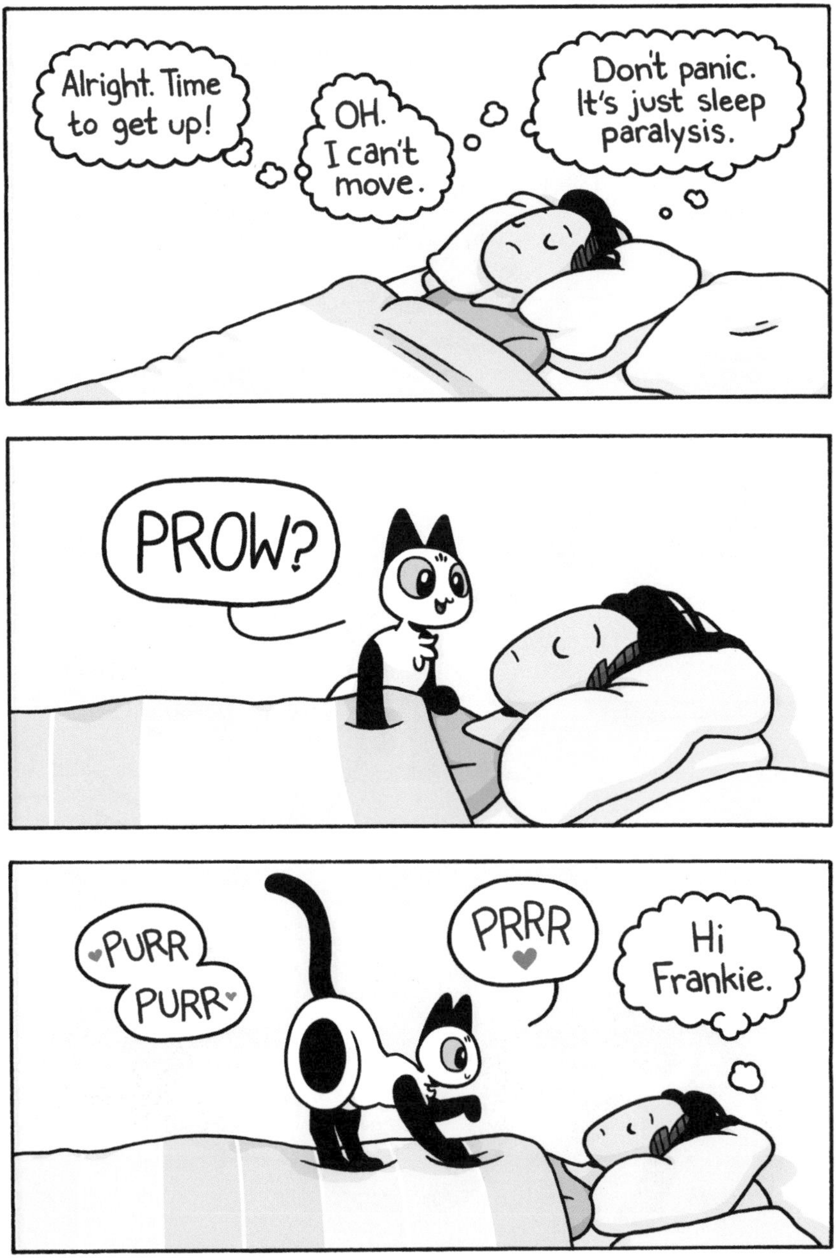
Alright. Time to get up!
OH. I can't move.
Don't panic. It's just sleep paralysis.
PROW?
PURR PURR
PRRR
Hi Frankie.

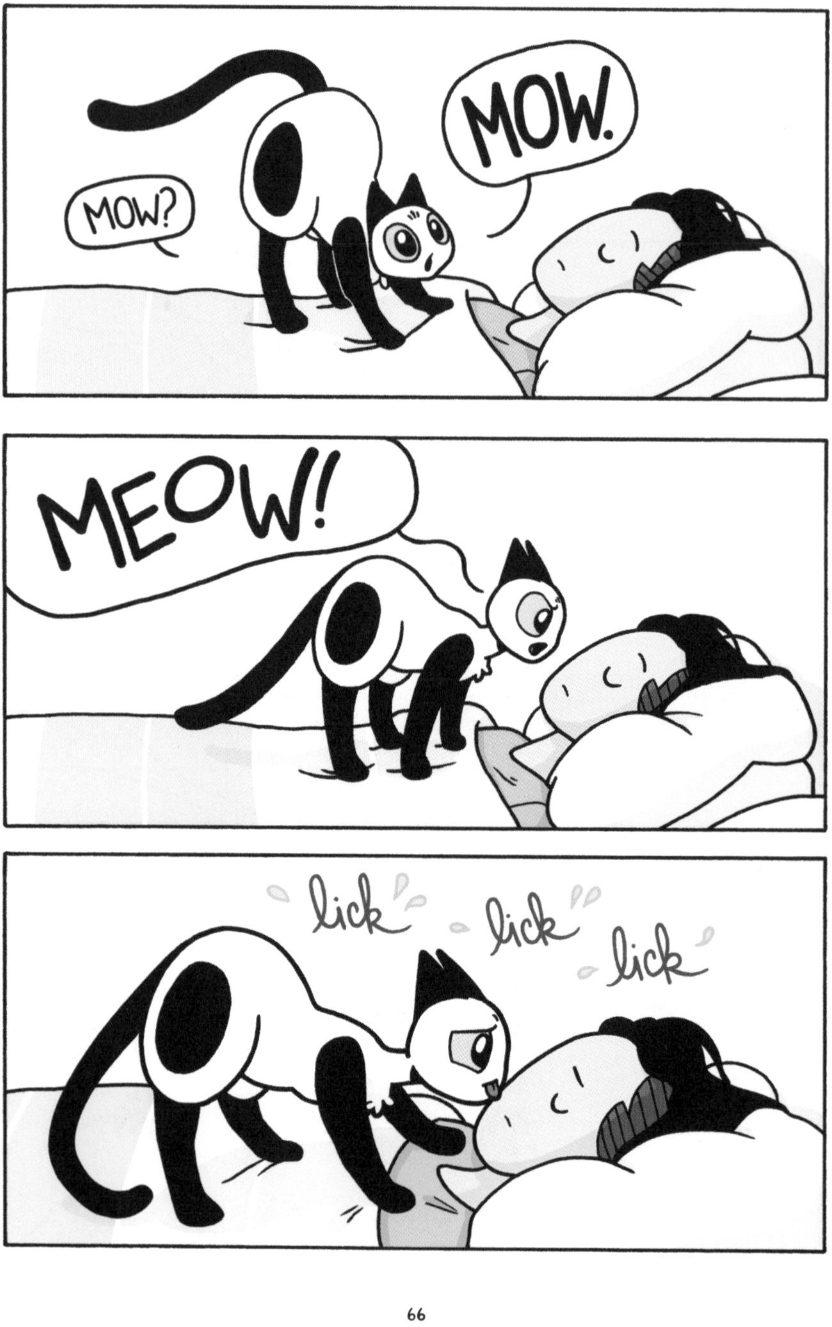
MOW?
MOW.
MEOW!
lick lick lick

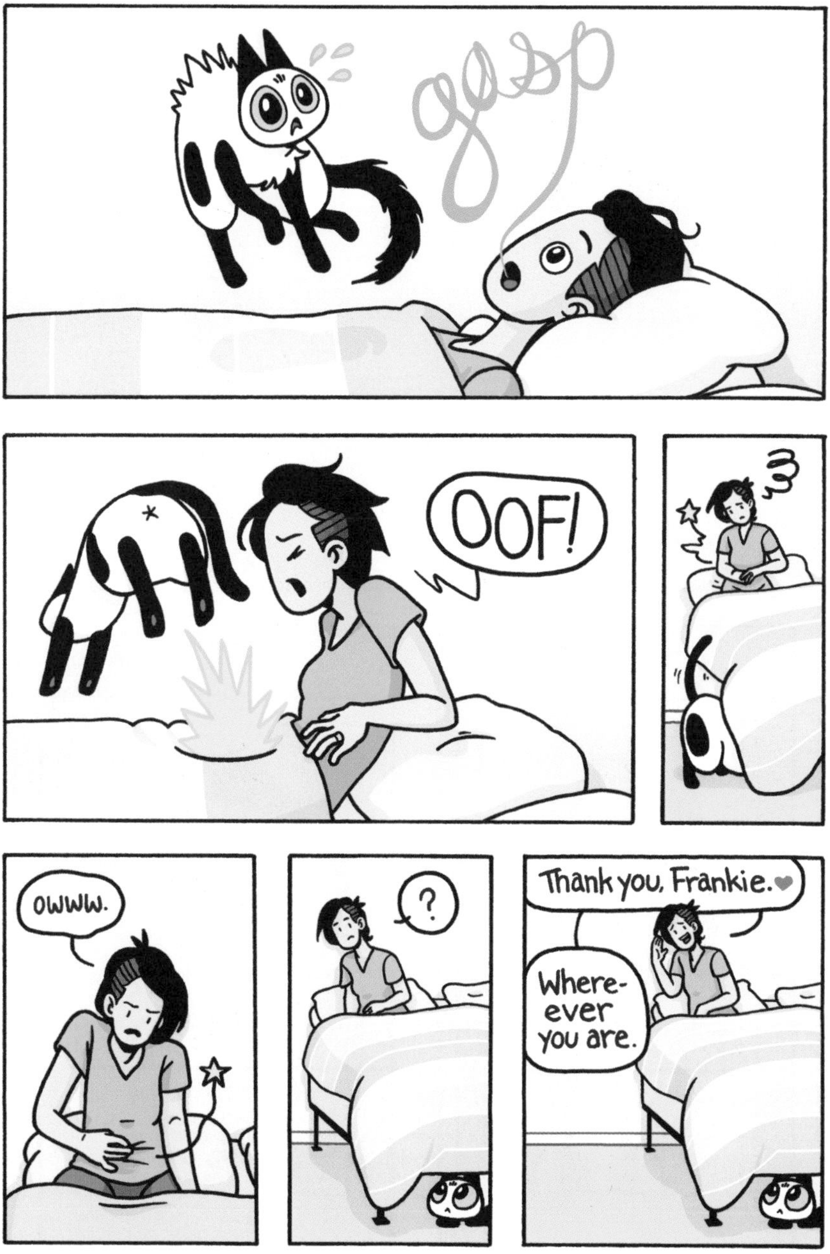
gasp
OOF!
OWWW.
?
Thank you, Frankie.
Where-ever you are.

"Cloud-watching"

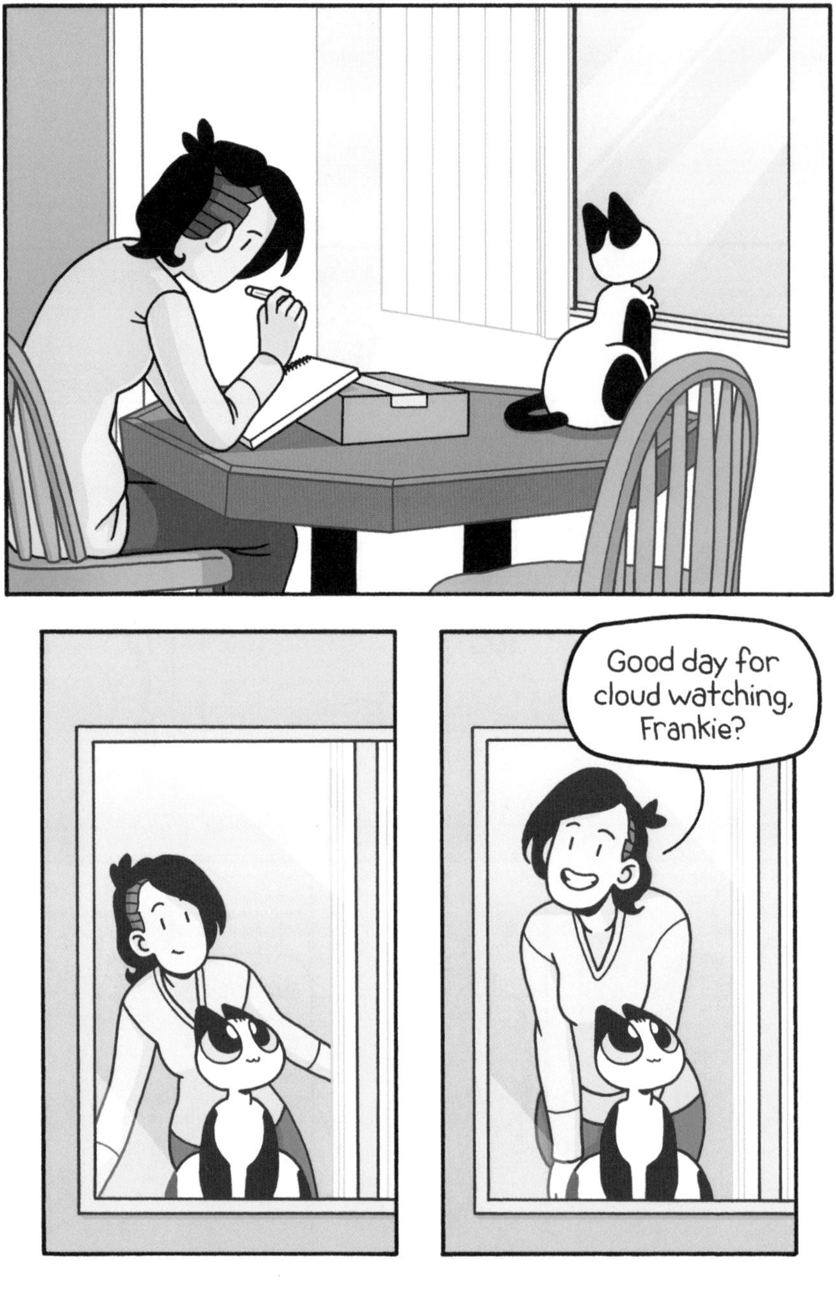
Good day for cloud watching, Frankie?

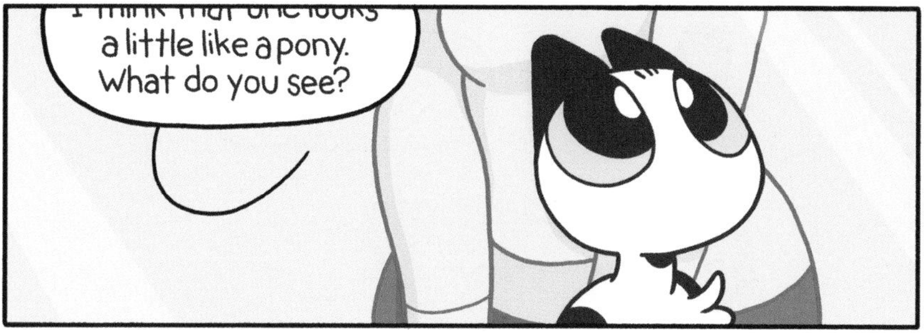
a little like a pony. What do you see?

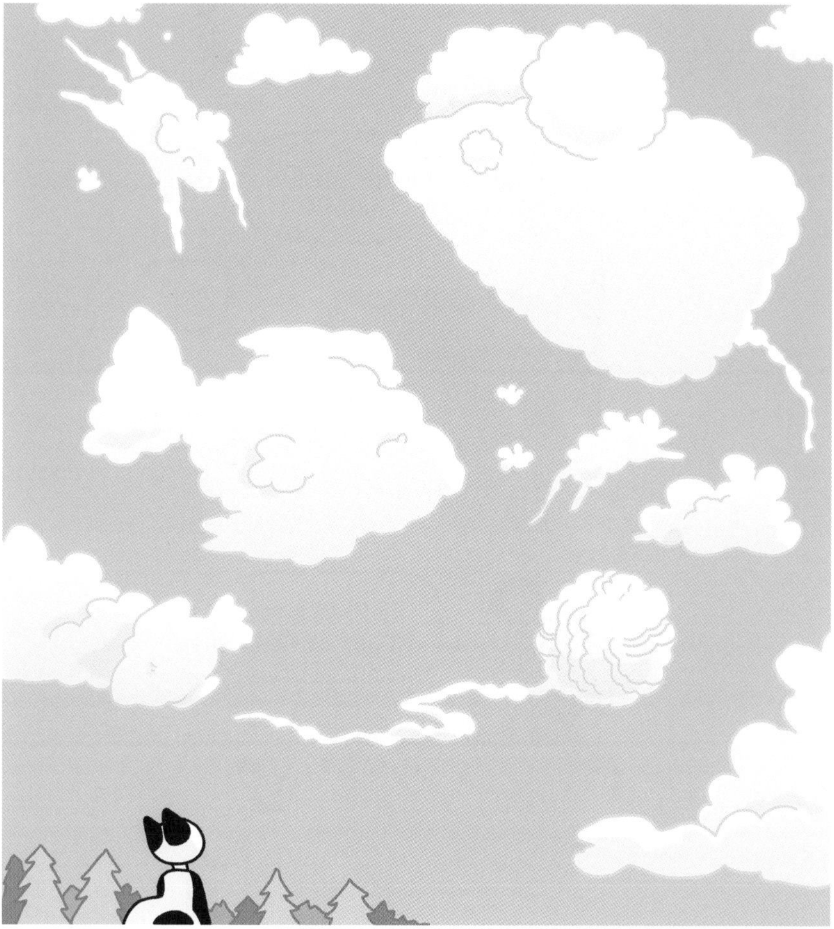

"The Box"

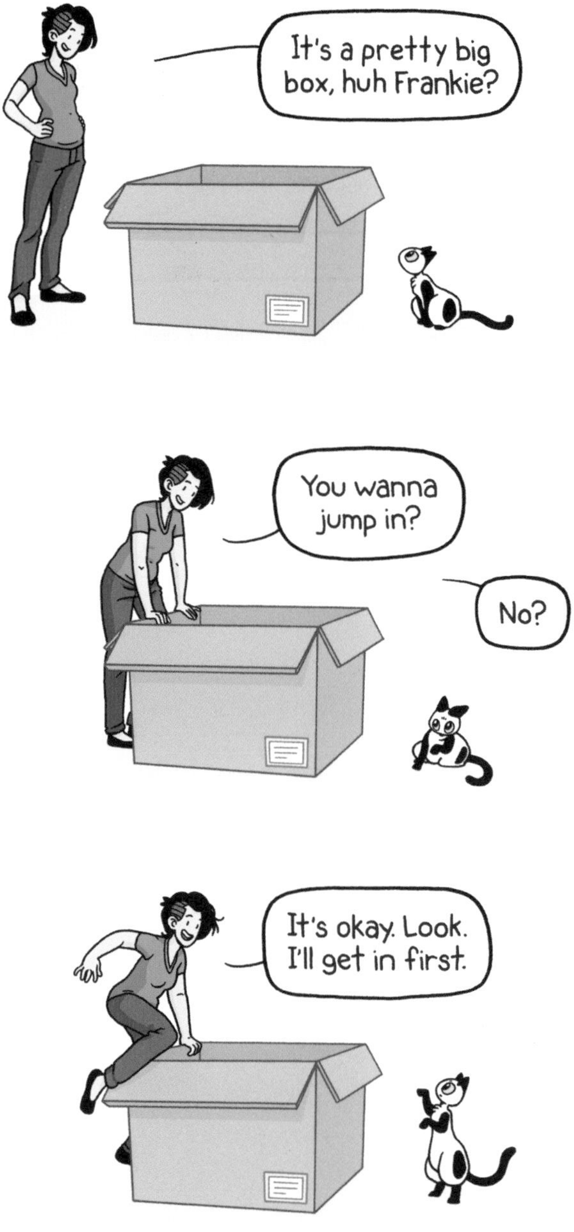

It's a pretty big box, huh Frankie?
You wanna jump in?
No?
It's okay. Look. I'll get in first.

See?
Frankie?
This is awesome.

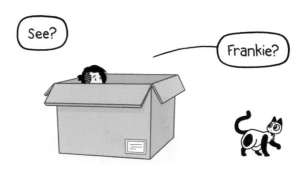

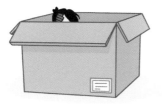

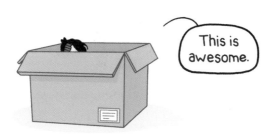

"All By Herself"

KICK KICK KICK
KICK KICK KICK KICK

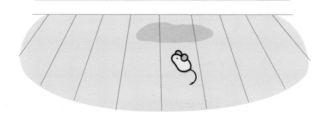

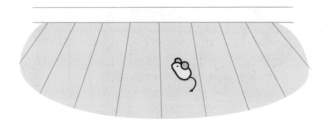

"Feline Follies"

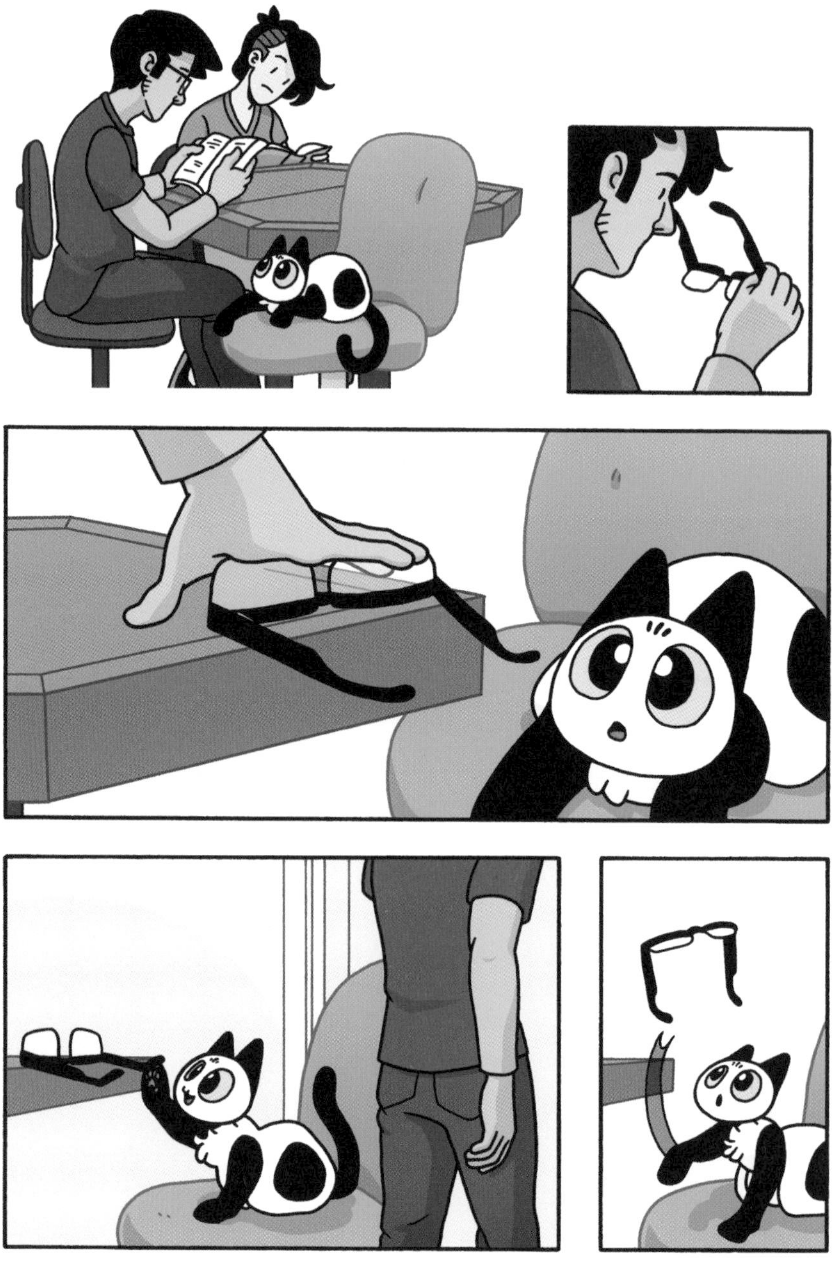

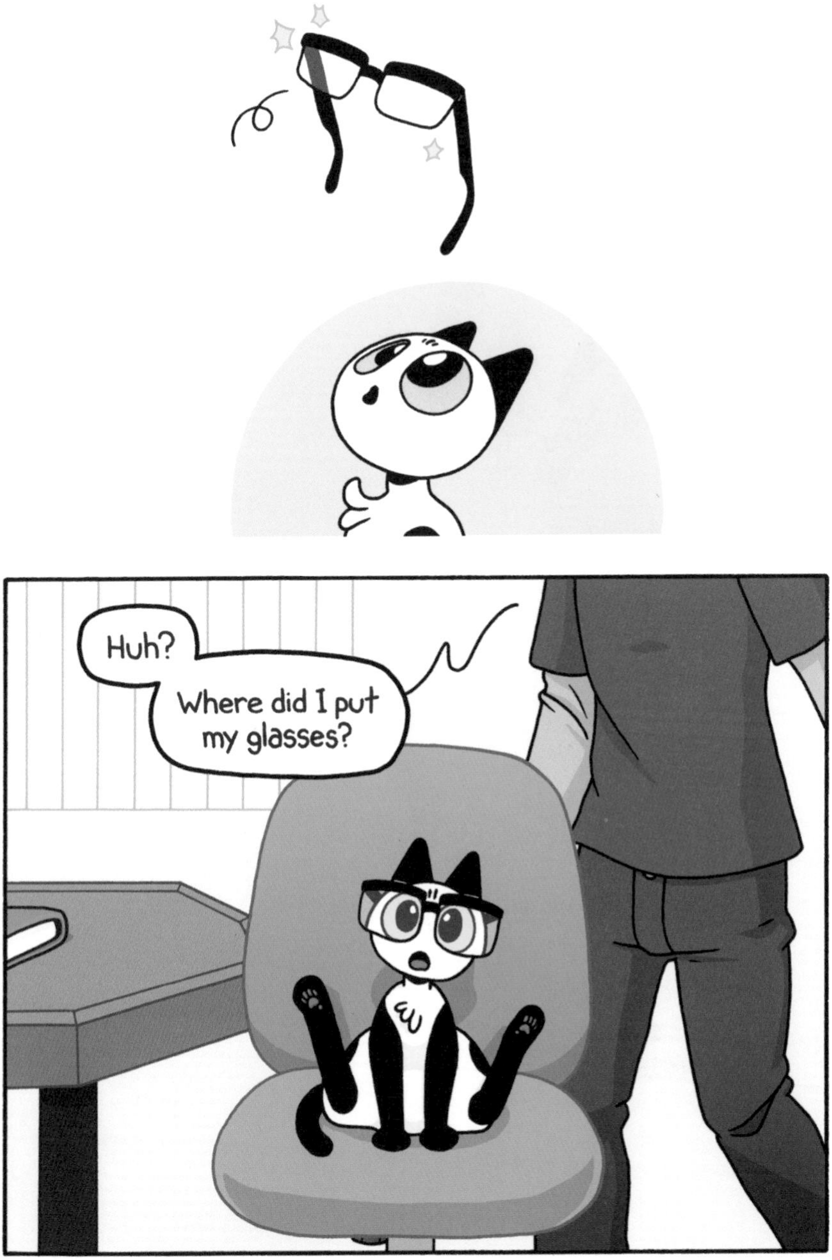
Huh?
Where did I put my glasses?

"Cat and Mouse"

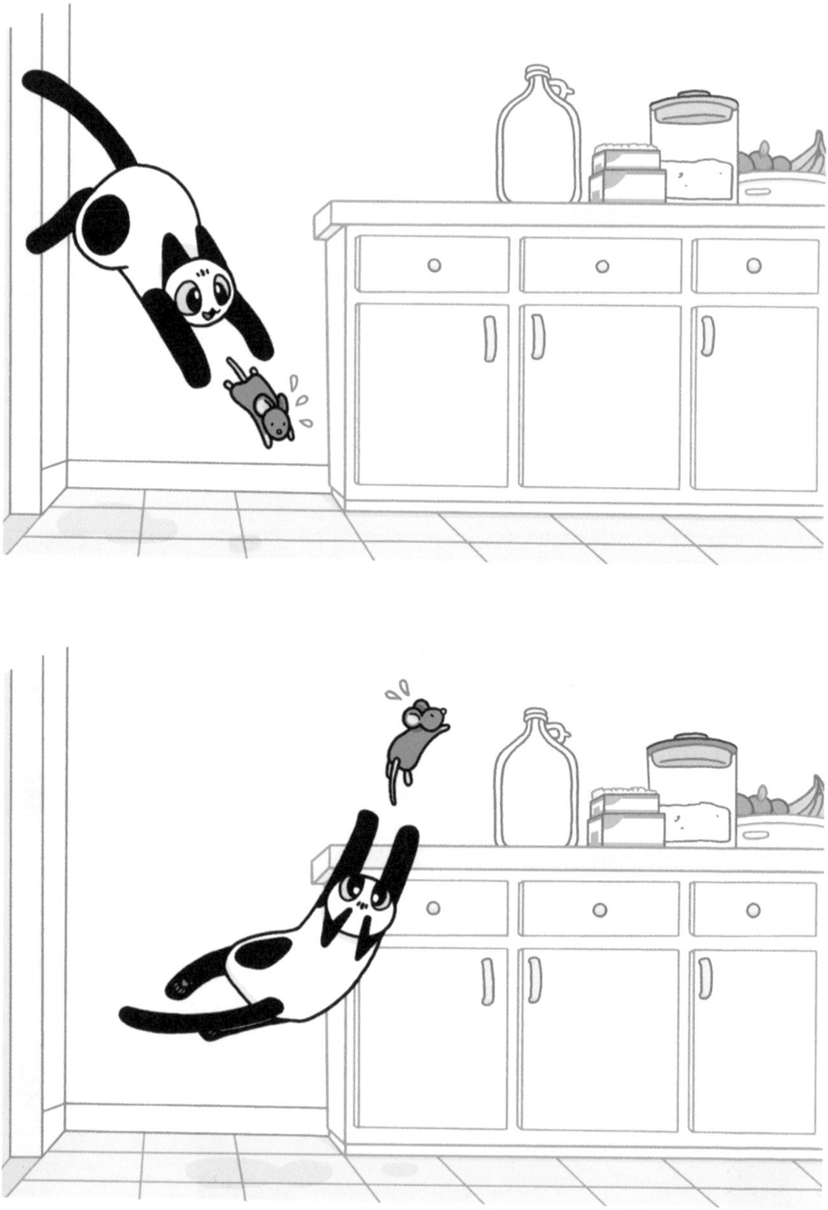

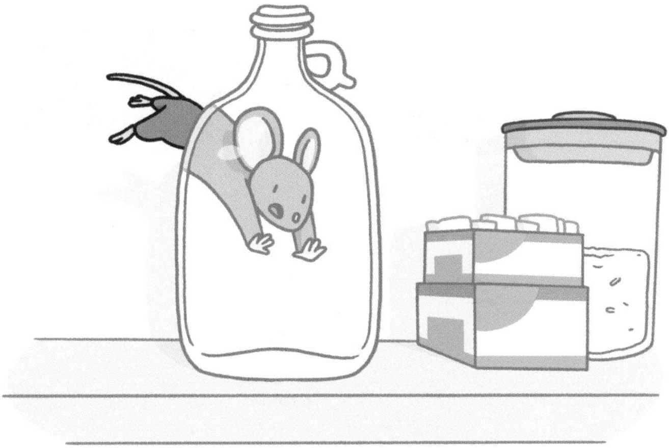

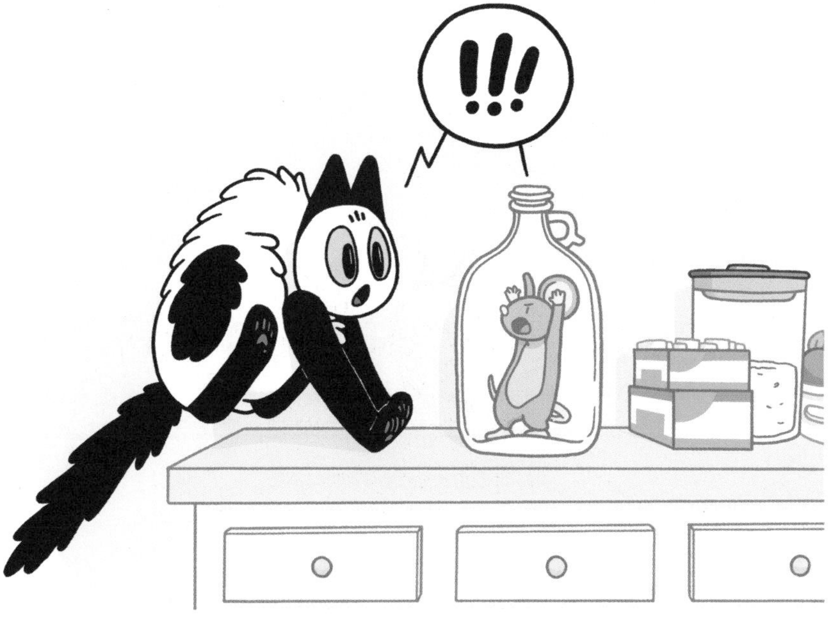
!!!

"Naptime"

Too hard.

Too soft.

Just right!

"Marco Polo"

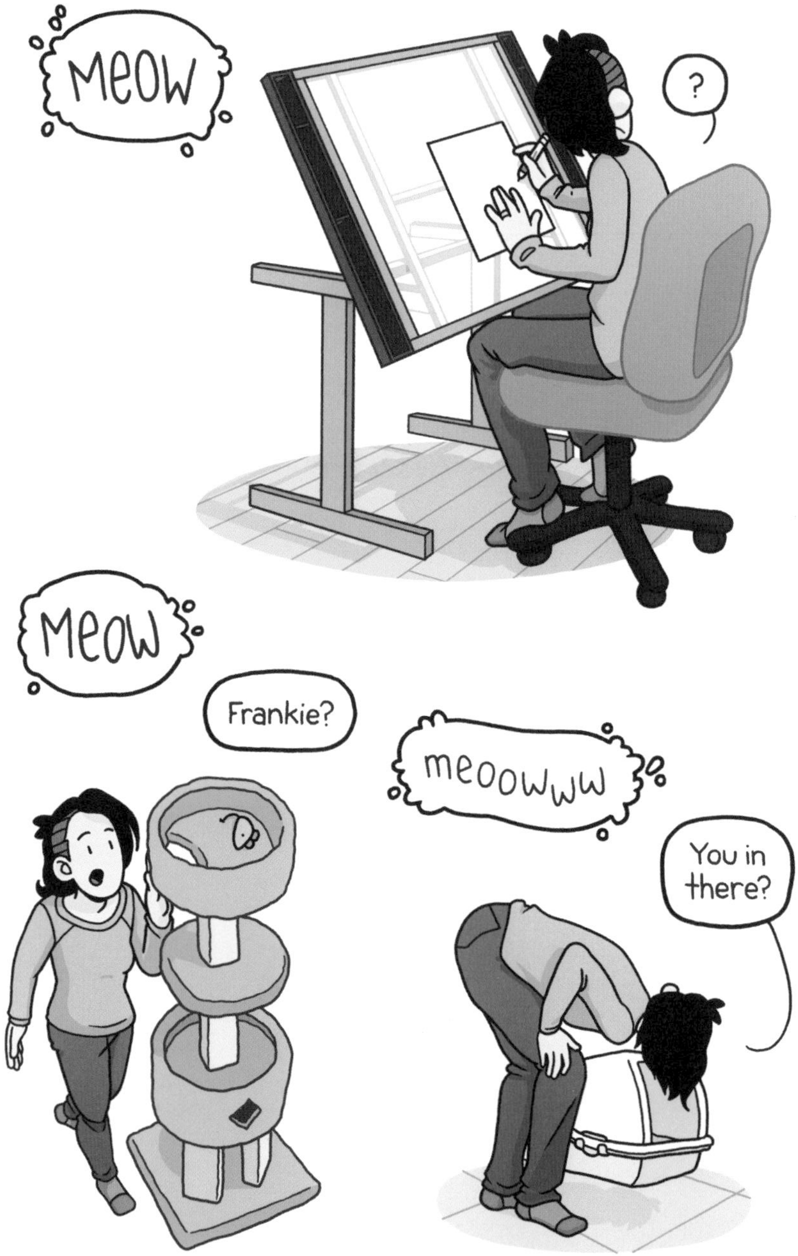
MEOW
?
MEOW
Frankie?
meoowwww
You in there?

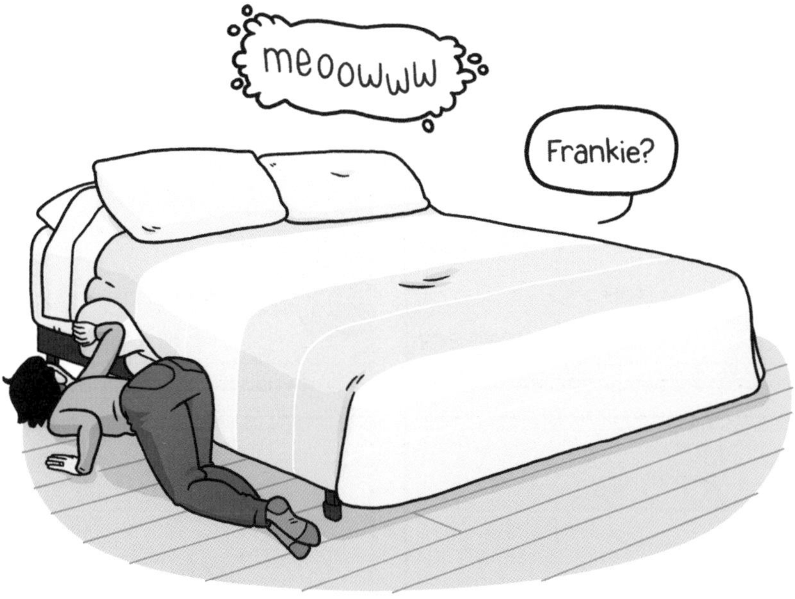
meoowww
Frankie?

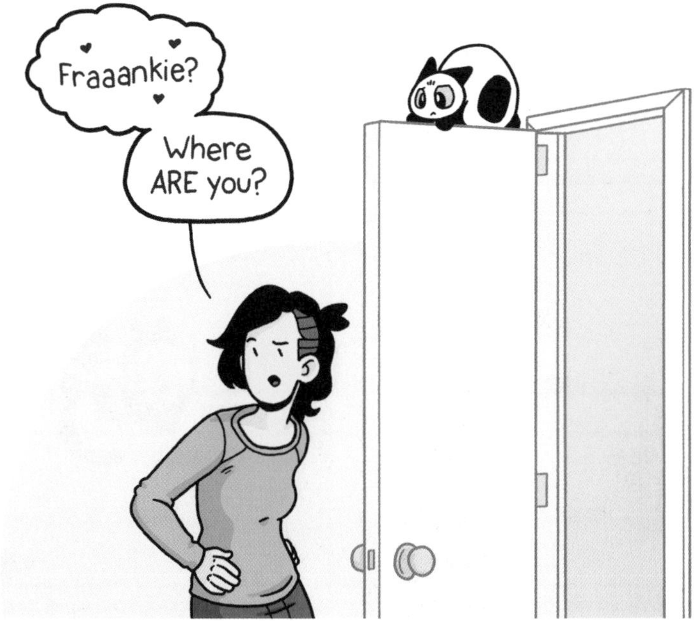
Fraaankie?
Where ARE you?

"Winter Warmth"

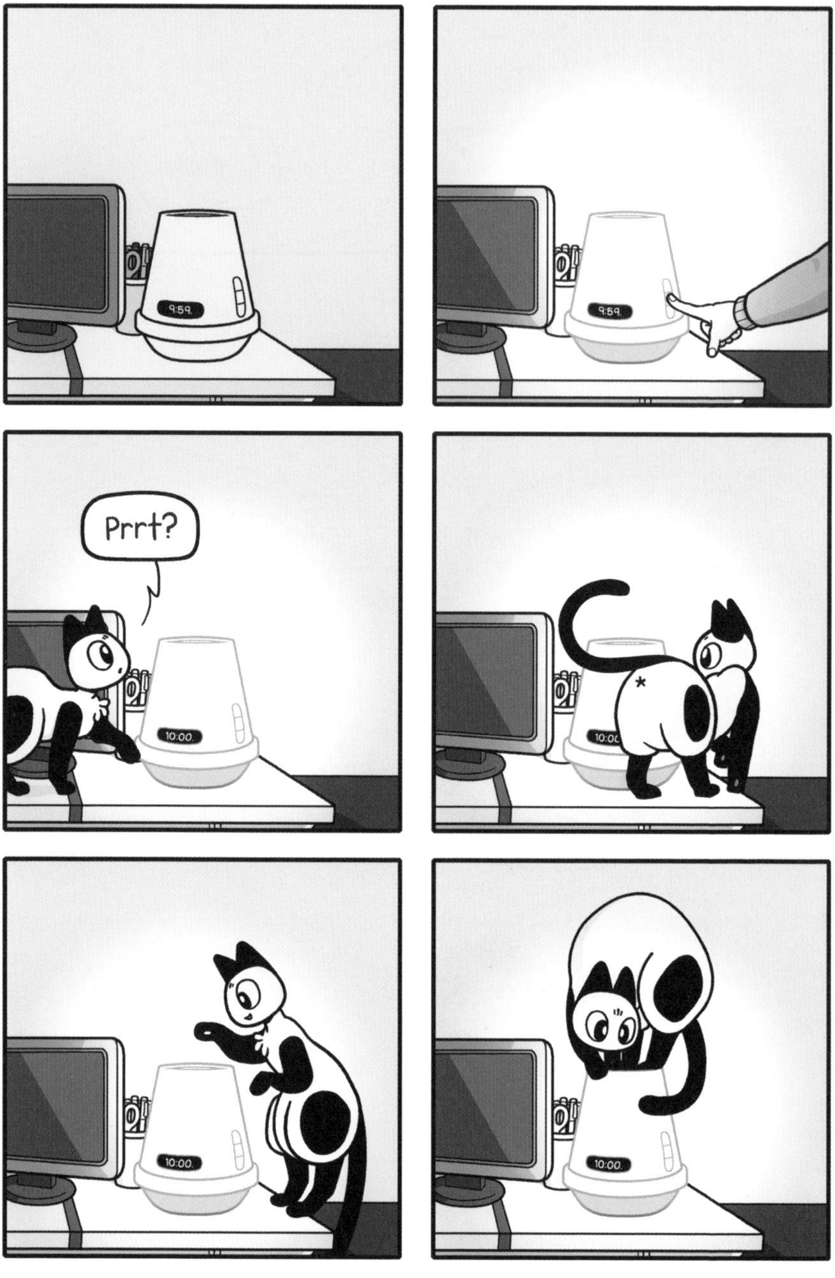
9:59.
9:59.
Prrt?
10:00.
*
10:00.
10:00.

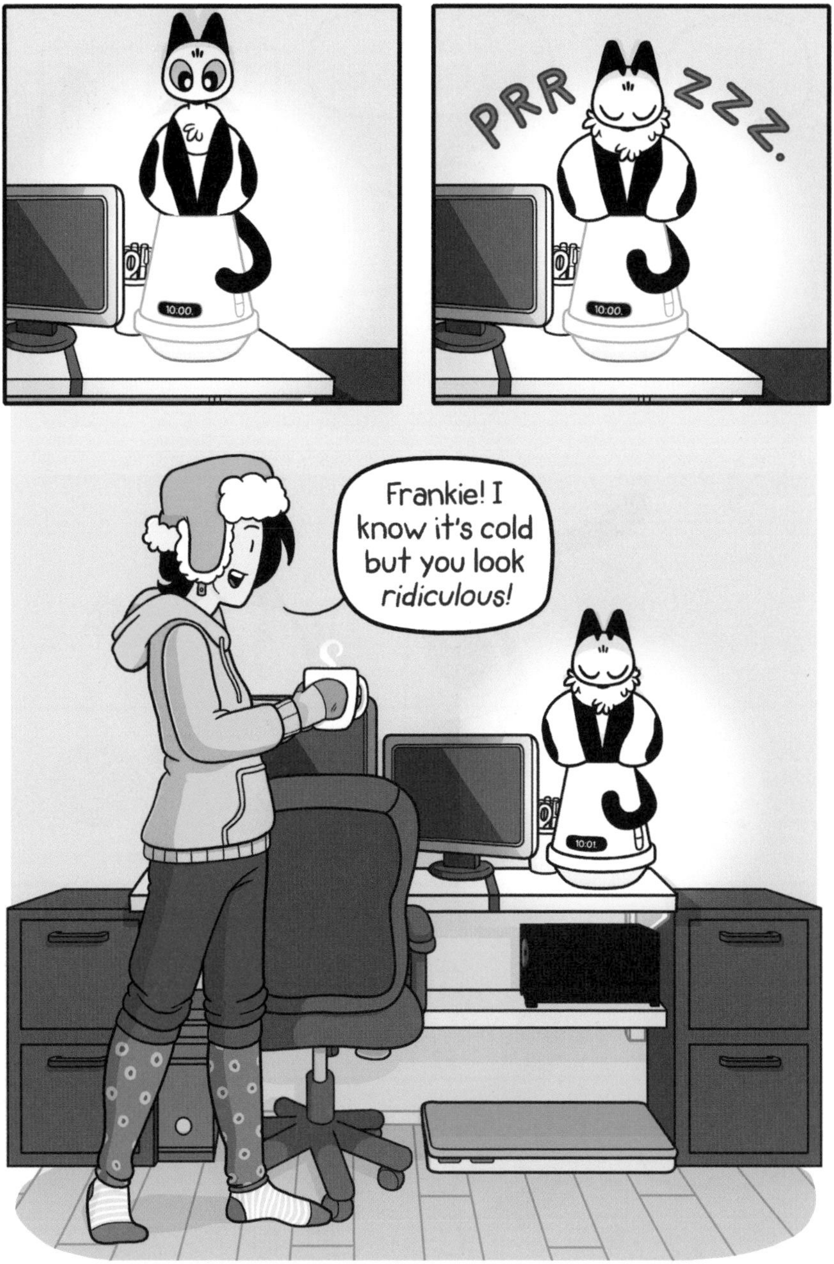
10:00.
PRR ZZZ.
10:00.
Frankie! I know it's cold but you look *ridiculous*!
10:01.

"A Day in the Life"

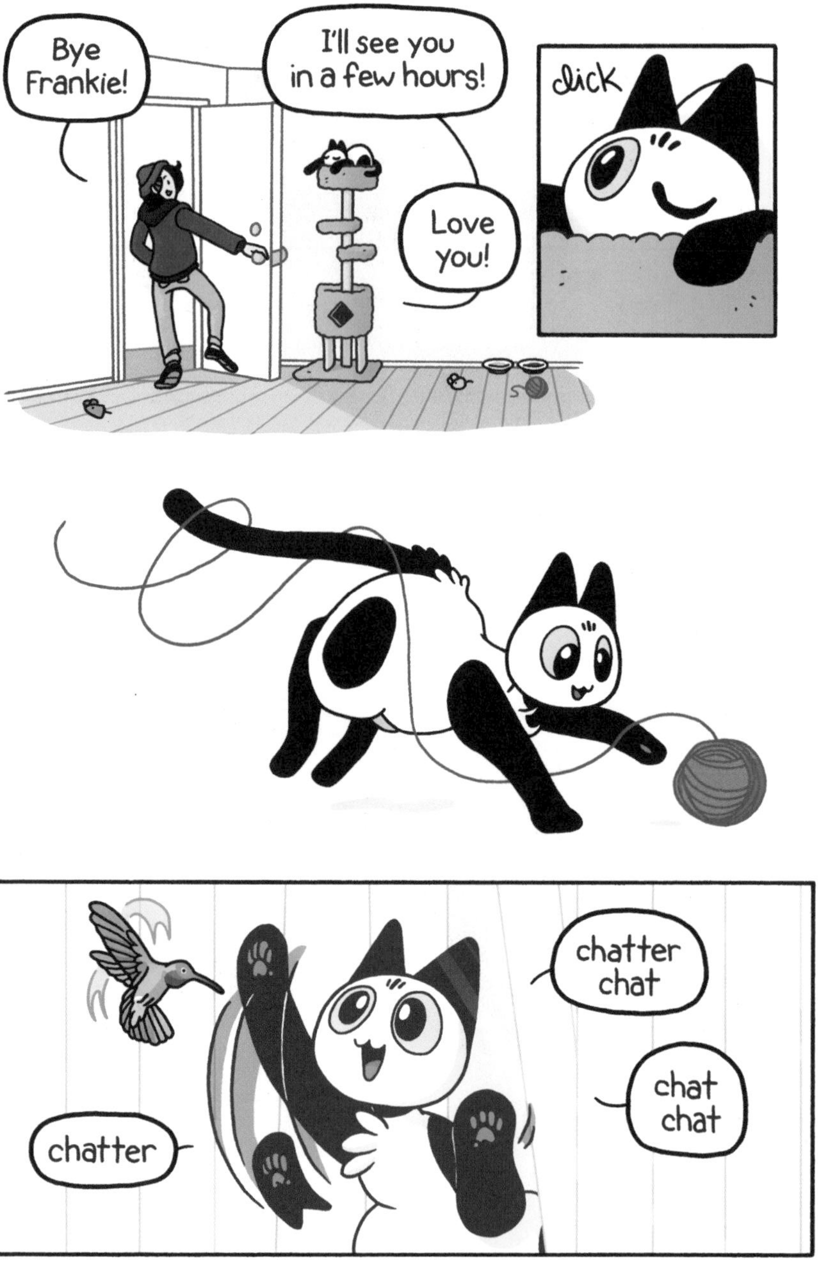
Bye Frankie!
I'll see you in a few hours!
Love you!
click
chatter
chatter chat
chat chat

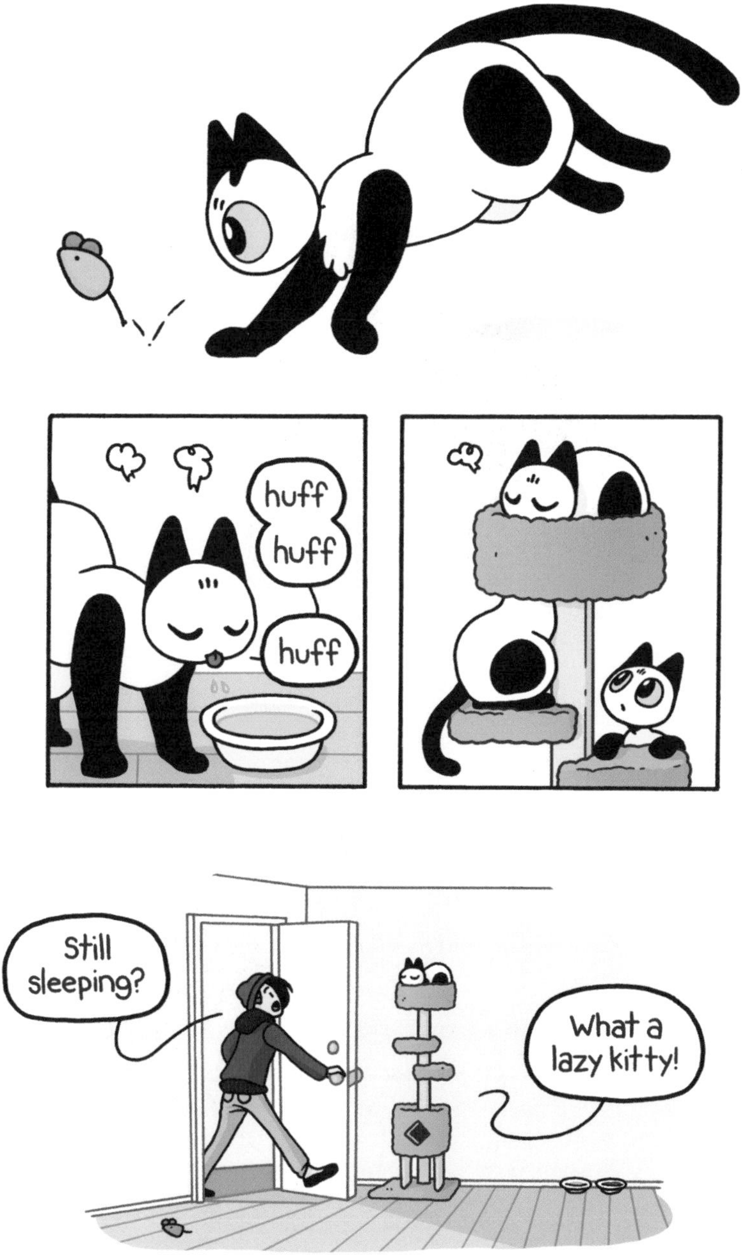
huff
huff
huff
Still sleeping?
What a lazy kitty!

"Teleportation"

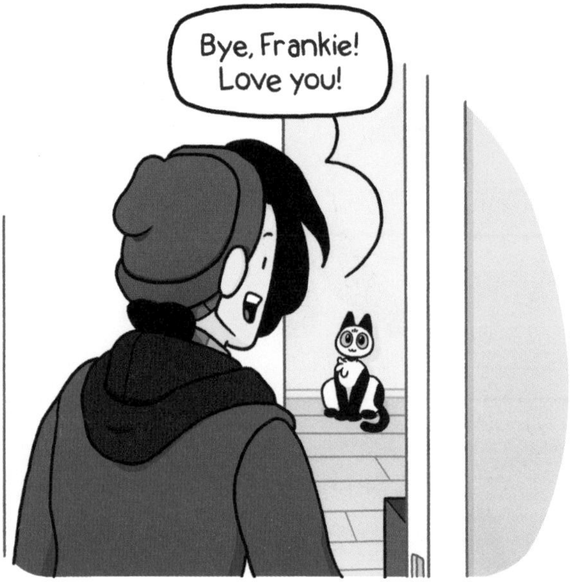
Bye, Frankie! Love you!

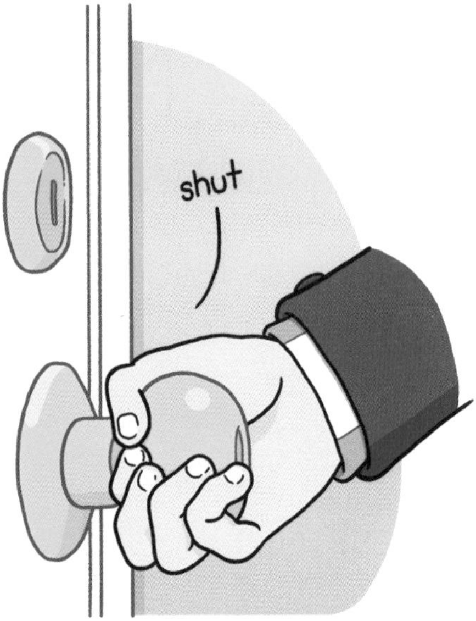
shut

How?!

"Sick Day With A Cat"

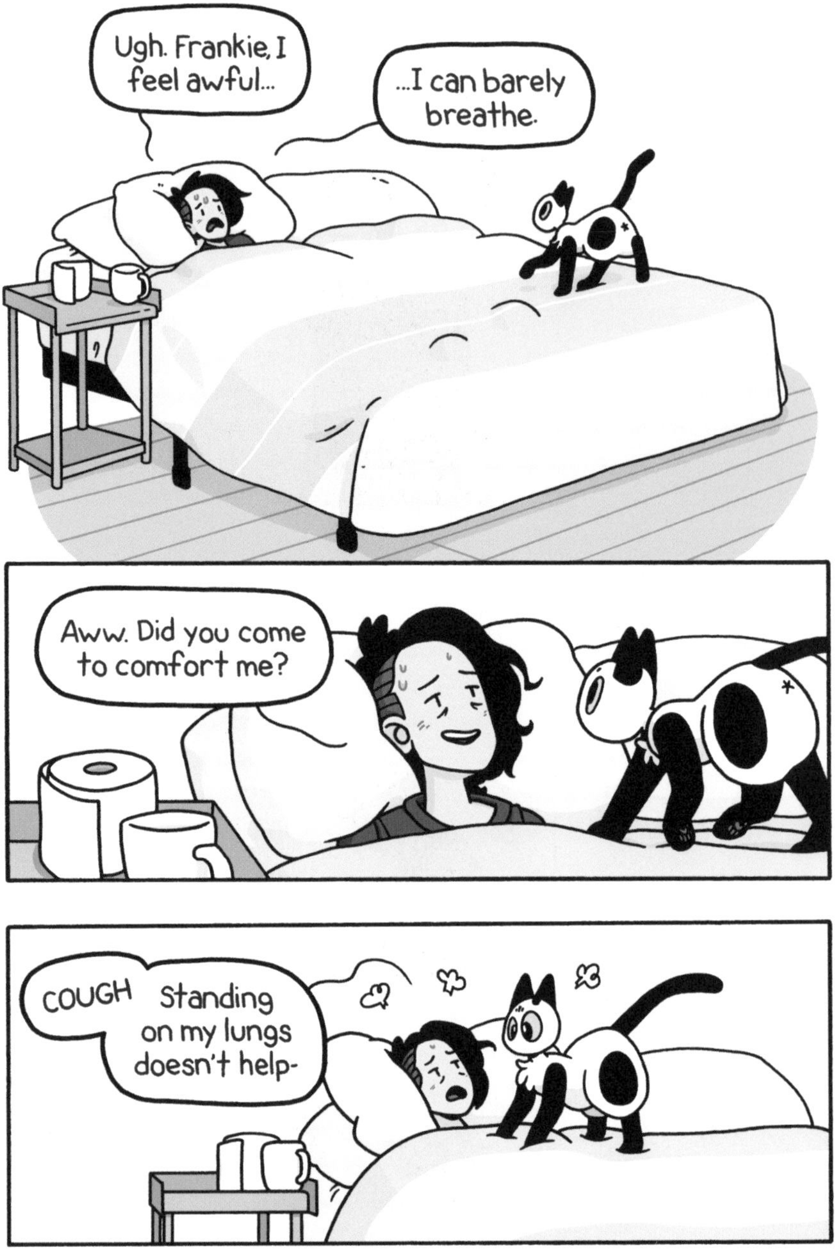
Ugh. Frankie, I feel awful...
...I can barely breathe.
Aww. Did you come to comfort me?
COUGH
Standing on my lungs doesn't help-

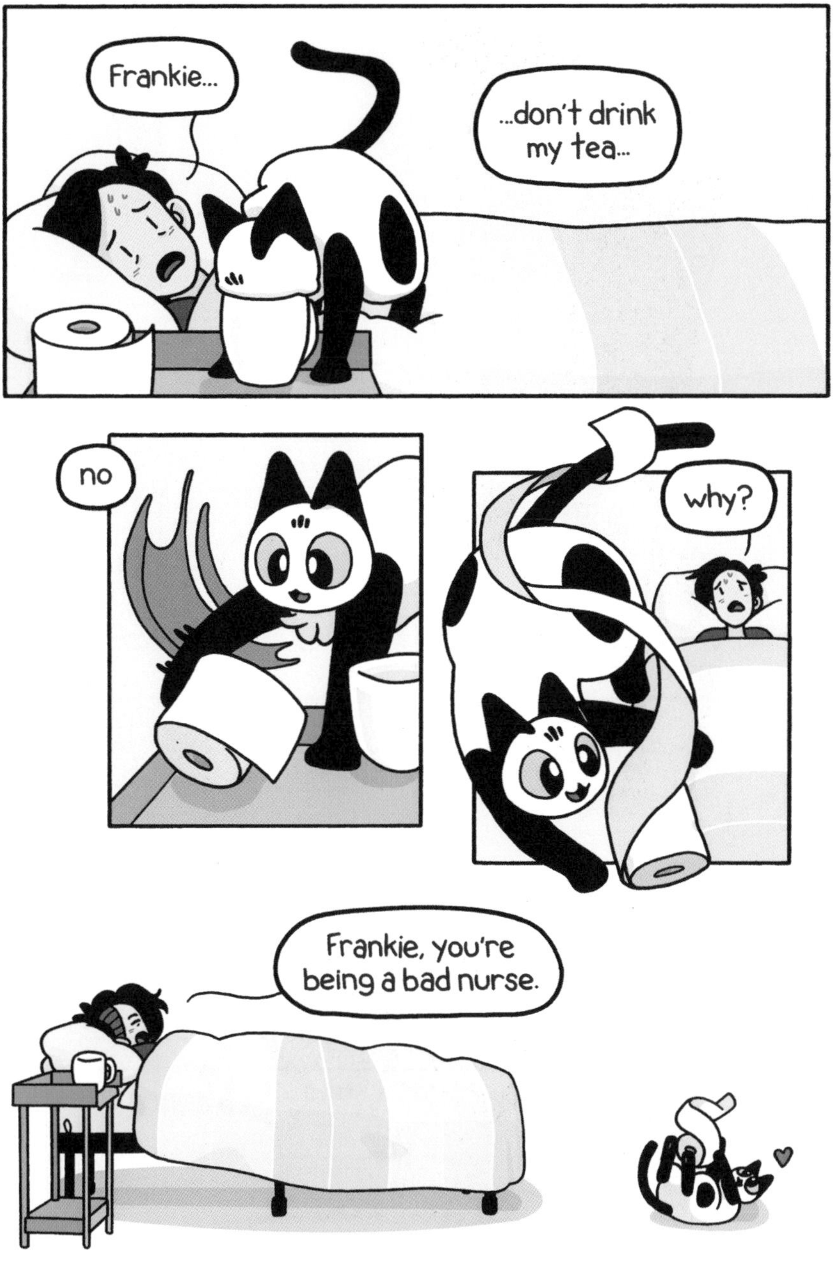
Frankie...
...don't drink my tea...
no
why?
Frankie, you're being a bad nurse.

"Hair-tie Season"

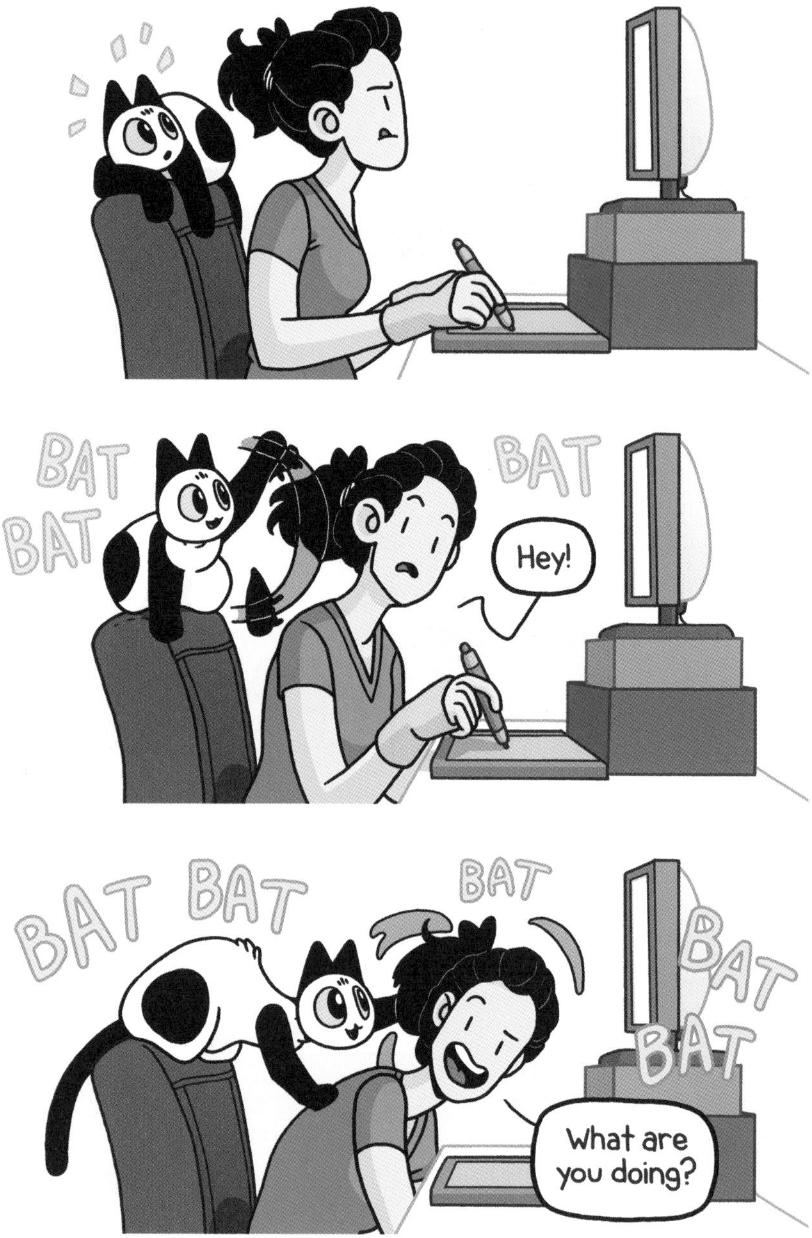
BAT
BAT
BAT
Hey!
BAT BAT
BAT
BAT
BAT
What are you doing?

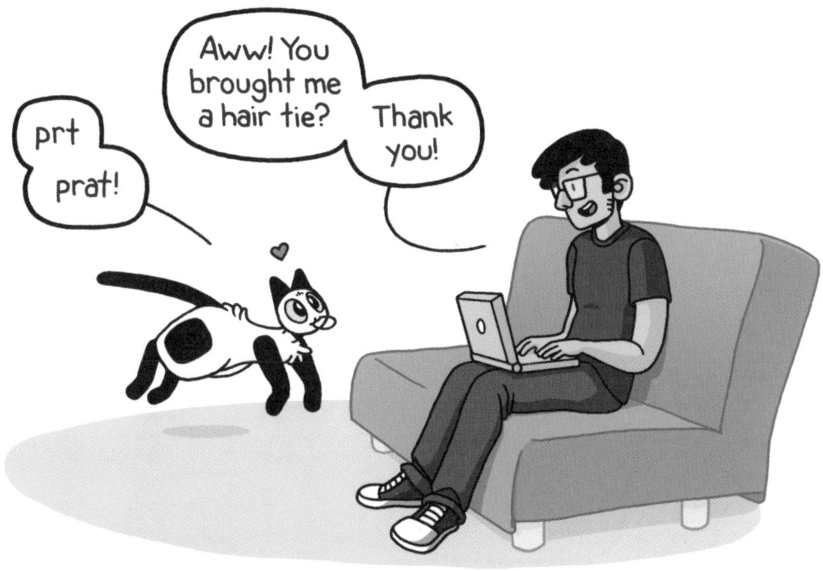
prrt
prat!
Aww! You brought me a hair tie?
Thank you!

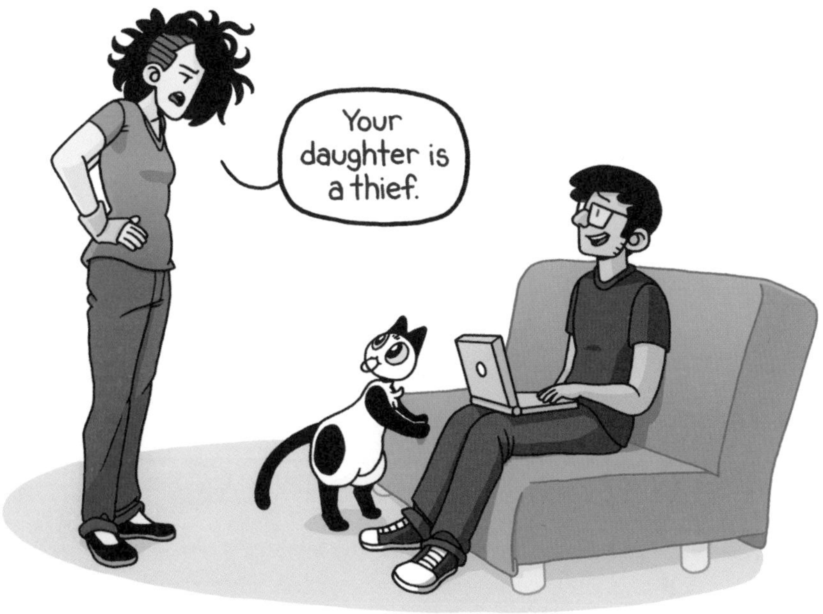
Your daughter is a thief.

"New Toys"

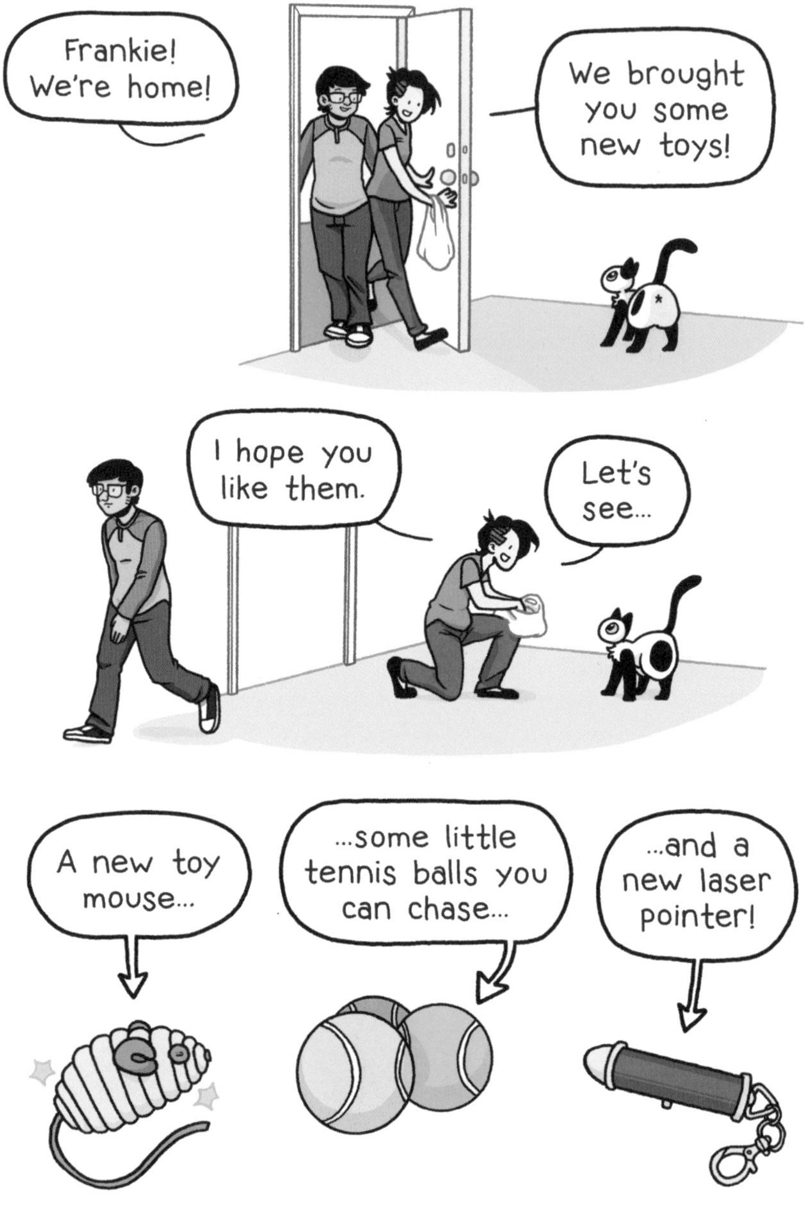
Frankie! We're home!
We brought you some new toys!
I hope you like them.
Let's see...
A new toy mouse...
...some little tennis balls you can chase...
...and a new laser pointer!

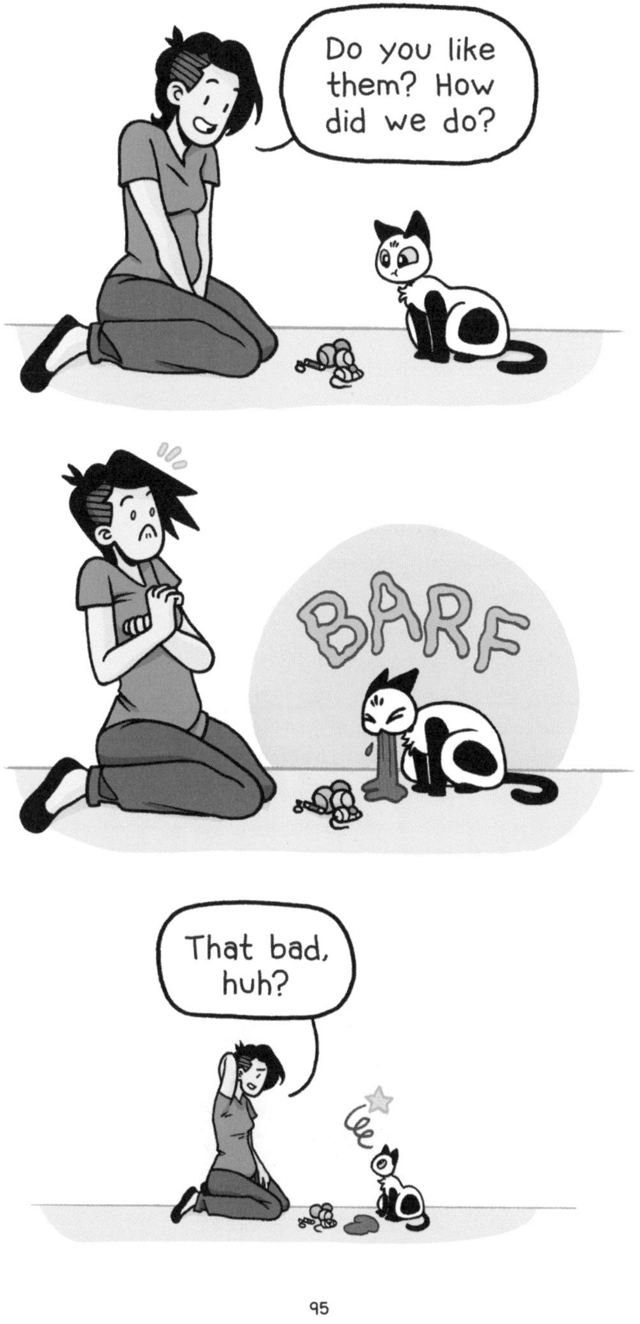
Do you like them? How did we do?
BARF
That bad, huh?

"Tea Time"

FWEEEEEEEEE
Oh! Tea's ready!
FWEEEEEEEEE

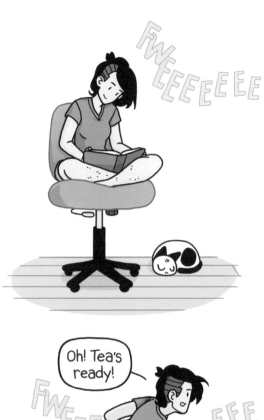

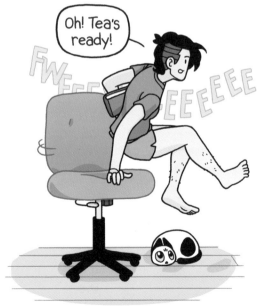

"Summer Bummer"

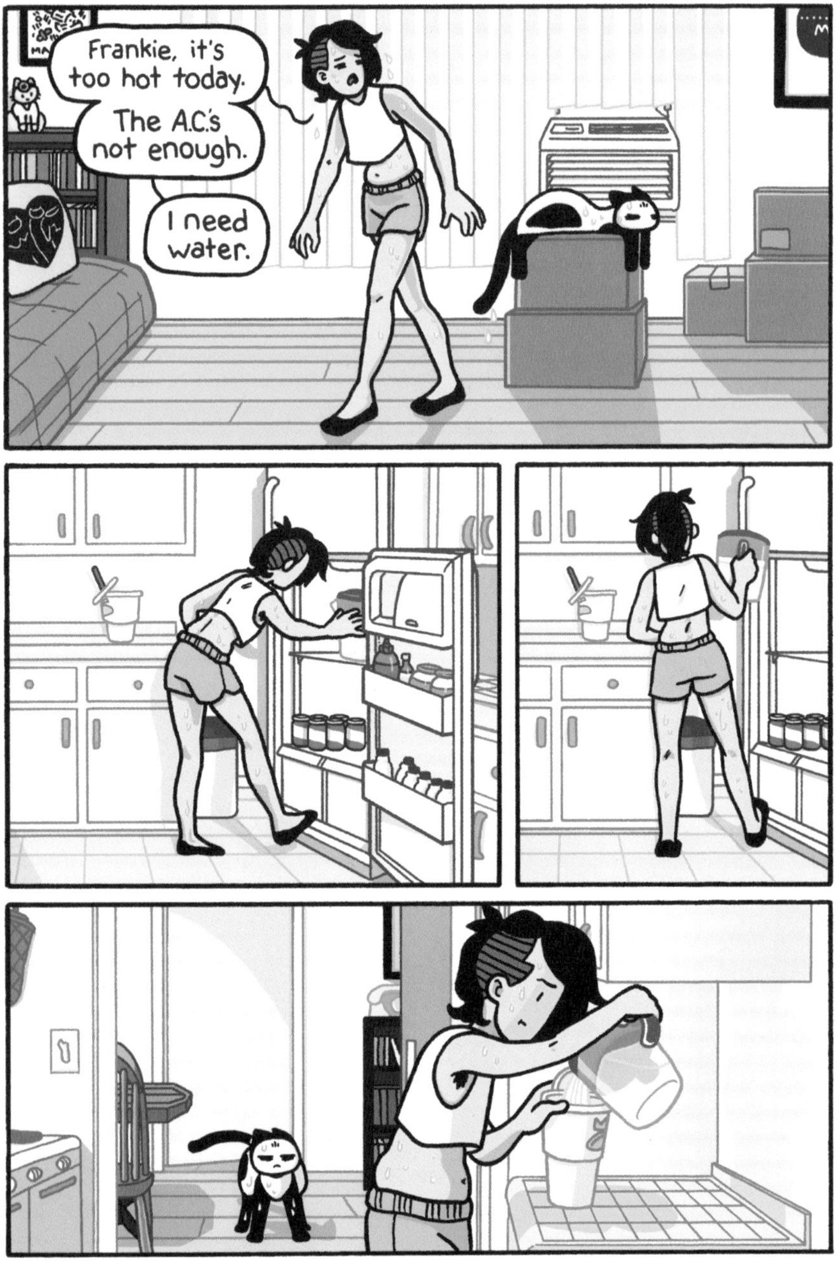

Frankie, it's too hot today.
The A.C.'s not enough.
I need water.

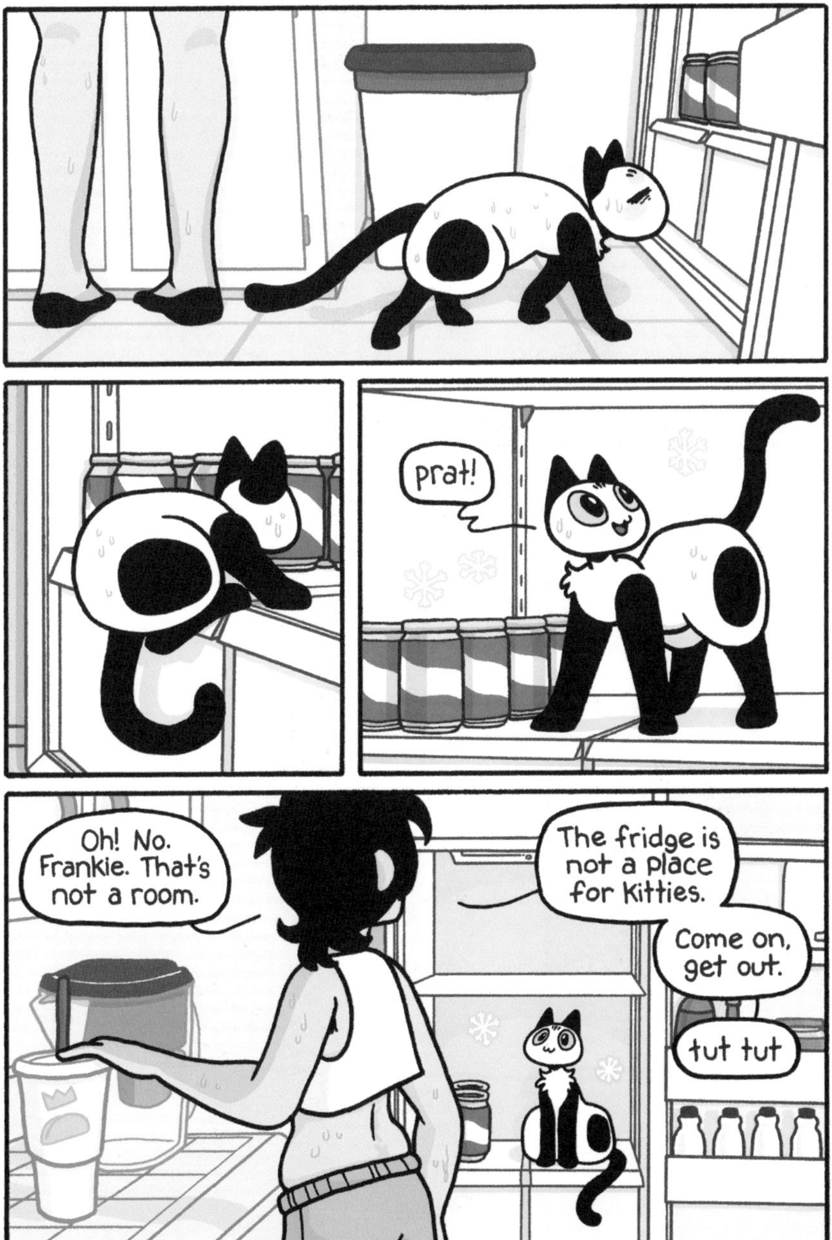
prat!
Oh! No. Frankie. That's not a room.
The fridge is not a place for Kitties.
Come on, get out.
tut tut

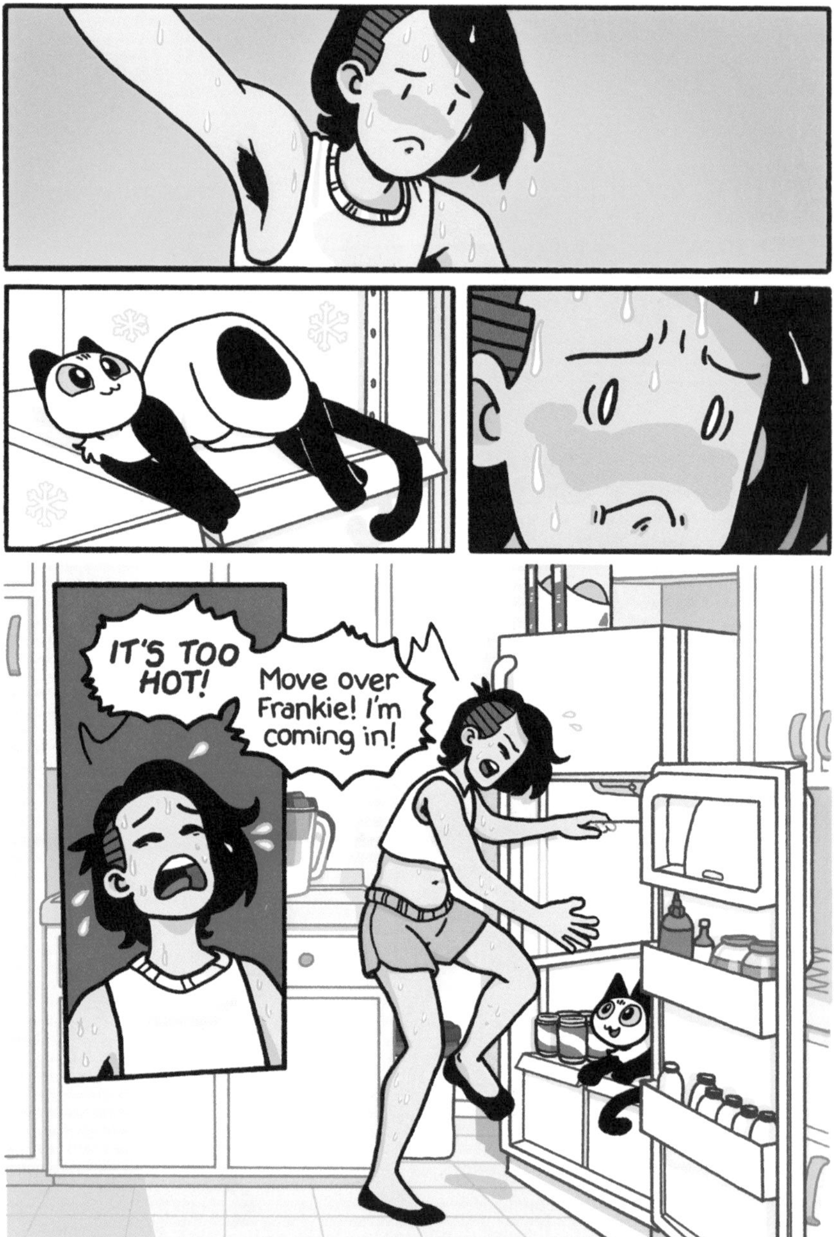
IT'S TOO HOT!
Move over Frankie! I'm coming in!

"Chasing Rainbows"

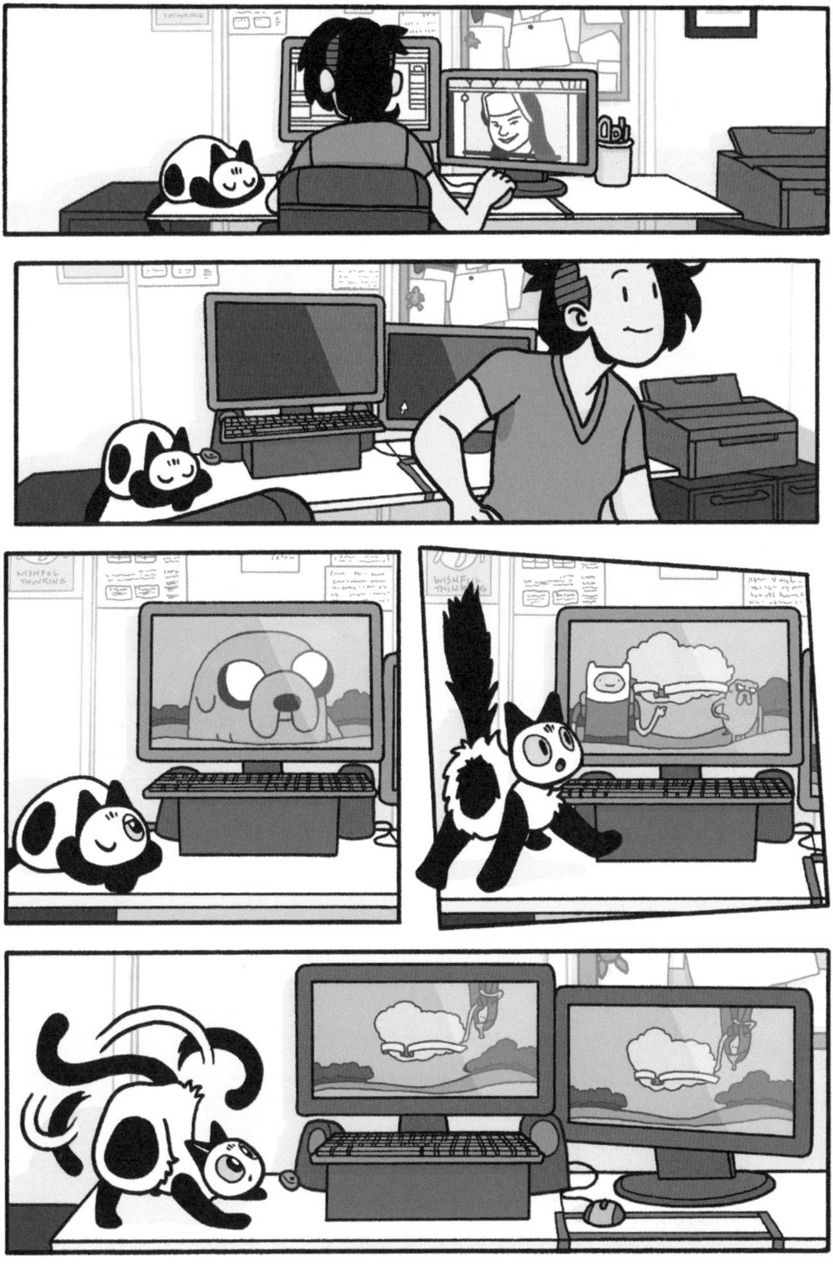
WISHFUL THINKING

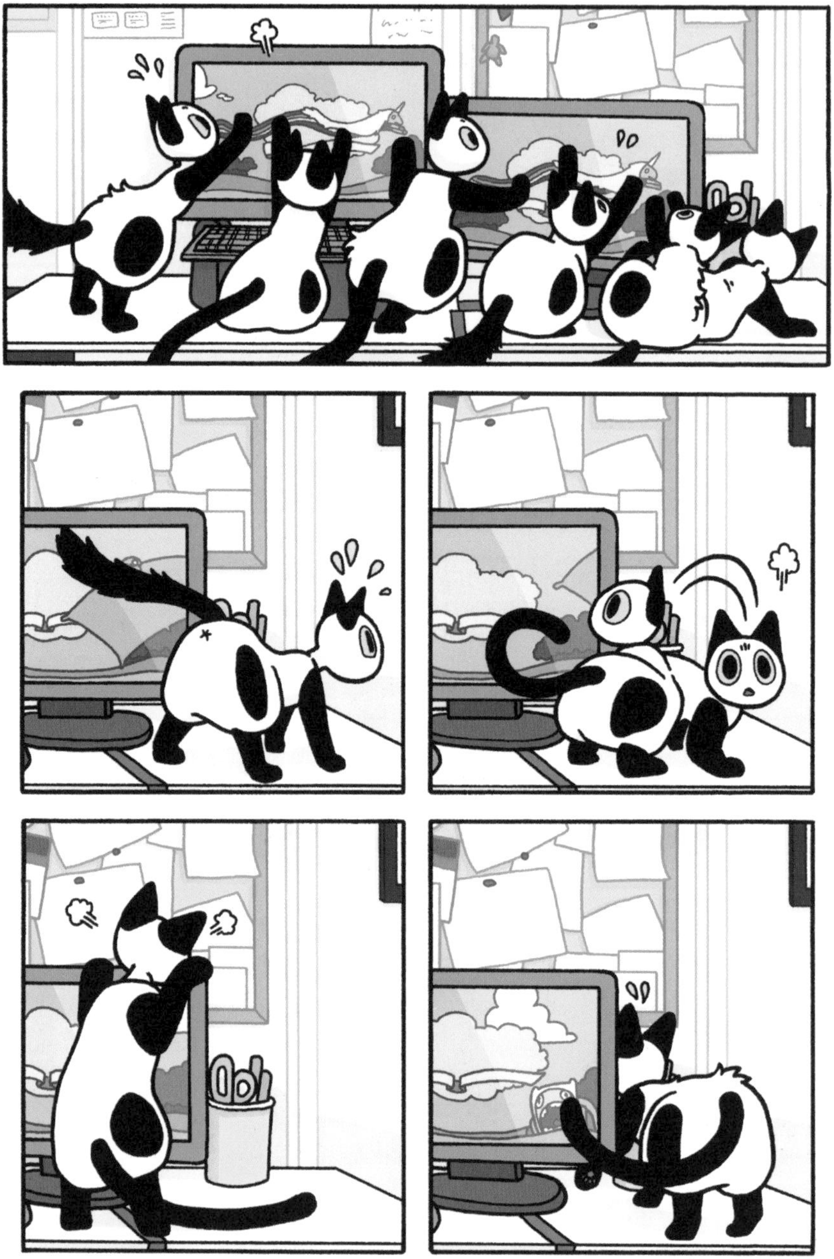

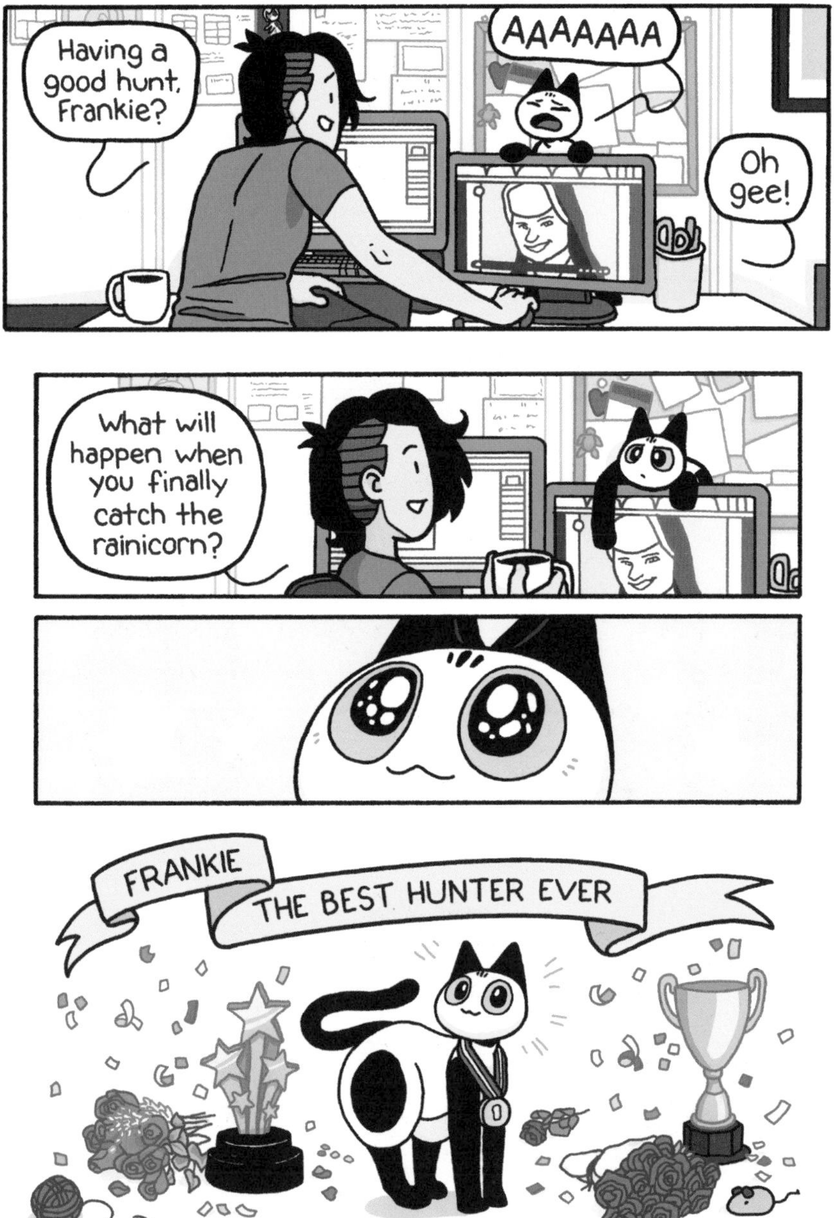
Having a good hunt, Frankie?
AAAAAAA
Oh gee!
What will happen when you finally catch the rainicorn?
FRANKIE
THE BEST HUNTER EVER

"Helping"

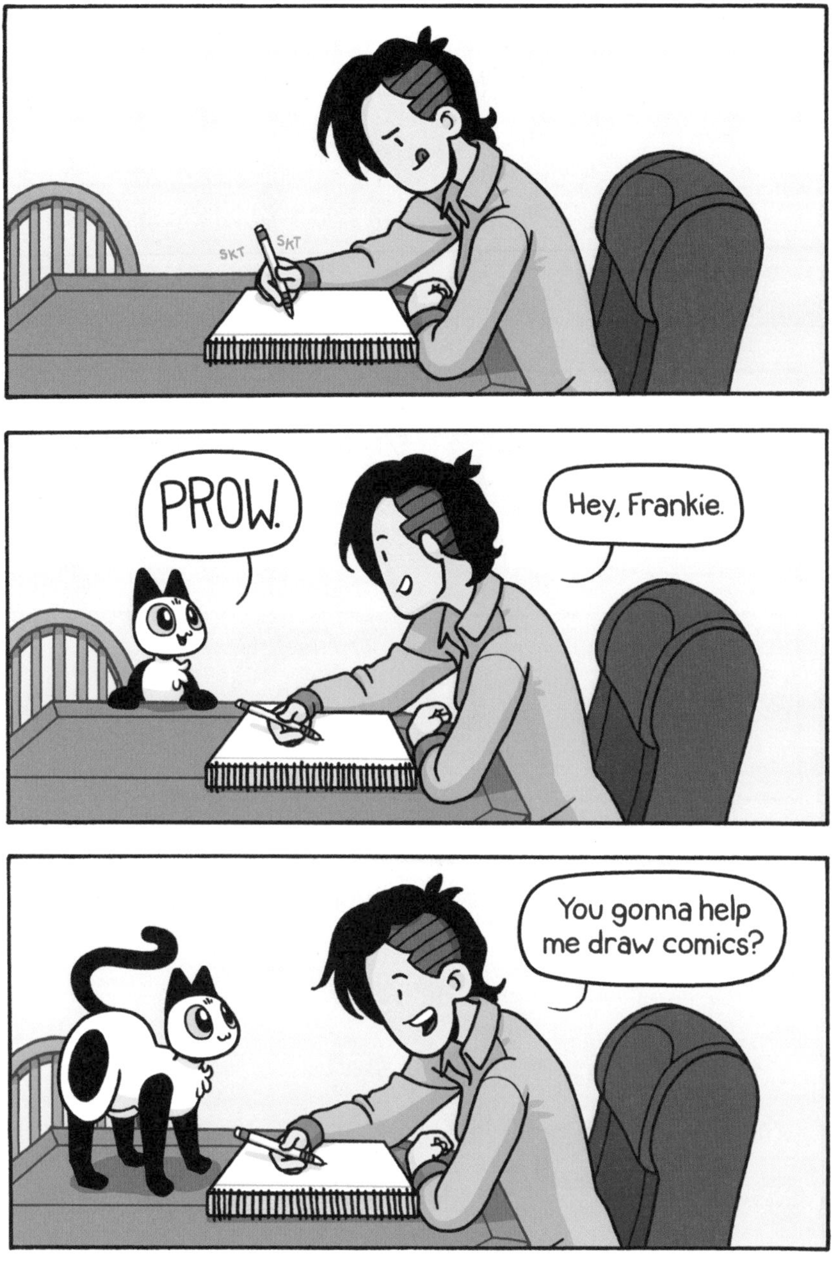
SKT
SKT
PROW.
Hey, Frankie.
You gonna help me draw comics?

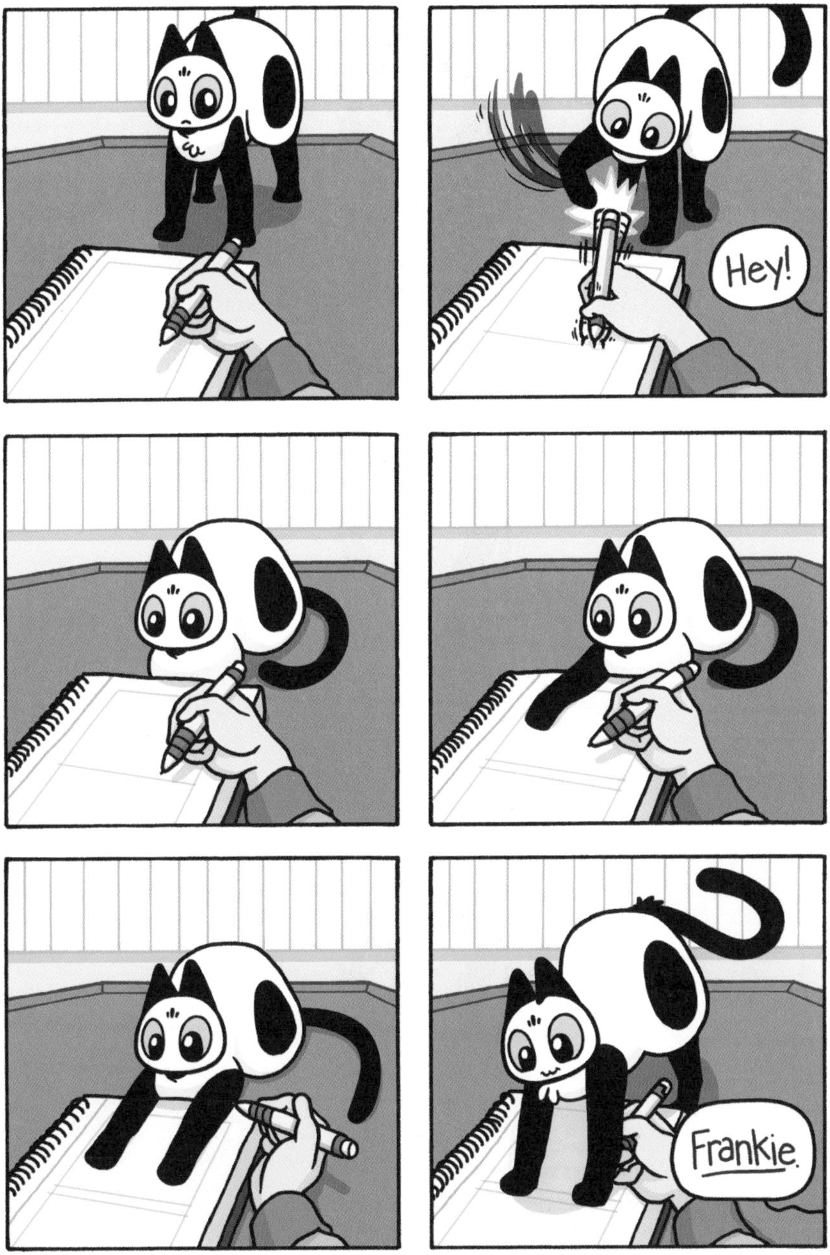
Hey!
Frankie.

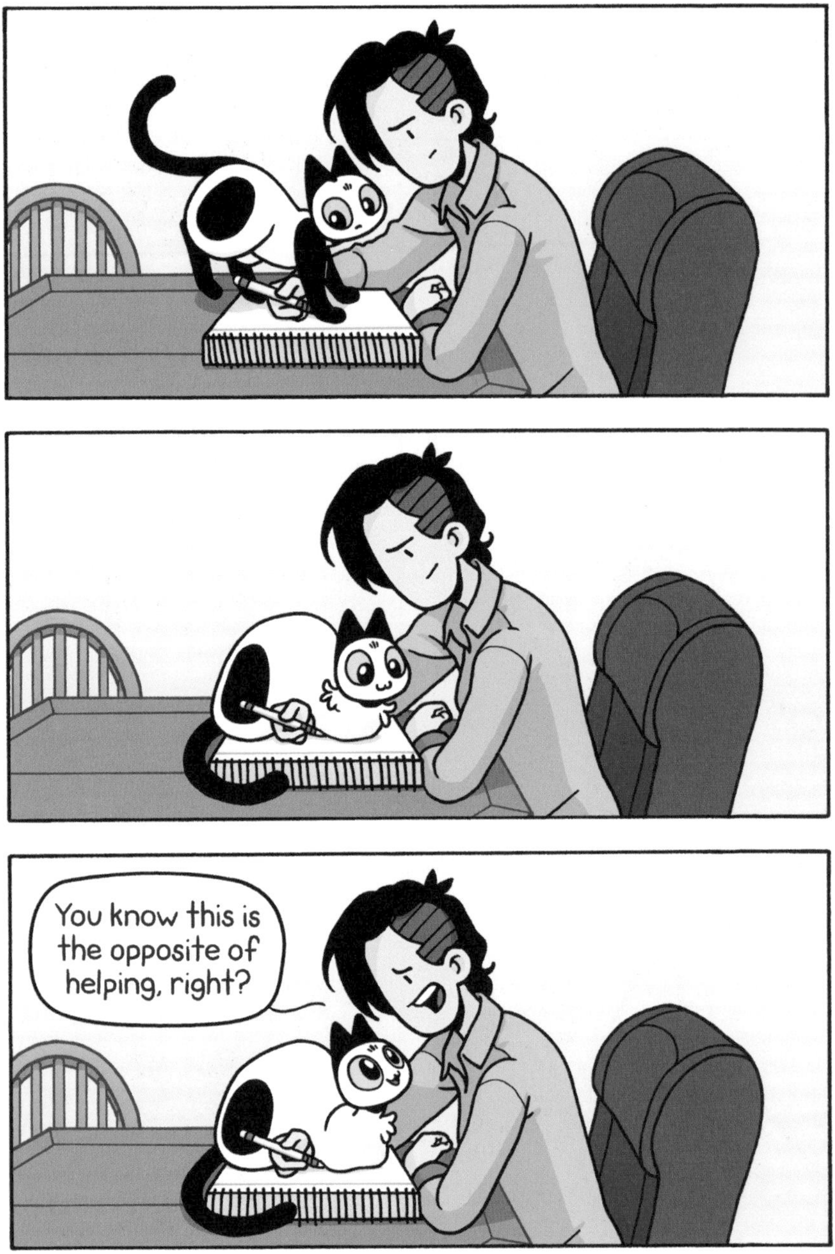
You know this is the opposite of helping, right?

"Call n' Return"

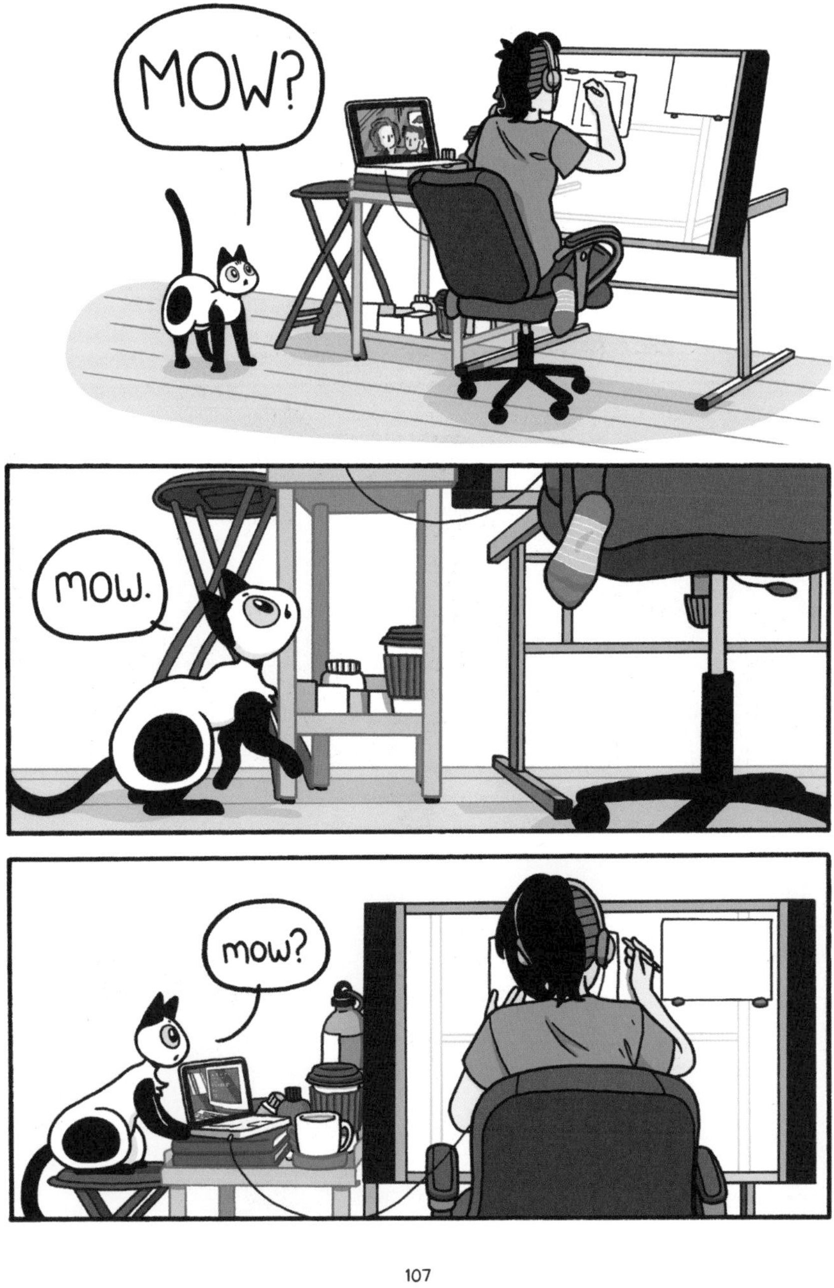
MOW?
mow.
mow?

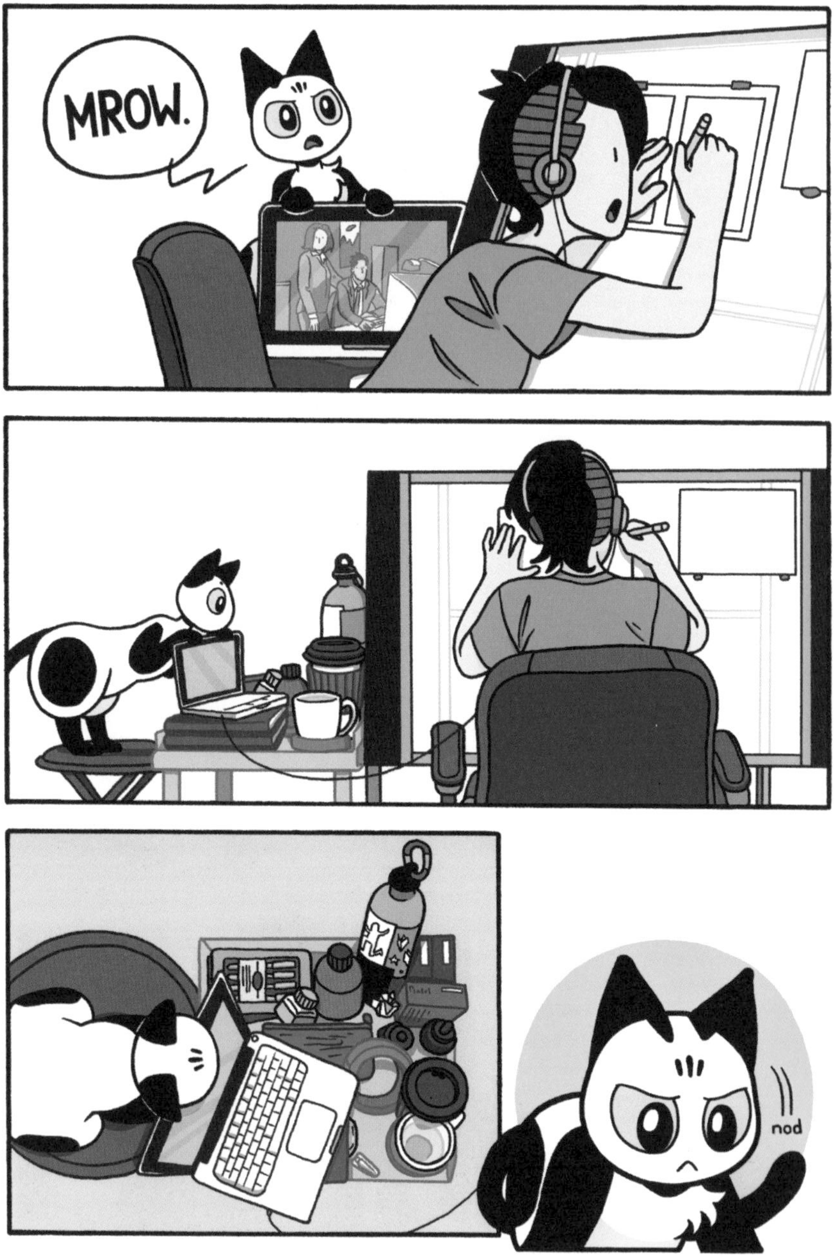
MROW.
nod

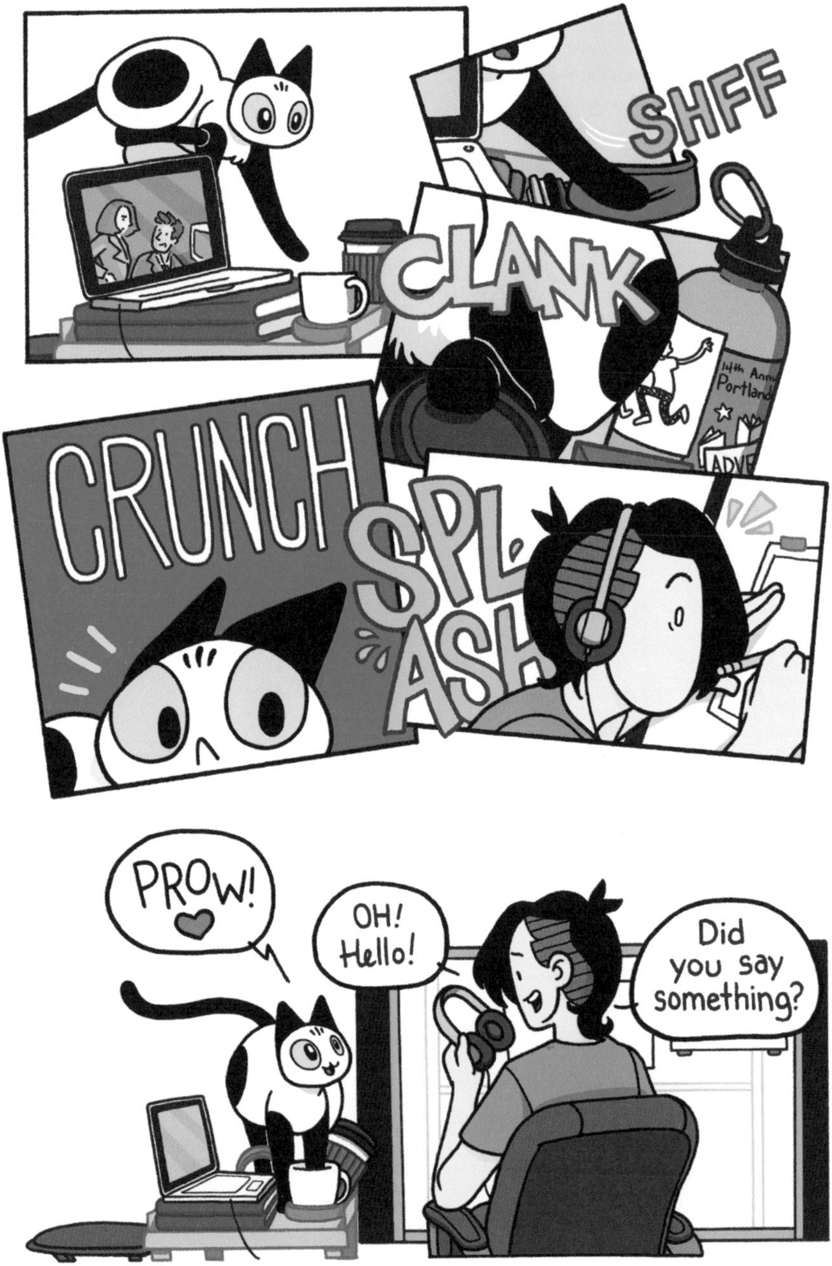
SHFF
CLANK
CRUNCH
SPLASH
PROW!
OH! Hello!
Did you say something?

"Fetch 1"

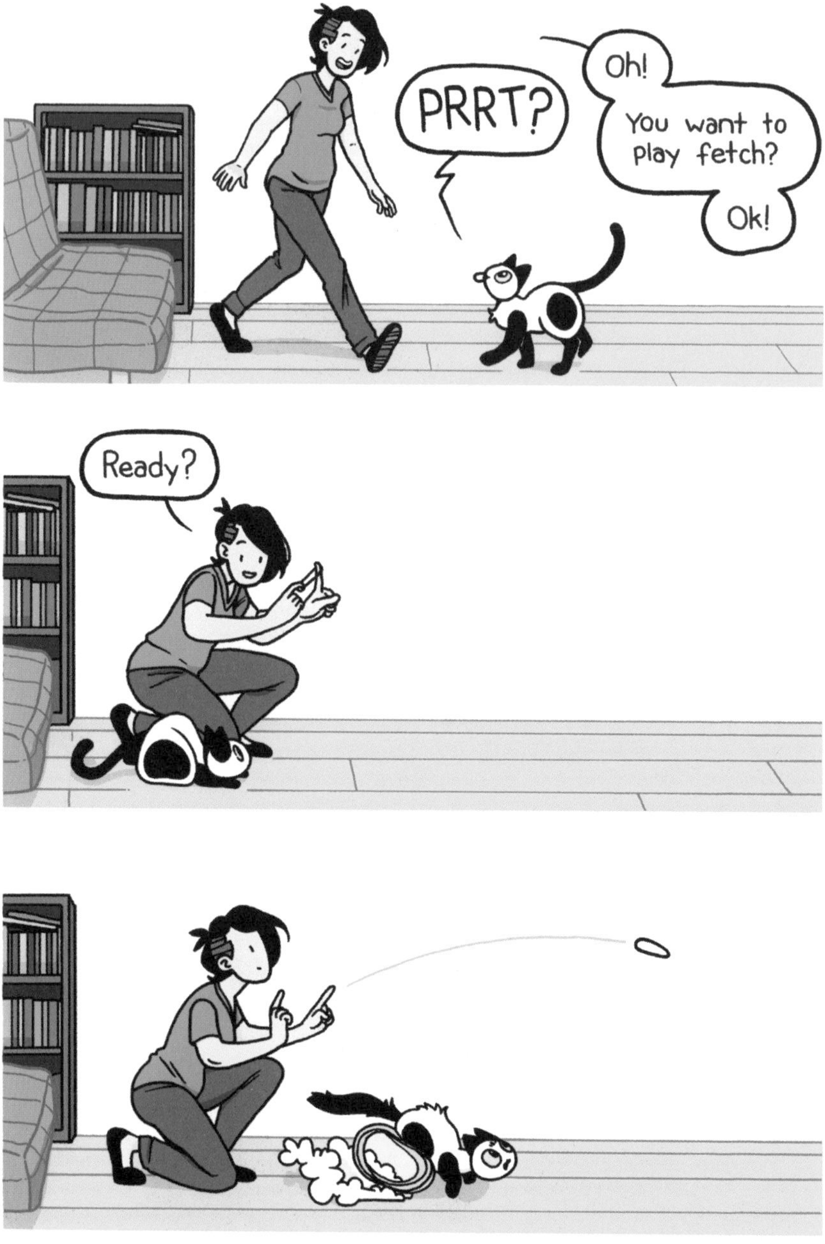
PRRT?
Oh!
You want to play fetch?
Ok!
Ready?

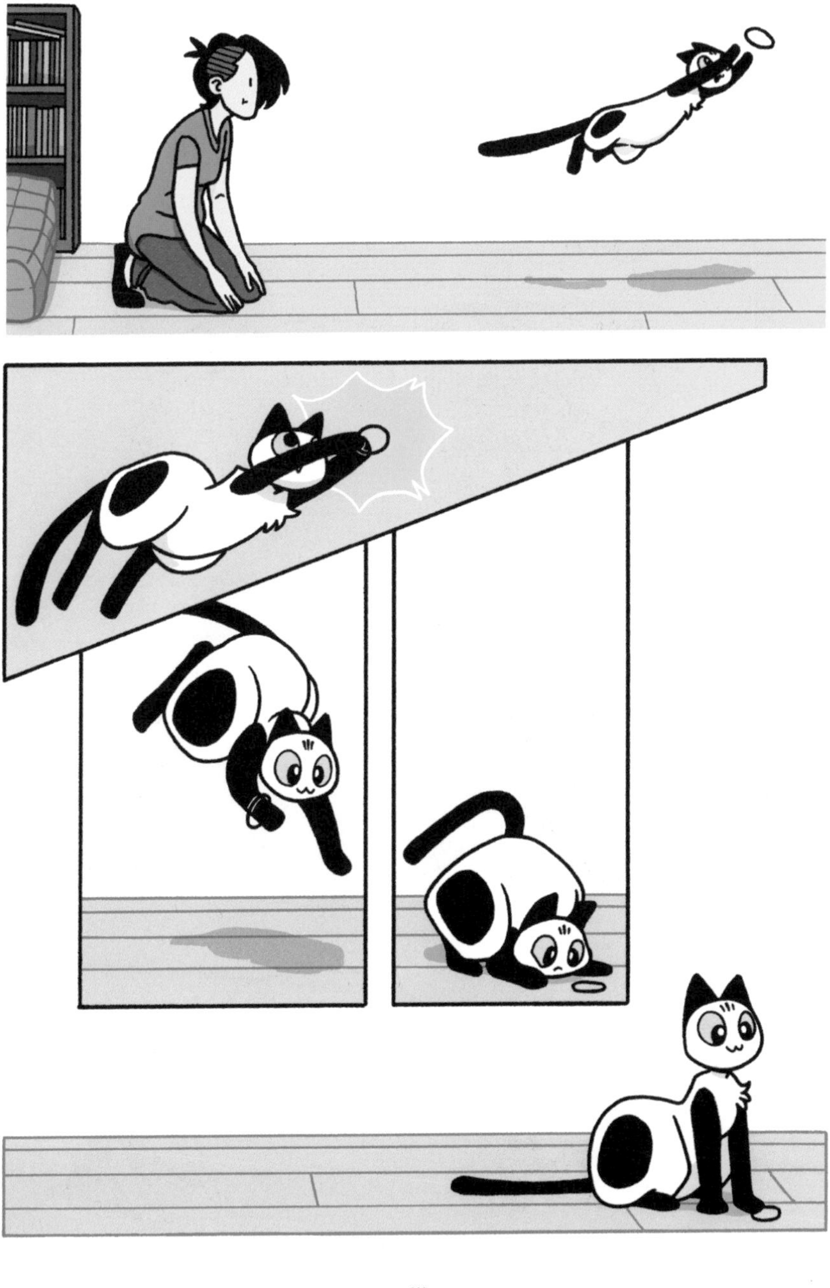

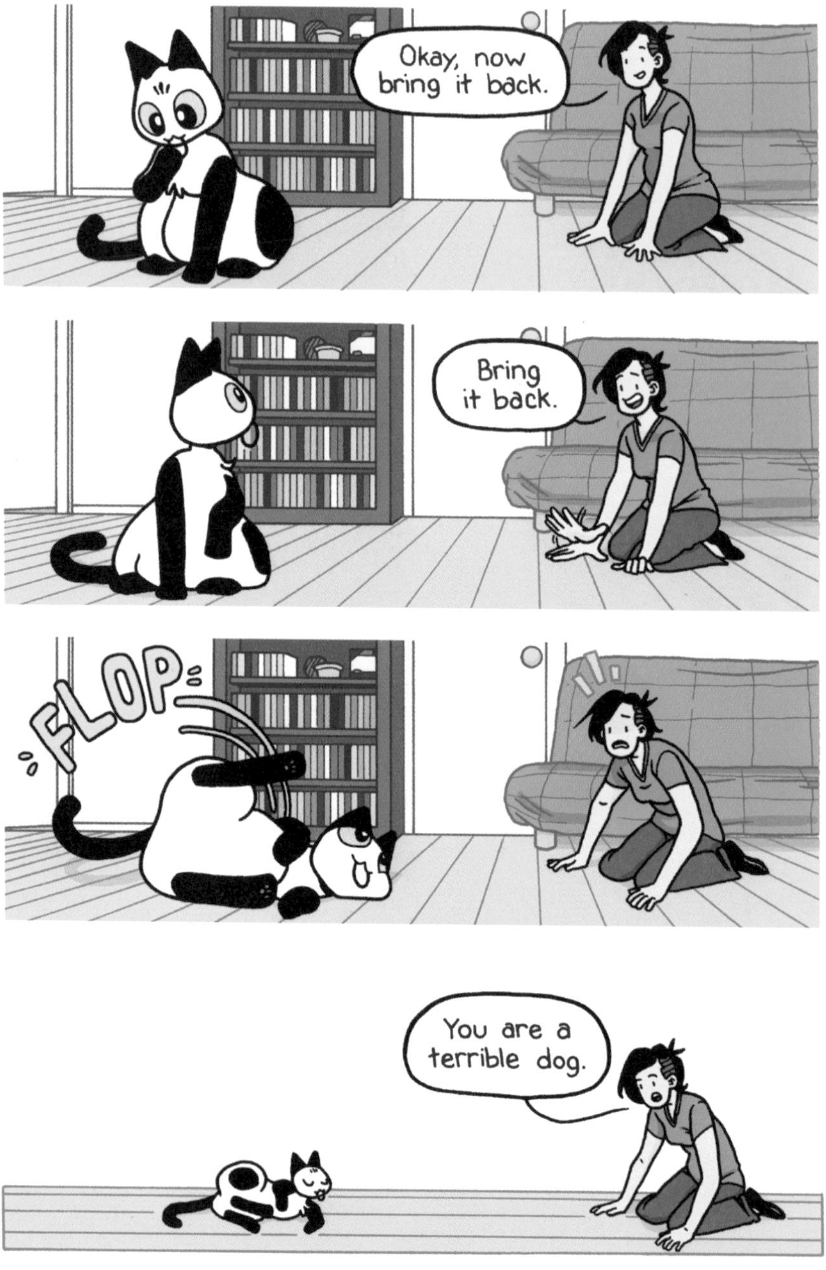
Okay, now bring it back.
Bring it back.
FLOP
You are a terrible dog.

"Booksmarts"

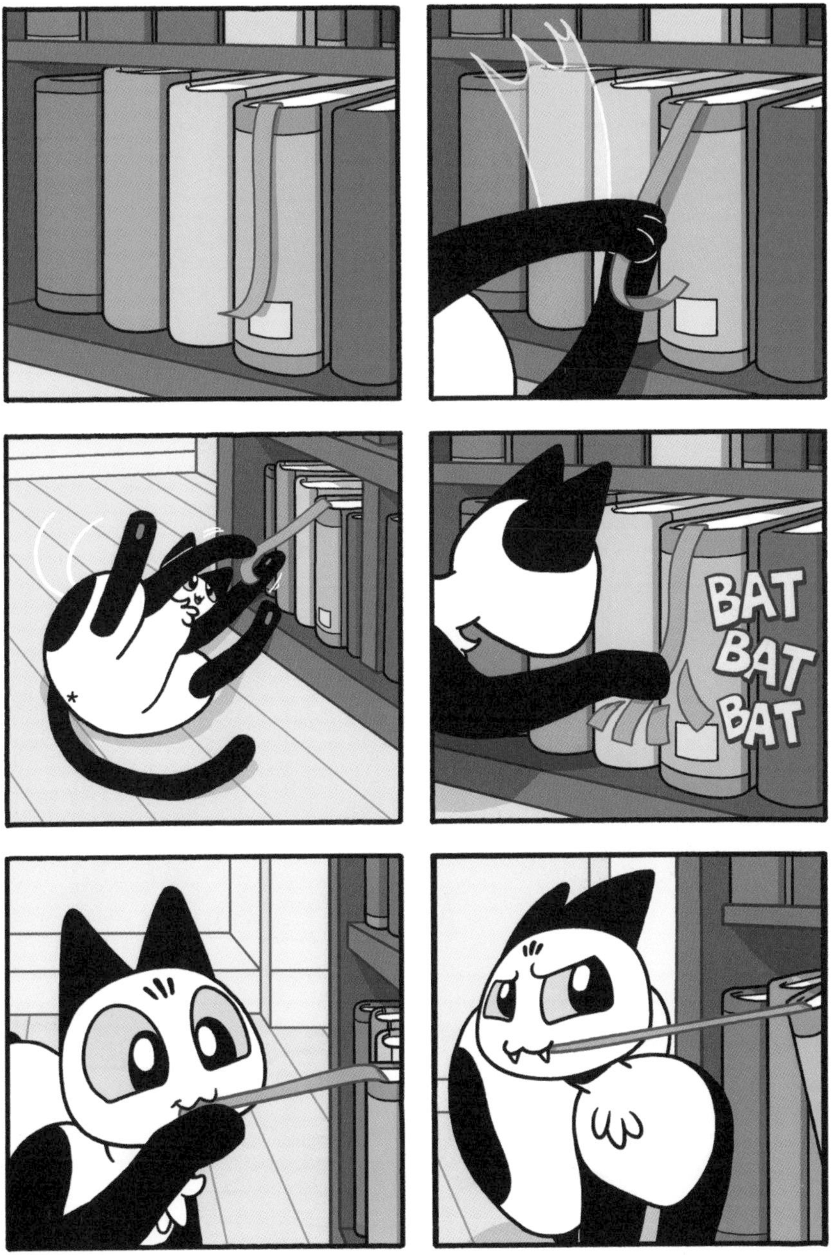
BAT
BAT
BAT

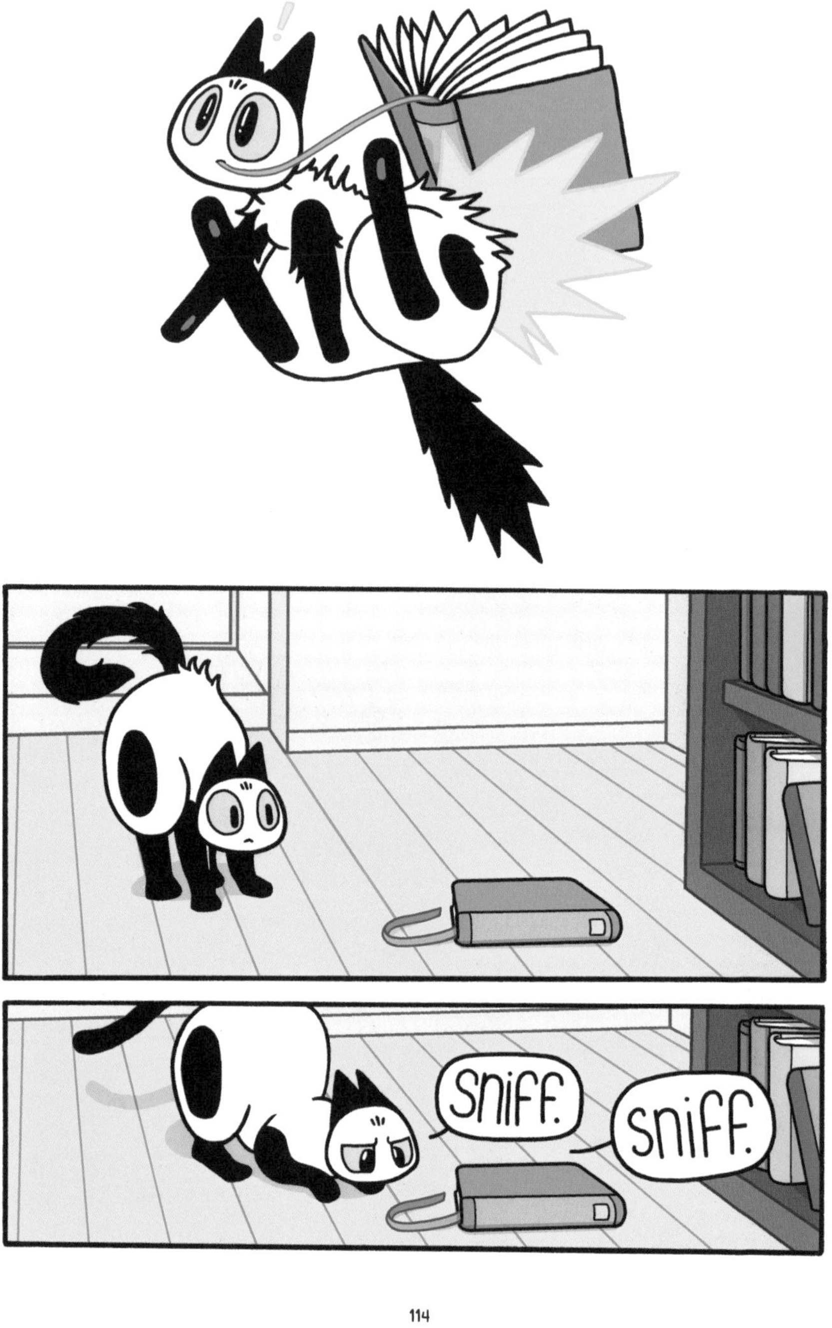
SNIFF.
SNIFF.

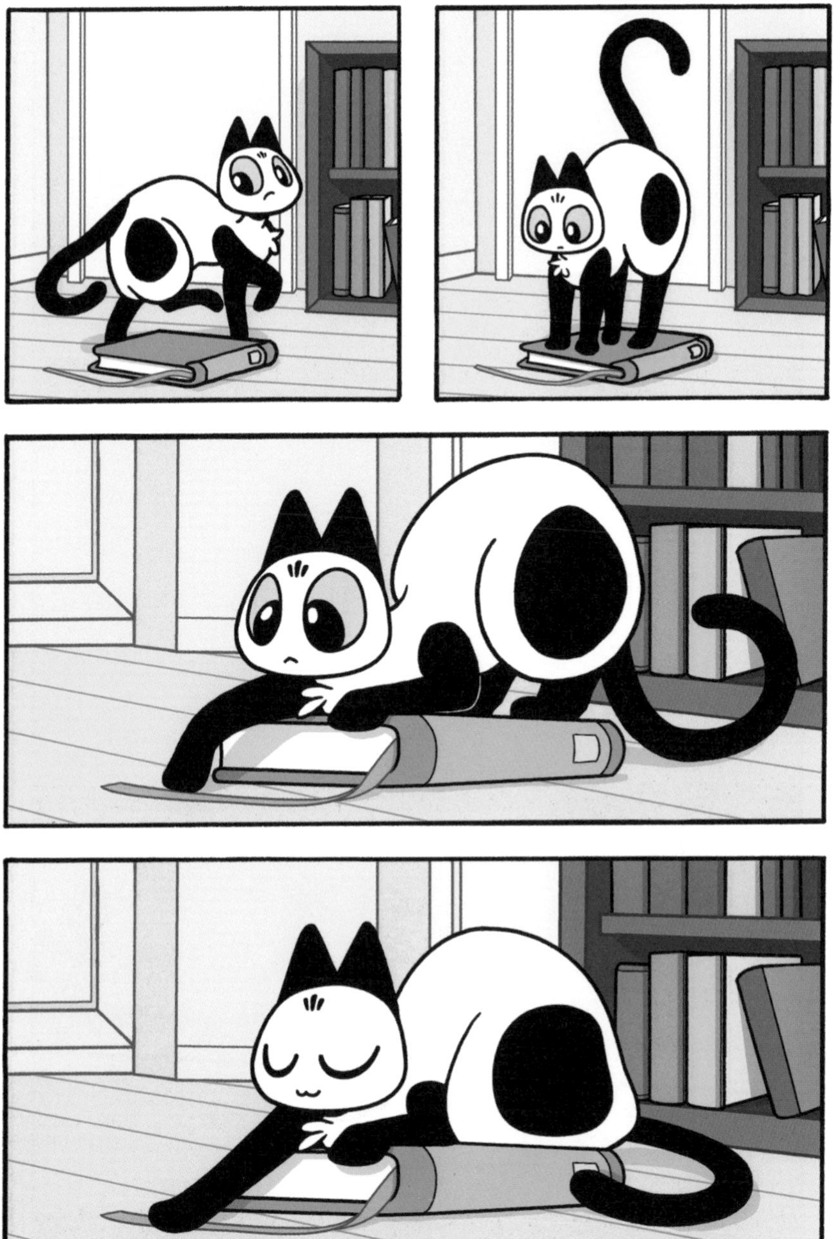

"Pigeon Party"

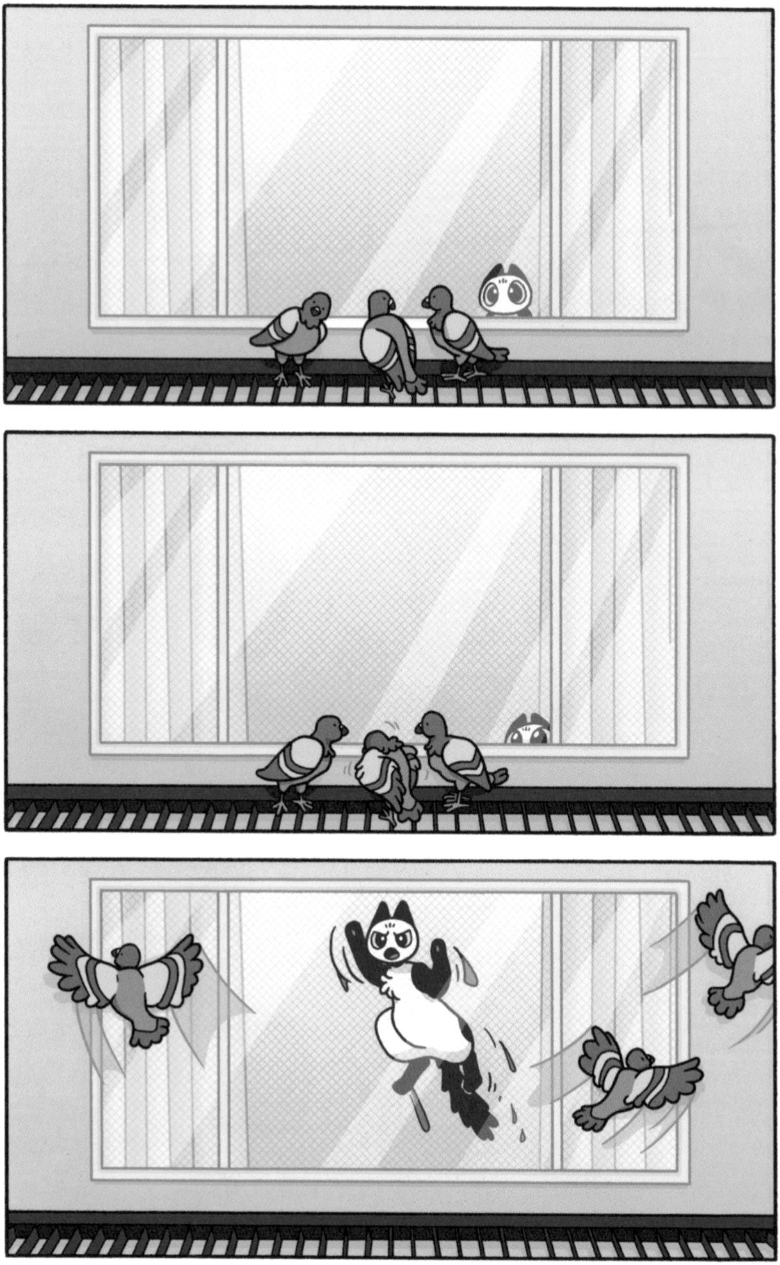

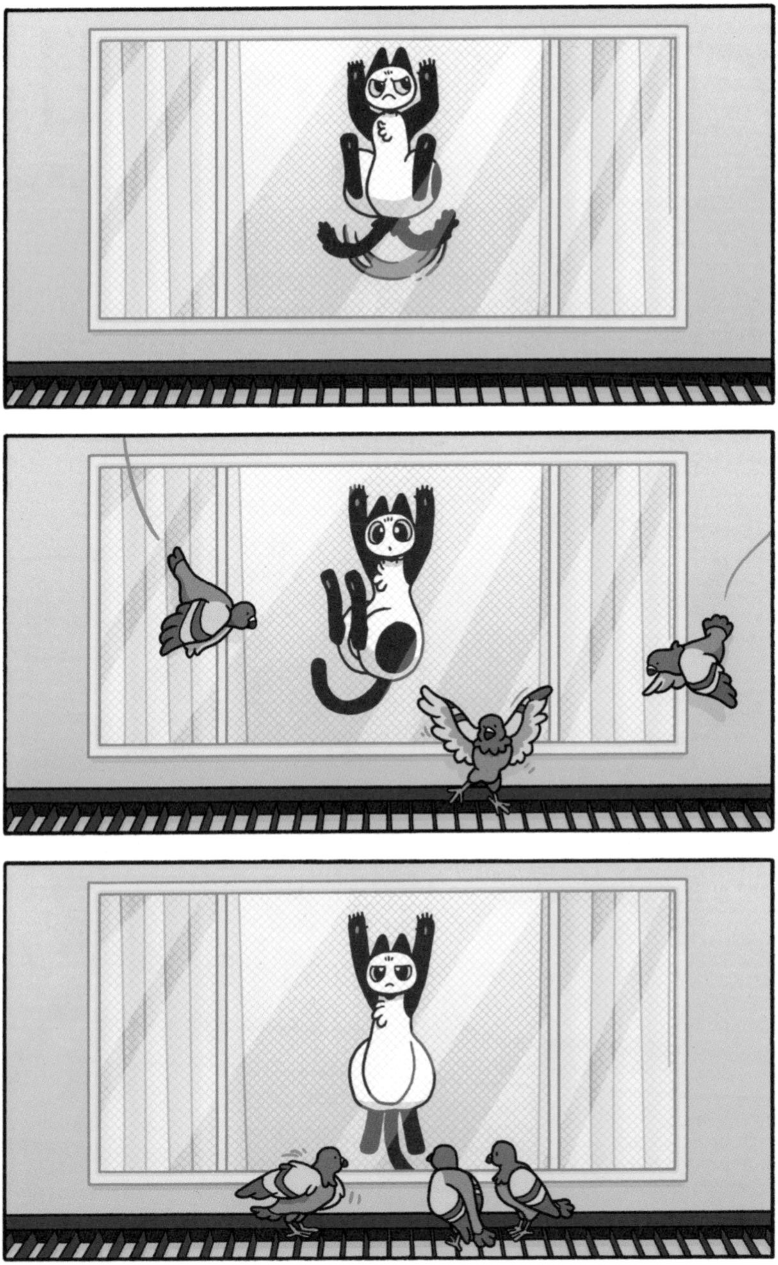

"Picture Perfect"

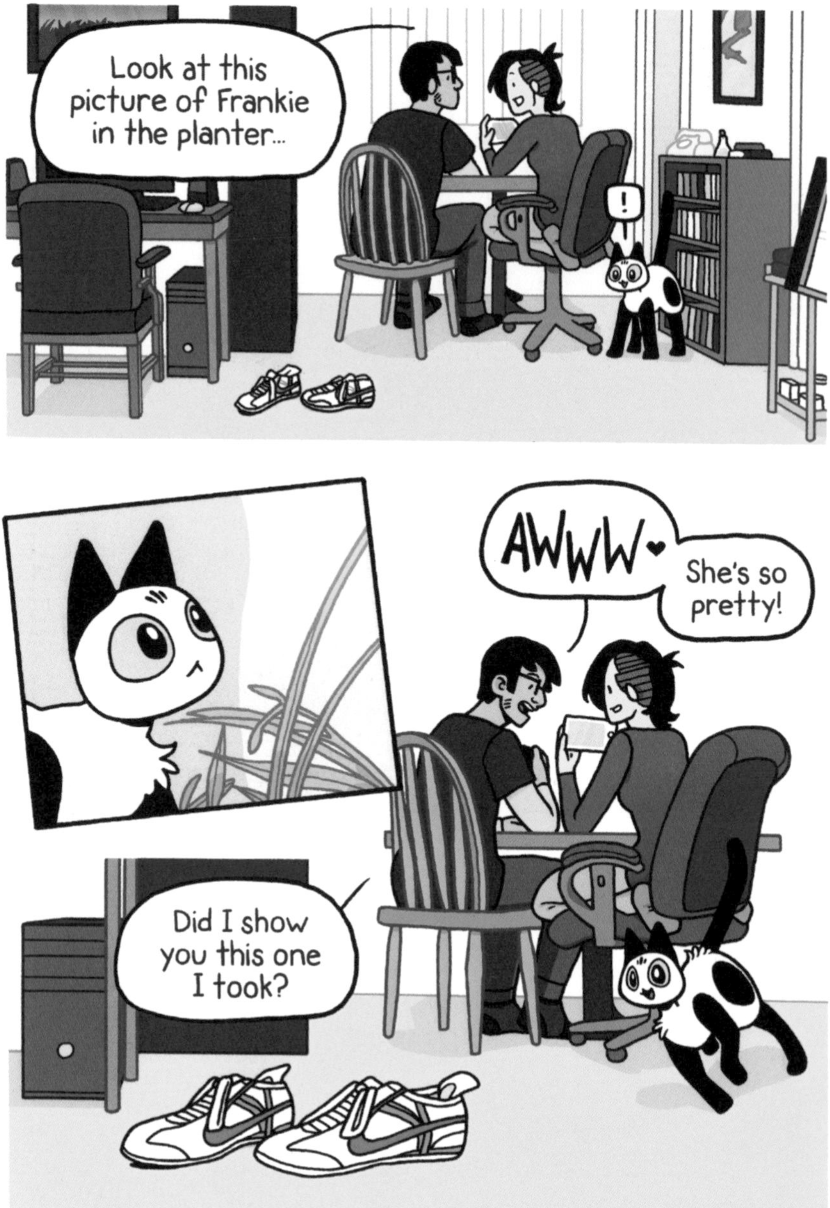
Look at this picture of Frankie in the planter...
!
AWWW
She's so pretty!
Did I show you this one I took?

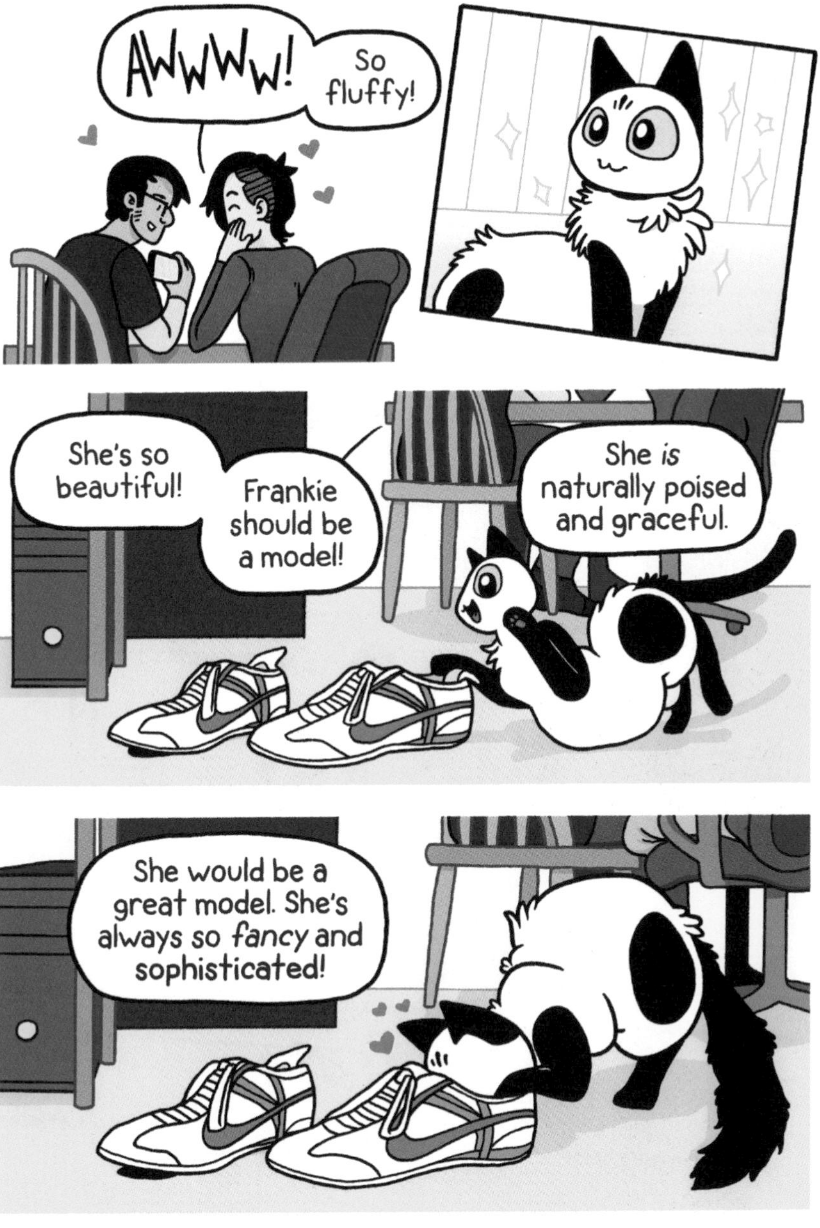
AWWWW!
So fluffy!
She's so beautiful!
Frankie should be a model!
She *is* naturally poised and graceful.
She would be a great model. She's always so *fancy* and sophisticated!

"Sweet Harmony"

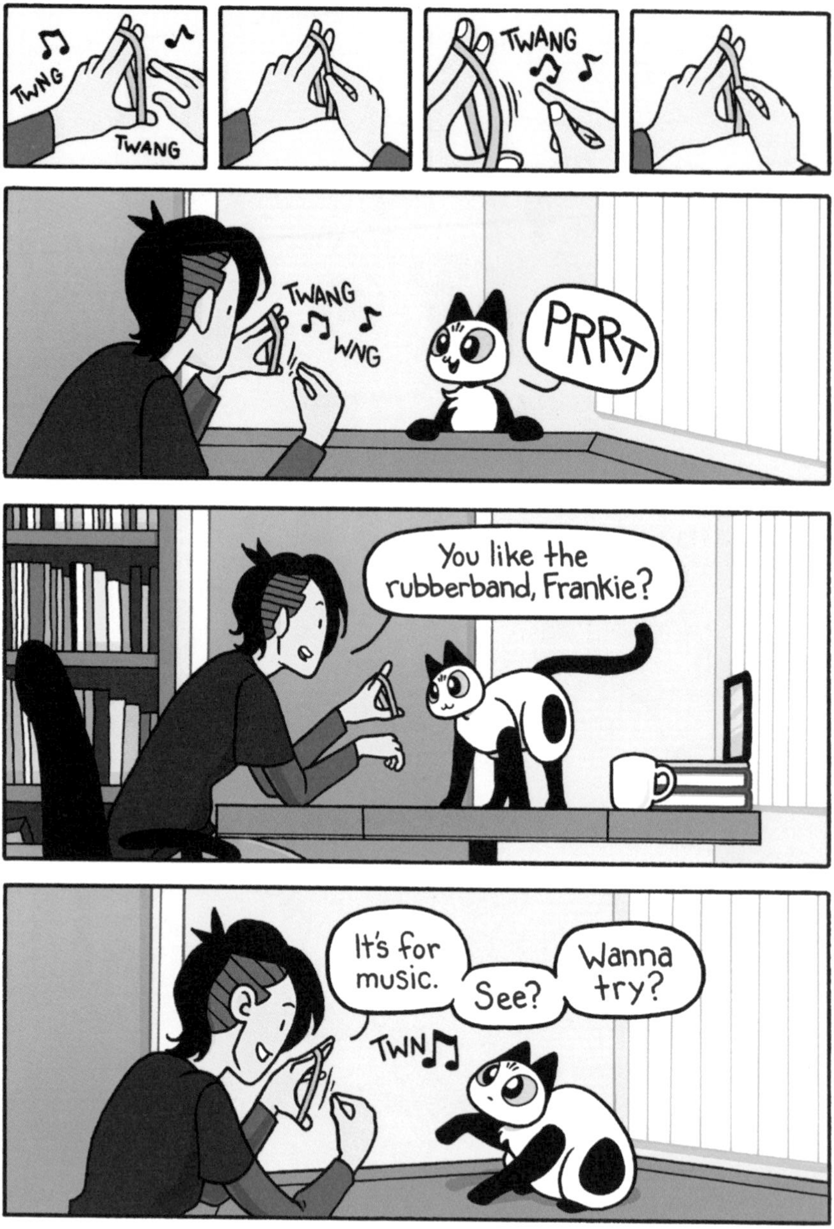
TWNG
TWANG
TWANG
TWANG
WNG
PRRT
You like the rubberband, Frankie?
It's for music.
See?
Wanna try?
TWN

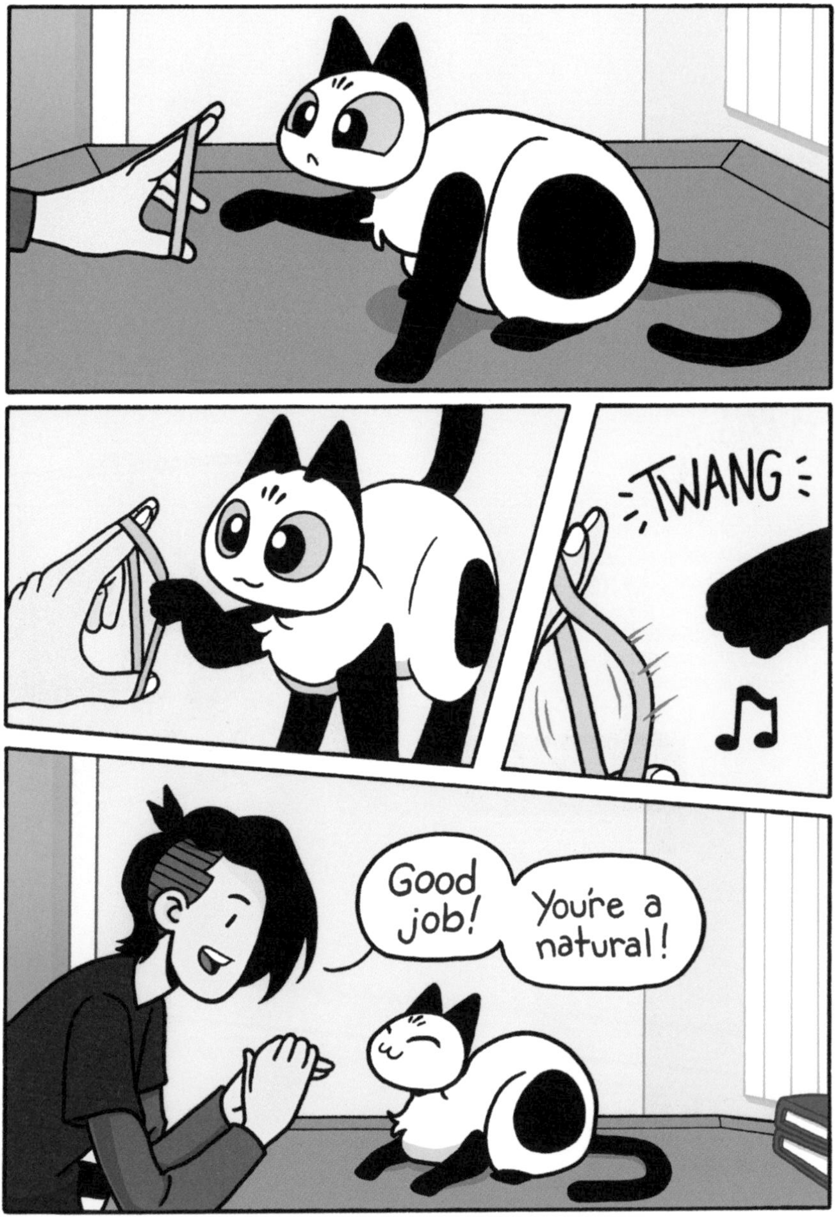
TWANG
Good job!
You're a natural!

Then:

"A bustling, impressive debut. The rubberband band is the genre we didn't know we needed."
- PunkMewsic ☆☆☆☆☆

"An influential album ahead of its time. Frankie raises the bar for all mewsicians."
- Meowximum Rocknroll ☆☆☆☆☆

Available on iTunes

PAWBREAKER

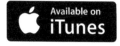

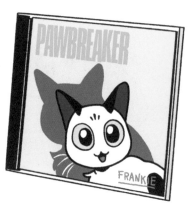

"Fetch 2"

GOOD CATCH!
Now bring it back.
Mrr.
Okay, fine.
Drop it.
Brrt.
Ready?

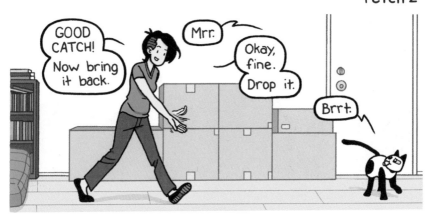

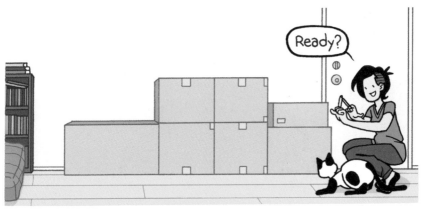

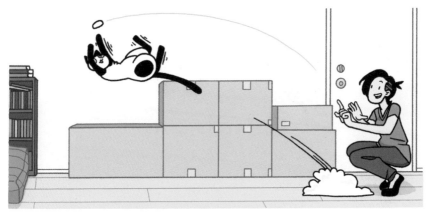

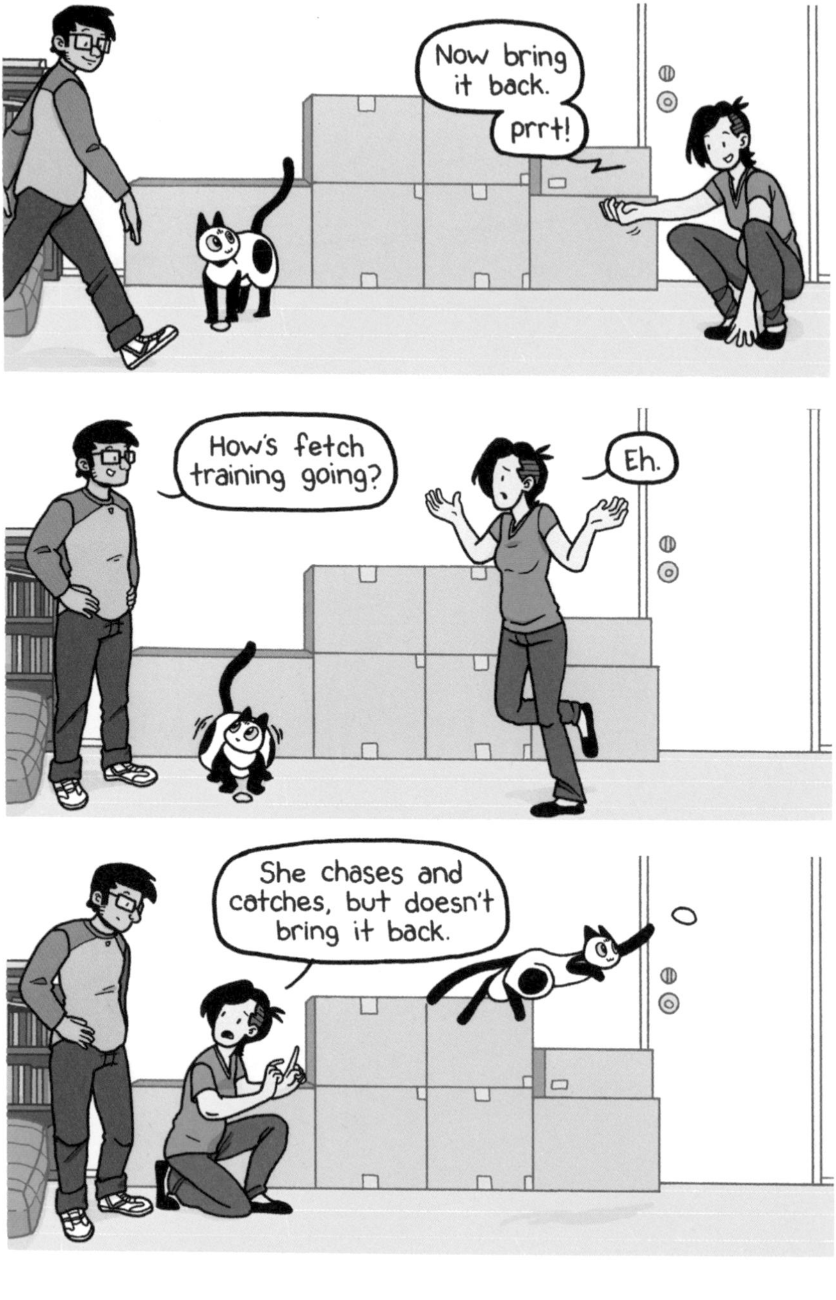
Now bring it back.
prrt!
How's fetch training going?
Eh.
She chases and catches, but doesn't bring it back.

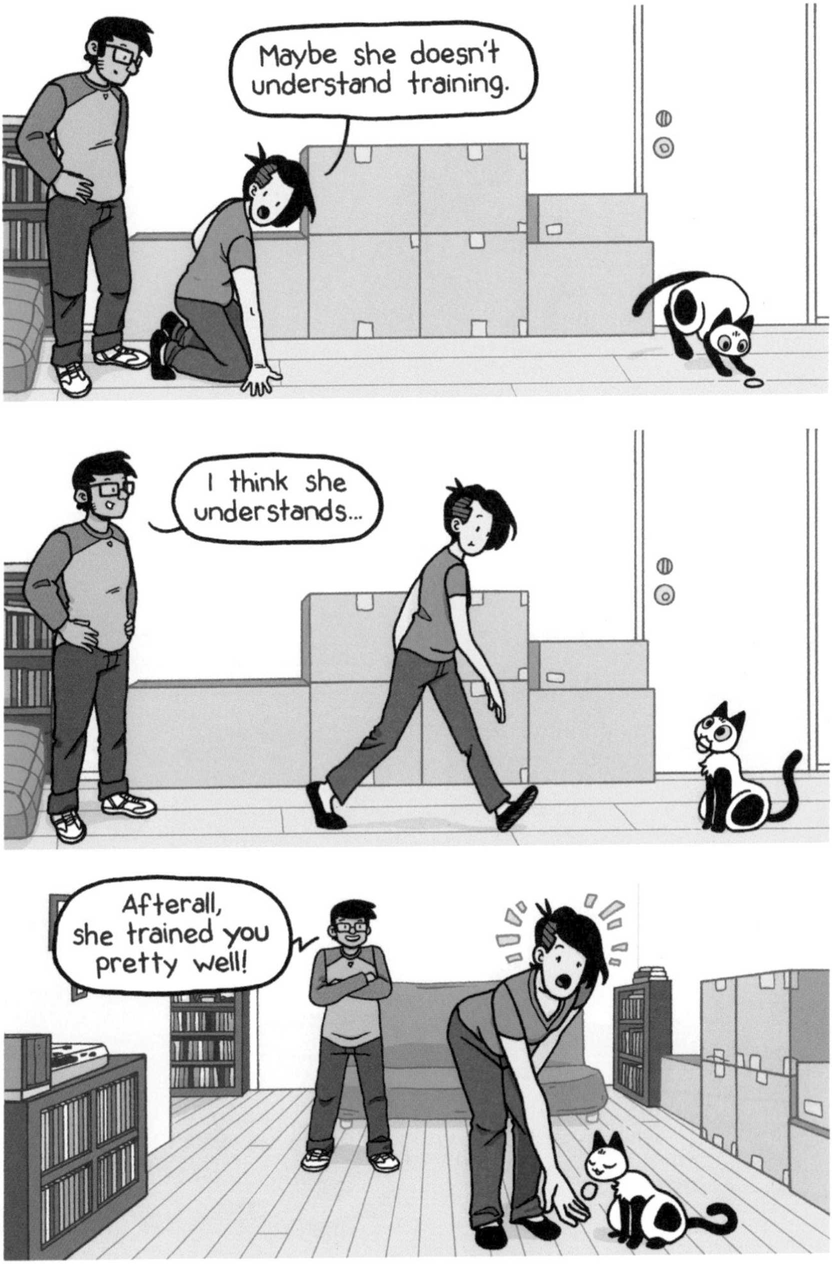
Maybe she doesn't understand training.
I think she understands...
Afterall, she trained you pretty well!

"Ugh, Bug"

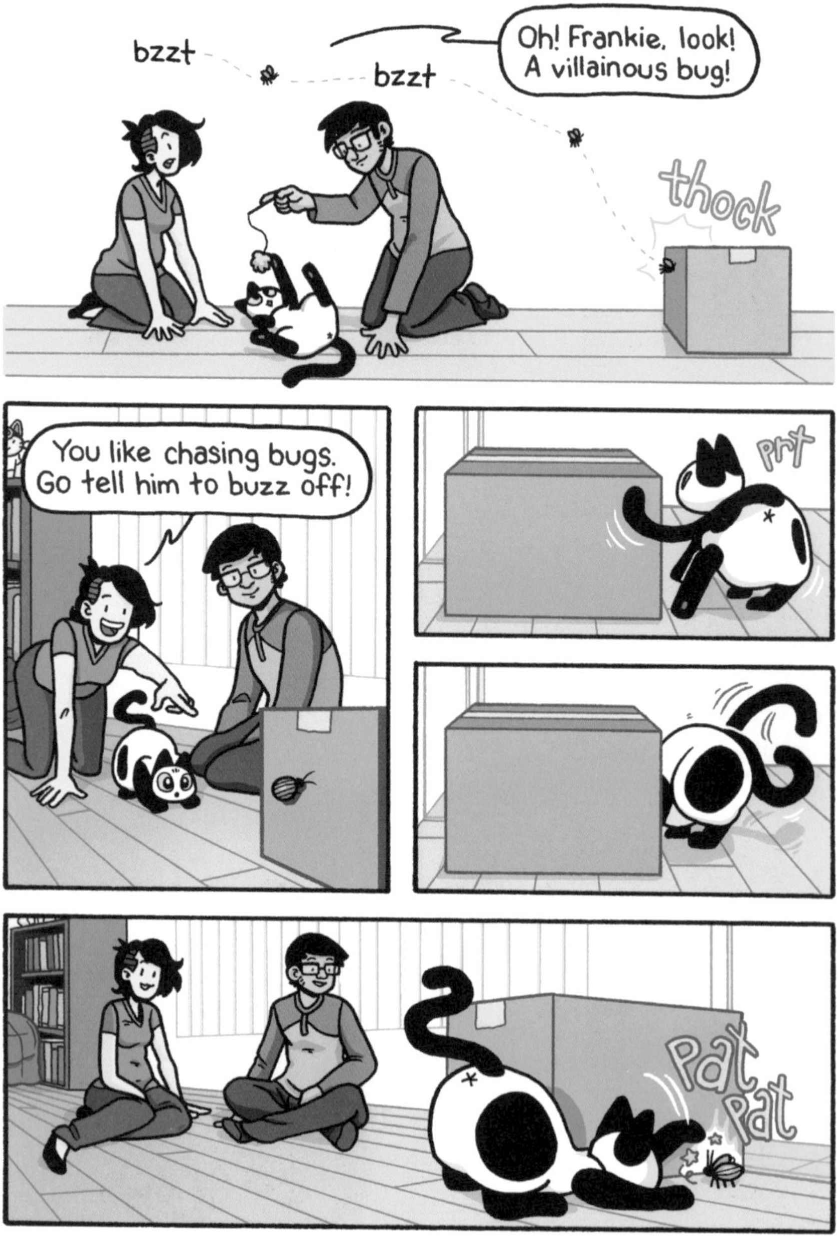

bzzt
bzzt
Oh! Frankie, look! A villainous bug!
thock
You like chasing bugs. Go tell him to buzz off!
prrt
Pat
Pat

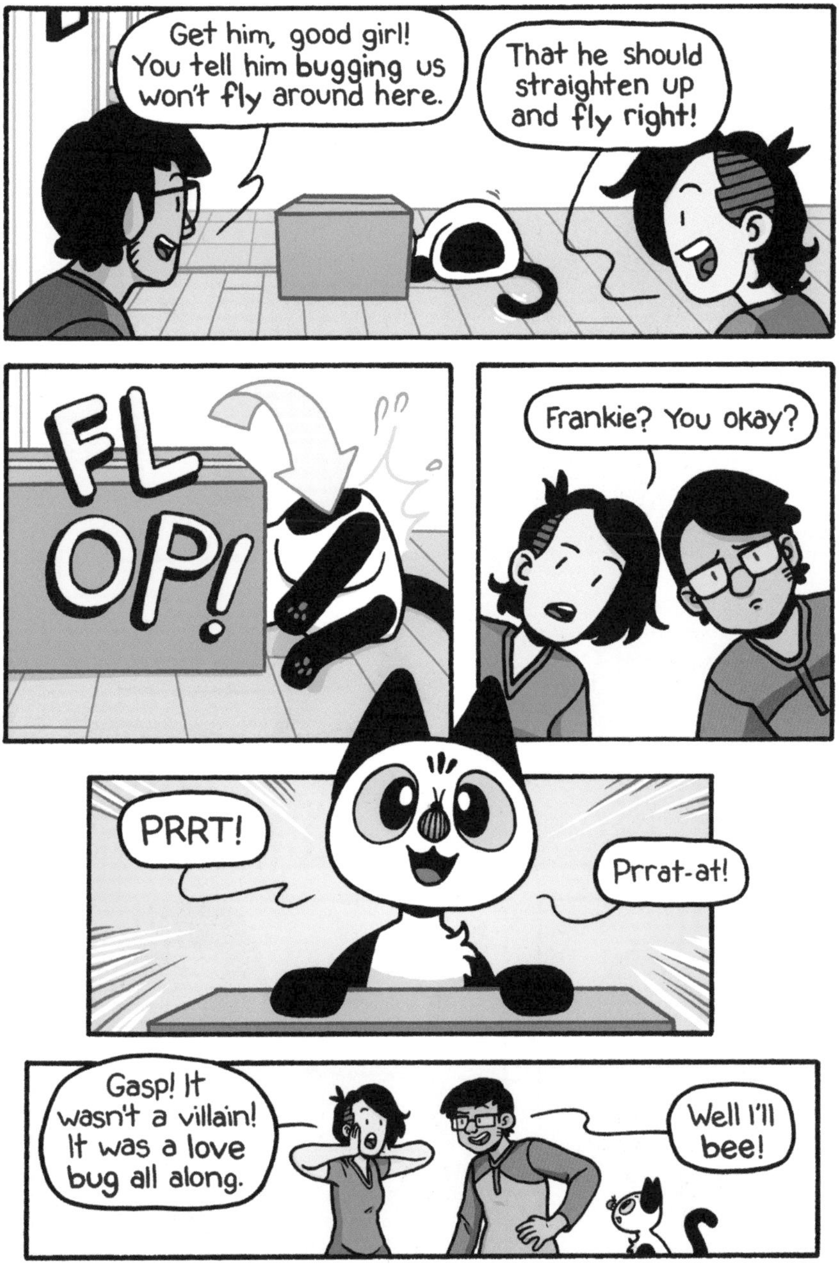
Get him, good girl! You tell him bugging us won't fly around here.
That he should straighten up and fly right!
FLOP!
Frankie? You okay?
PRRT!
Prrat-at!
Gasp! It wasn't a villain! It was a love bug all along.
Well I'll bee!

"Feeding Frankie"

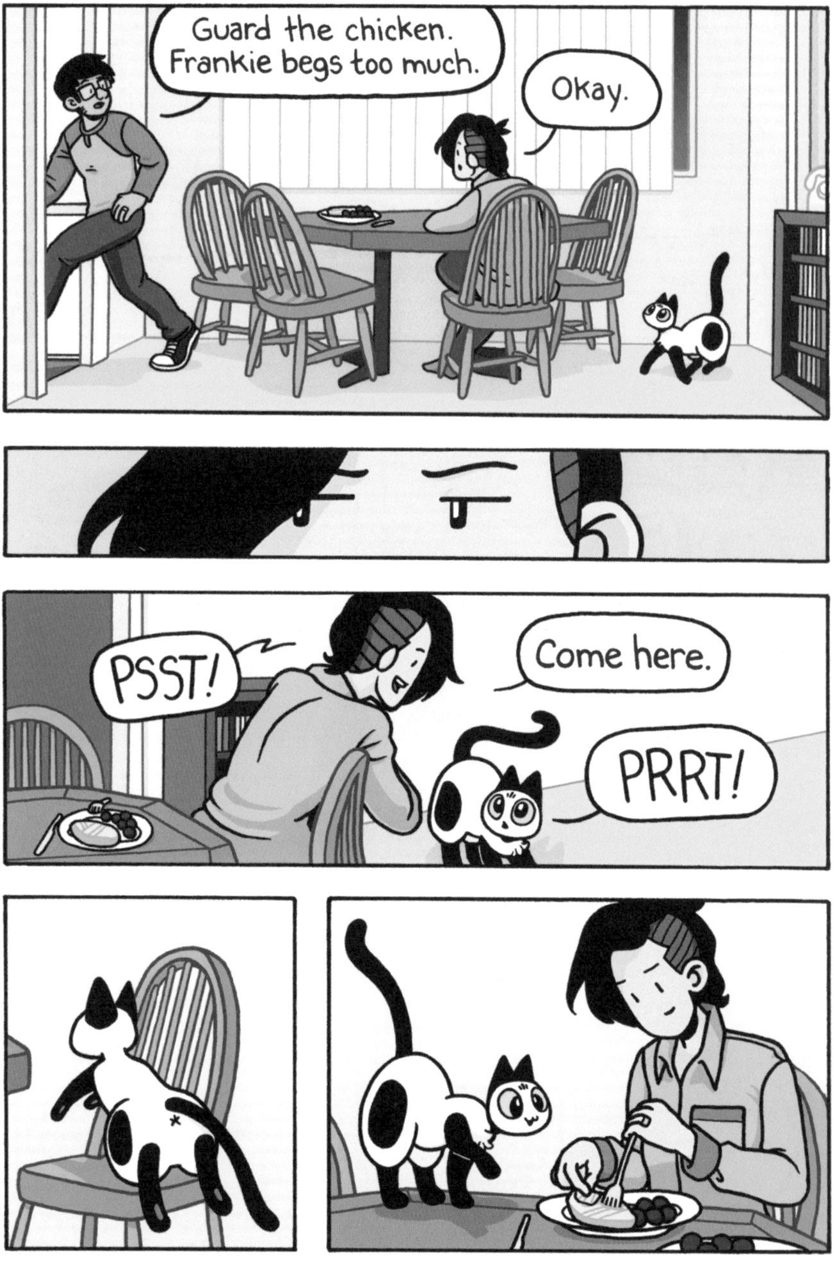

Guard the chicken. Frankie begs too much.
Okay.
PSST!
Come here.
PRRT!

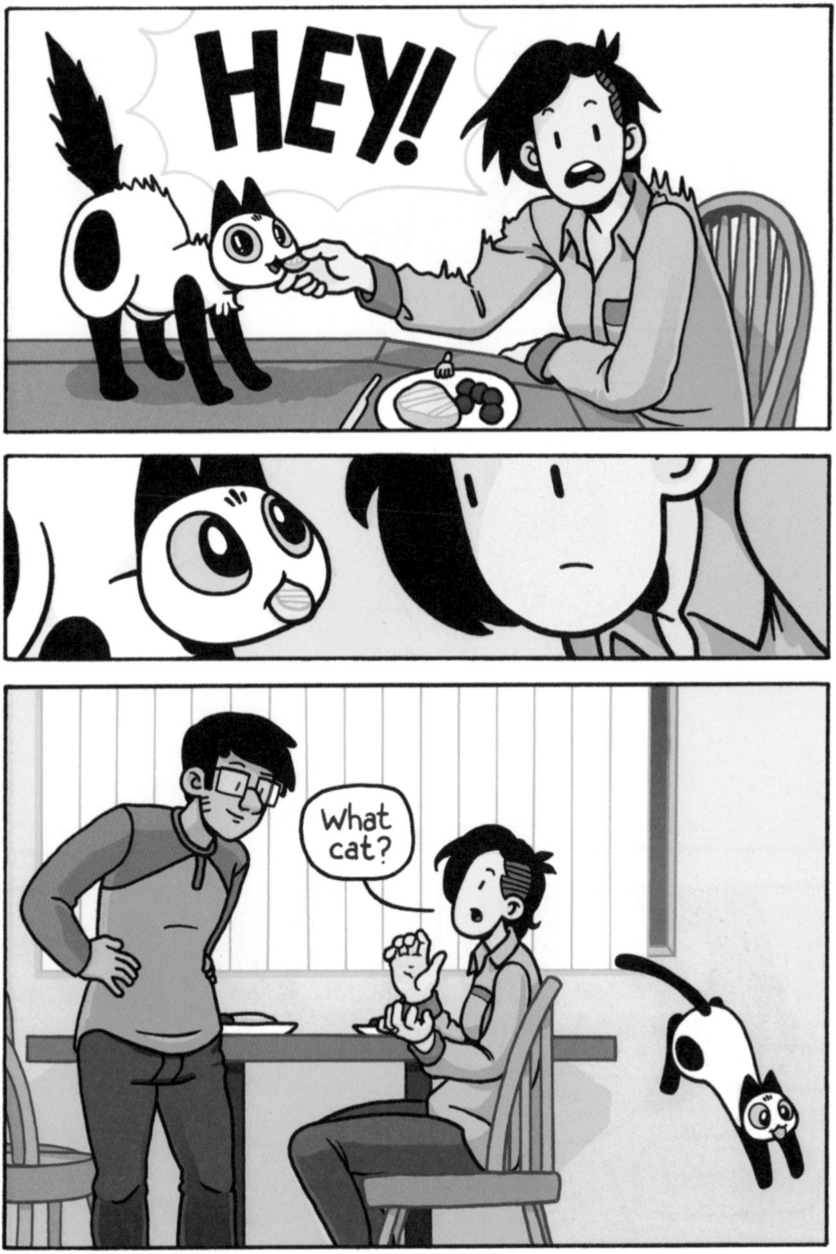
HEY!
What cat?

"Bathtime 3"

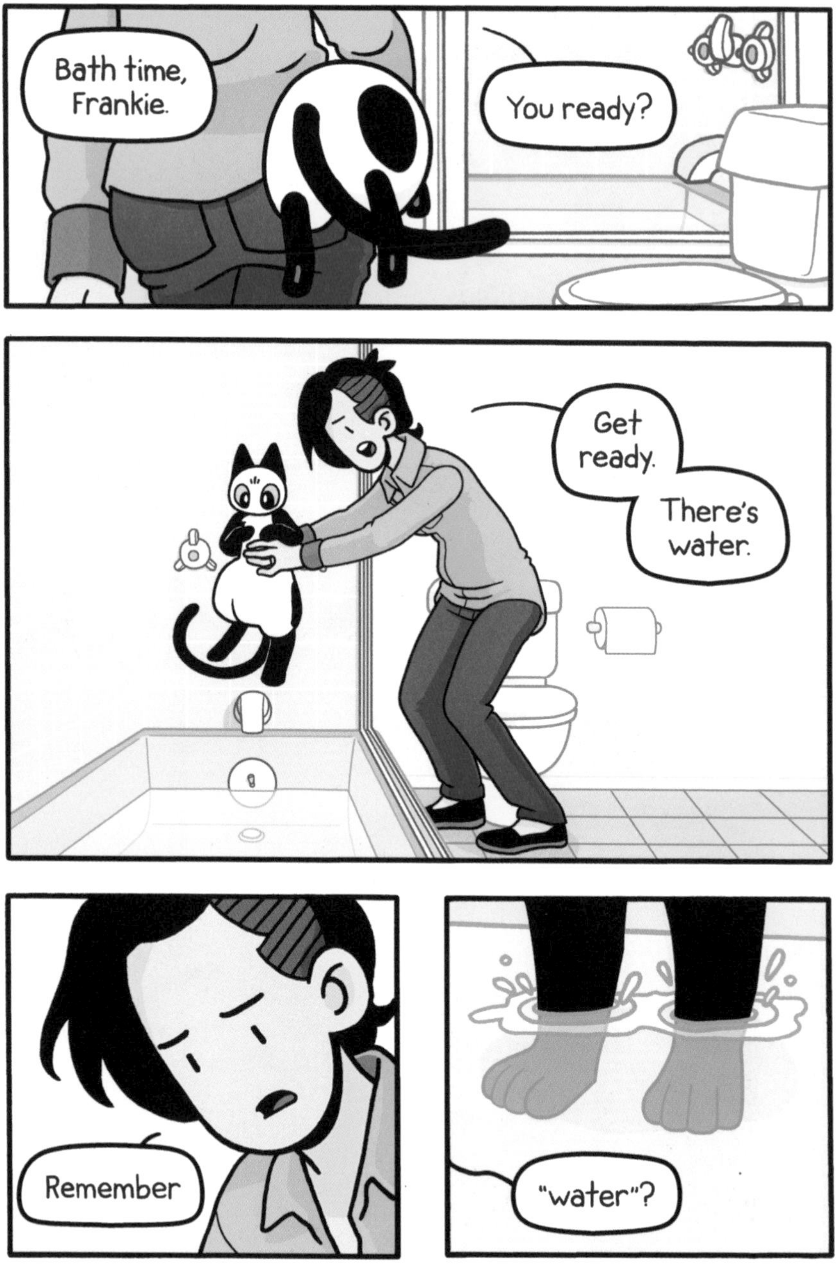
Bath time, Frankie.
You ready?
Get ready.
There's water.
Remember
"water"?

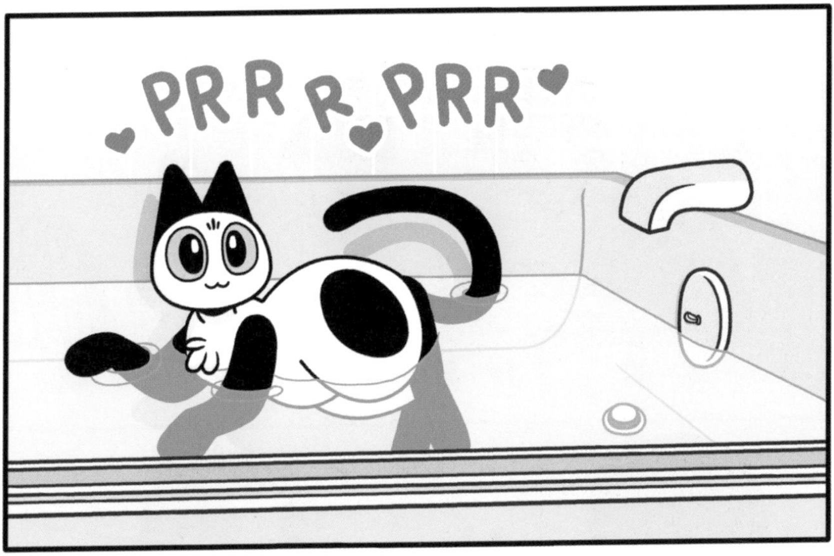
PRRR PRRR

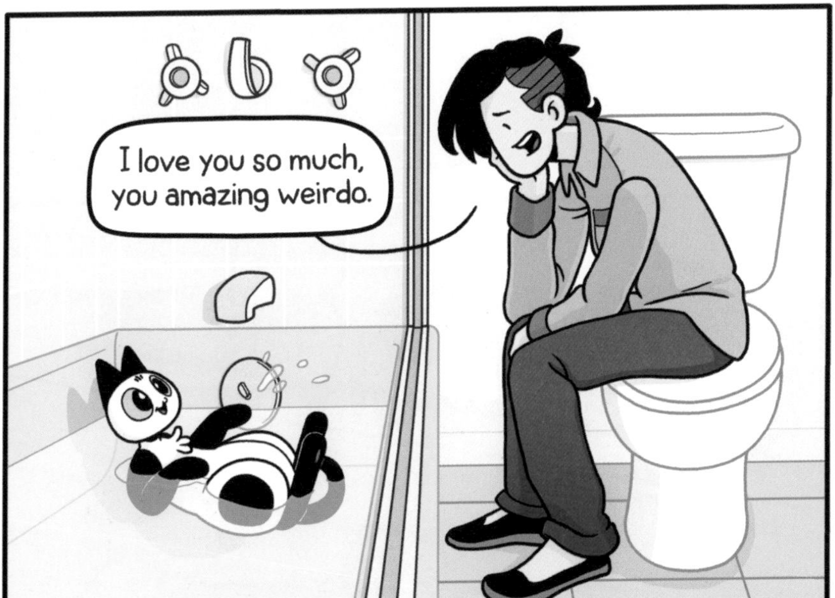
I love you so much, you amazing weirdo.

"Looking Good"

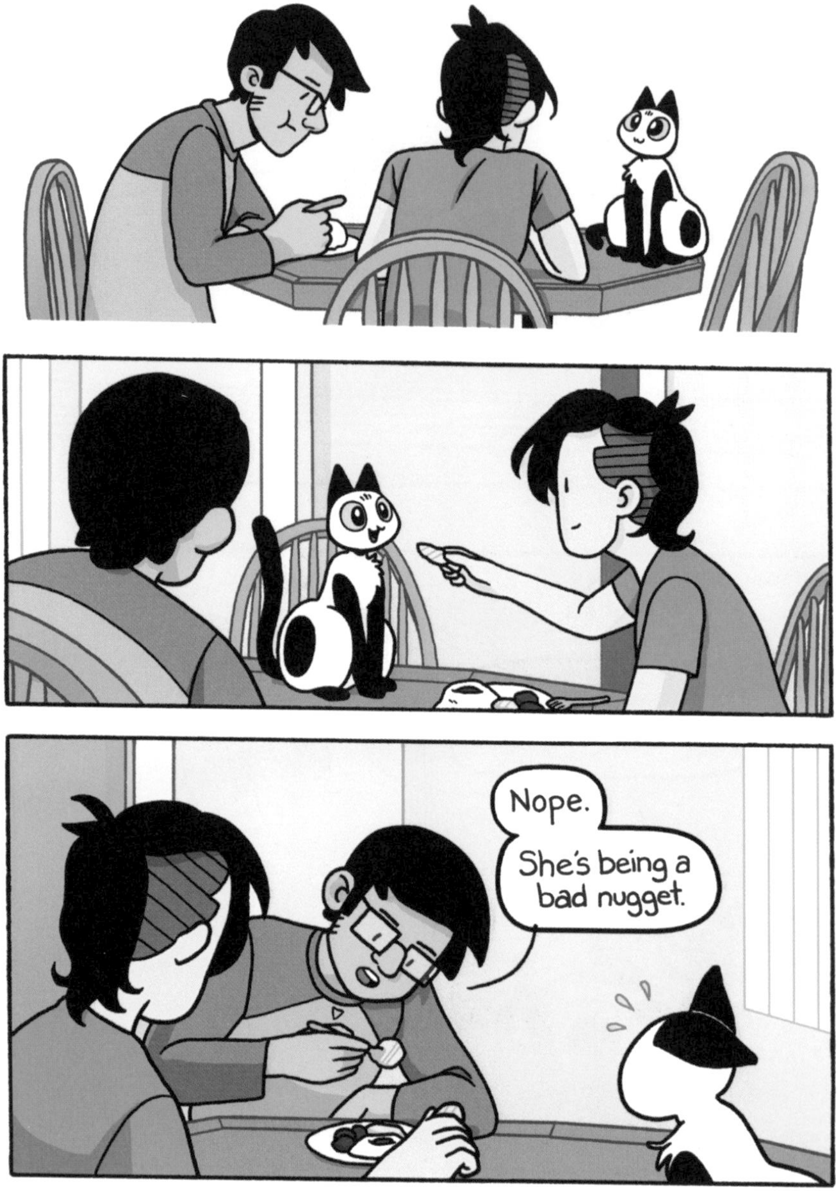
Nope.
She's being a bad nugget.

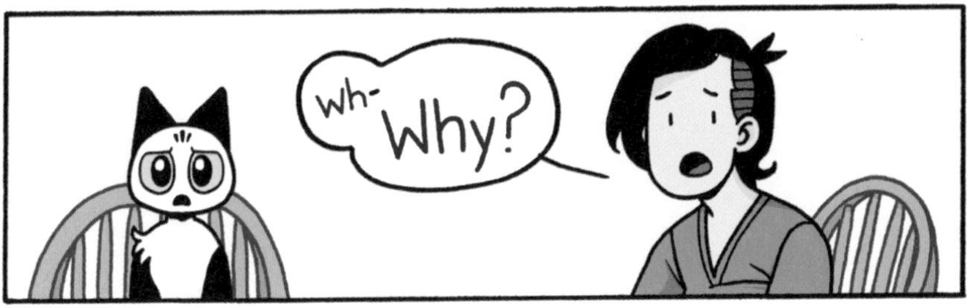
wh-
Why?
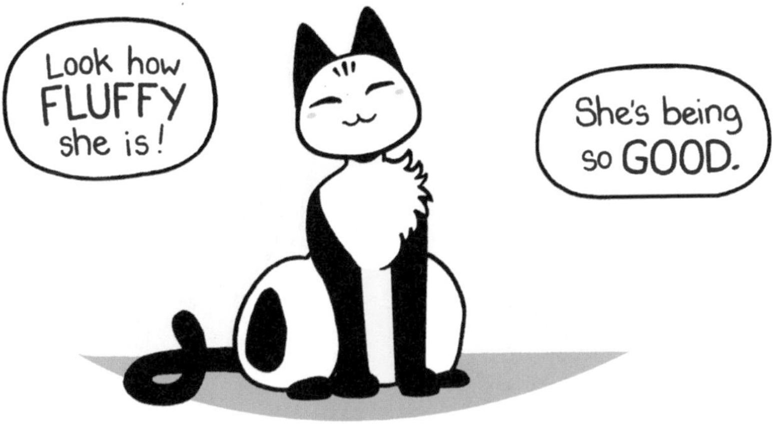
Look how FLUFFY she is!
She's being so GOOD.
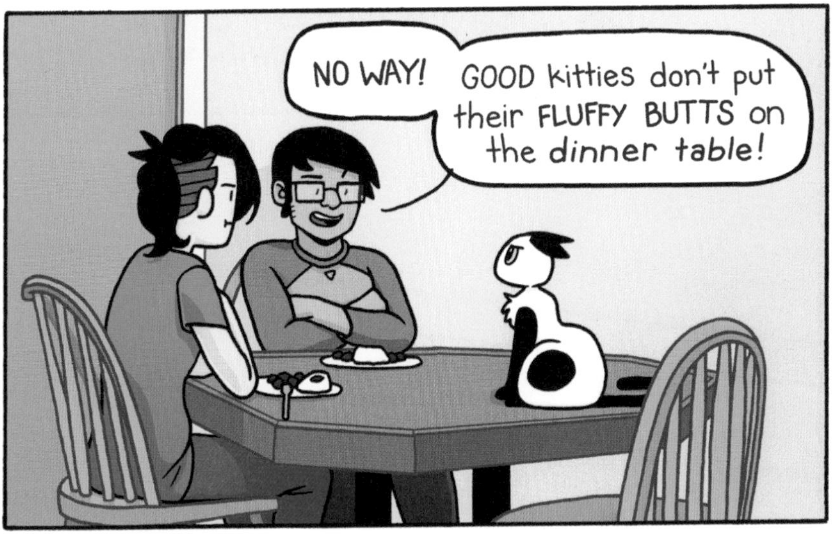
NO WAY! GOOD kitties don't put their FLUFFY BUTTS on the dinner table!

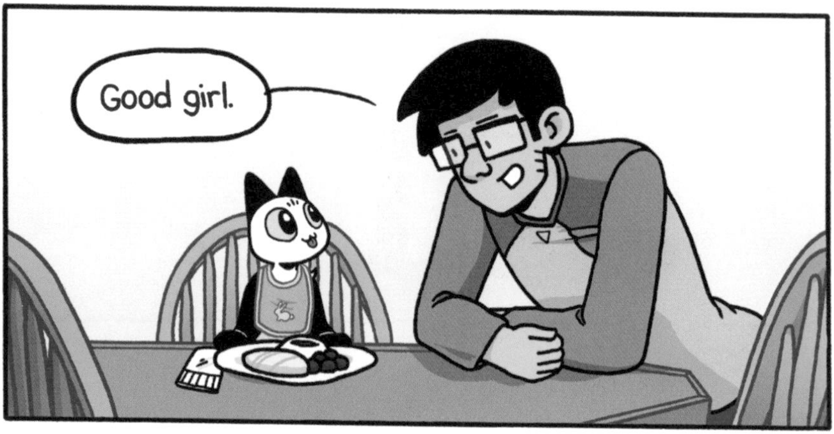
Good girl.

"Outside"

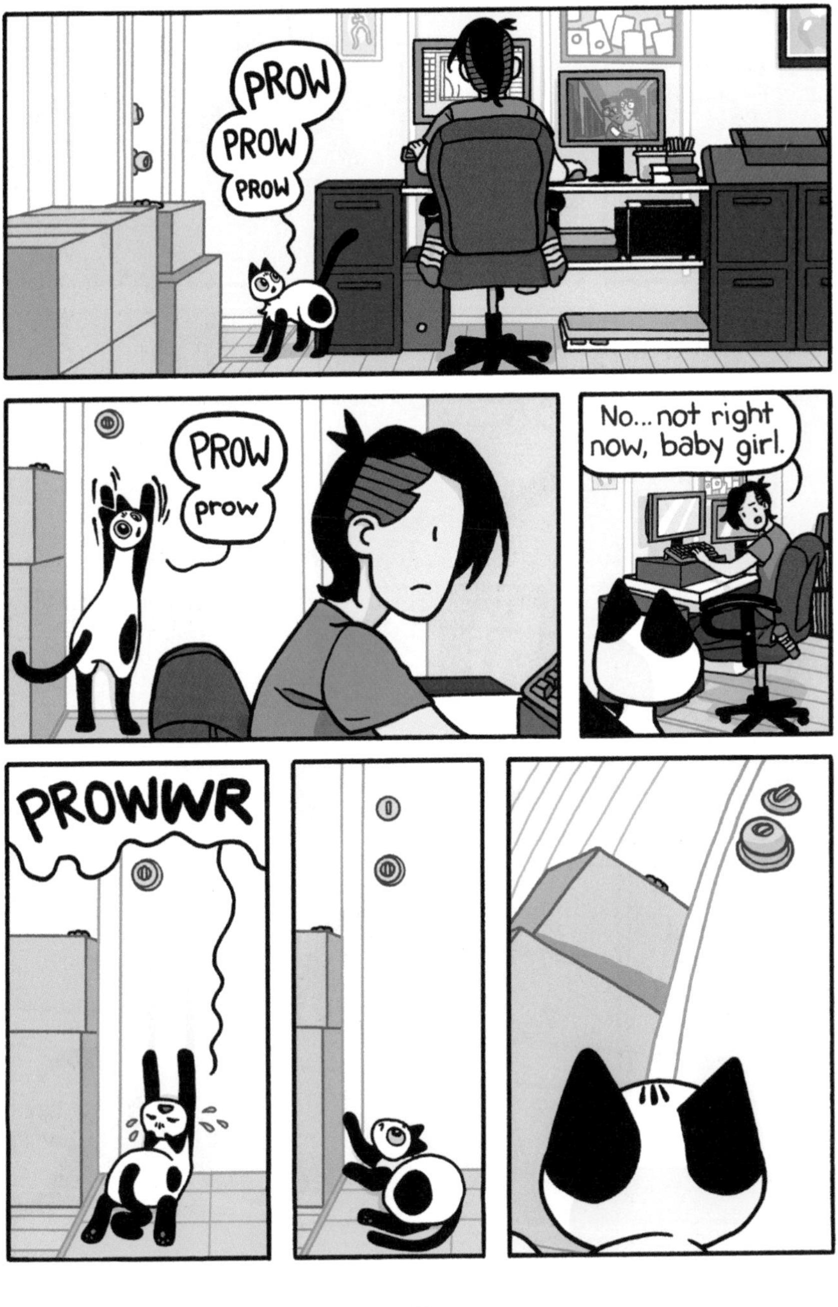
PROW
PROW
PROW
PROW
prow
No... not right now, baby girl.
PROWWR

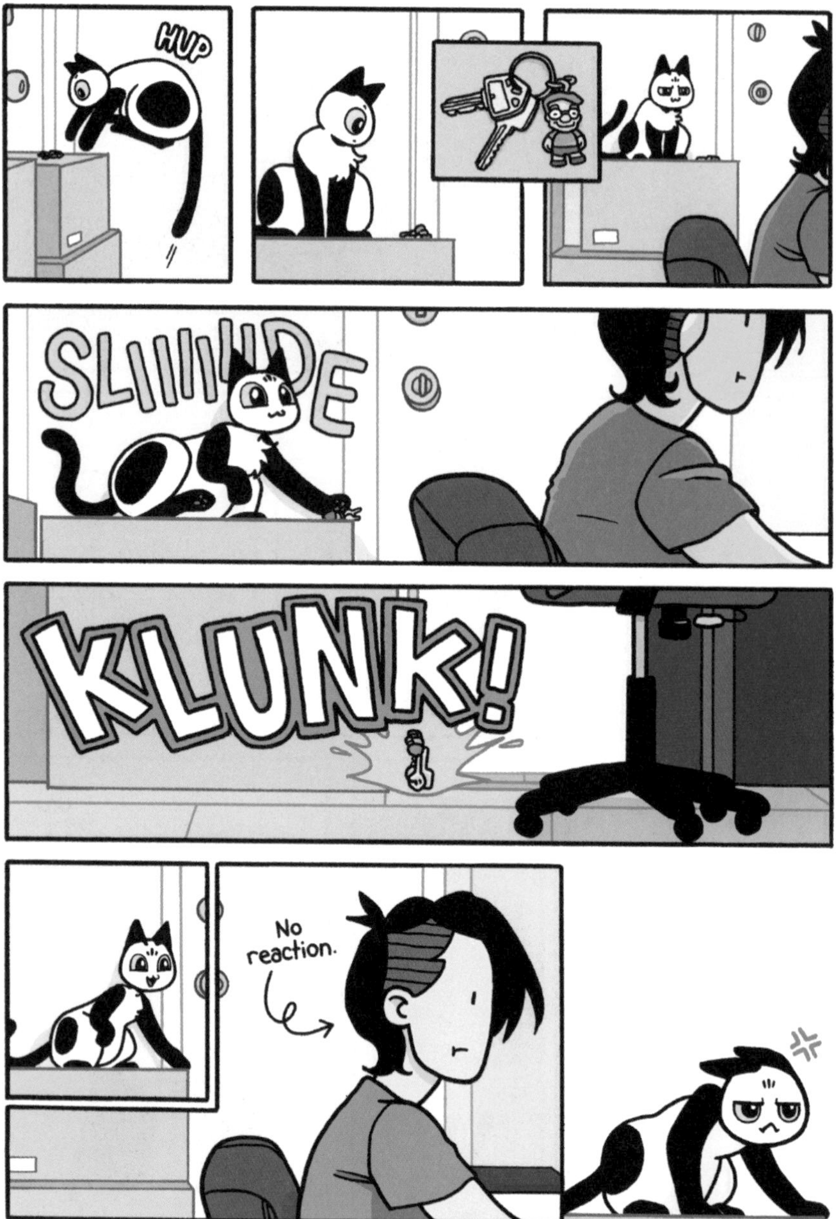
HUP
SLIIIIIDE
KLUNK!
No reaction.

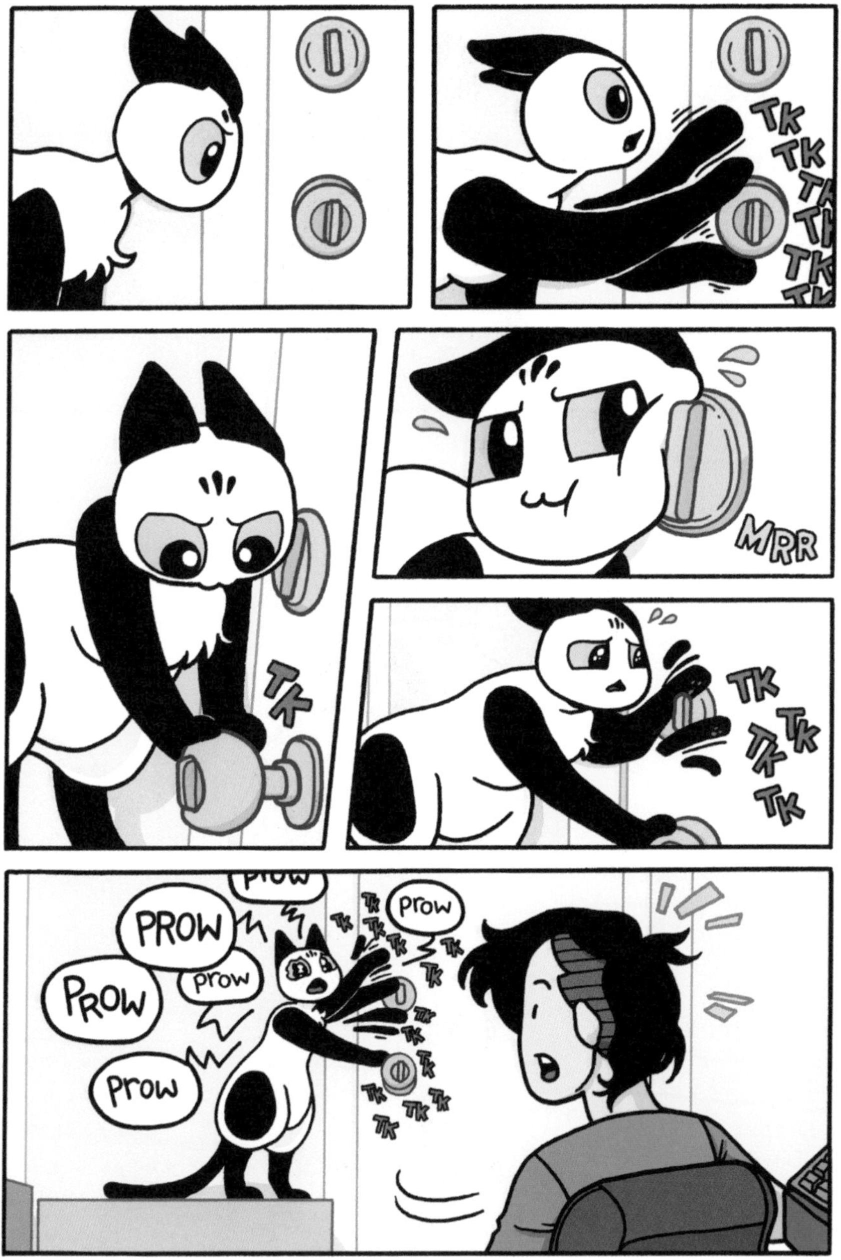
TK TK TK TK TK TK
TK
MRR
TK TK TK TK
PROW
PROW
prow
prow
prow
TK TK TK TK TK TK TK TK TK TK TK TK TK TK

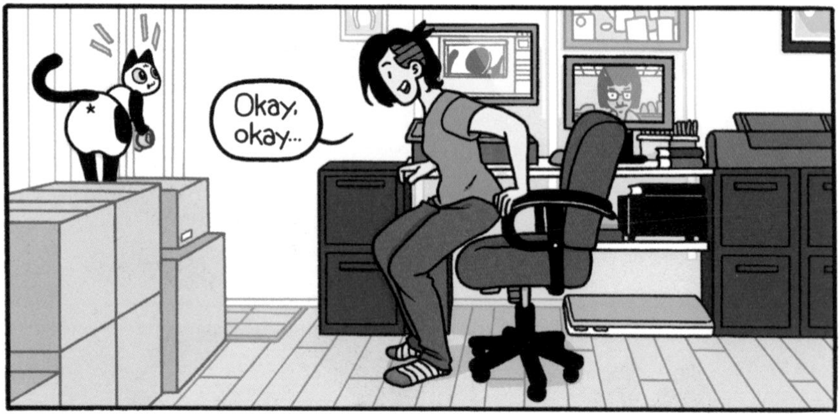
Okay, okay...

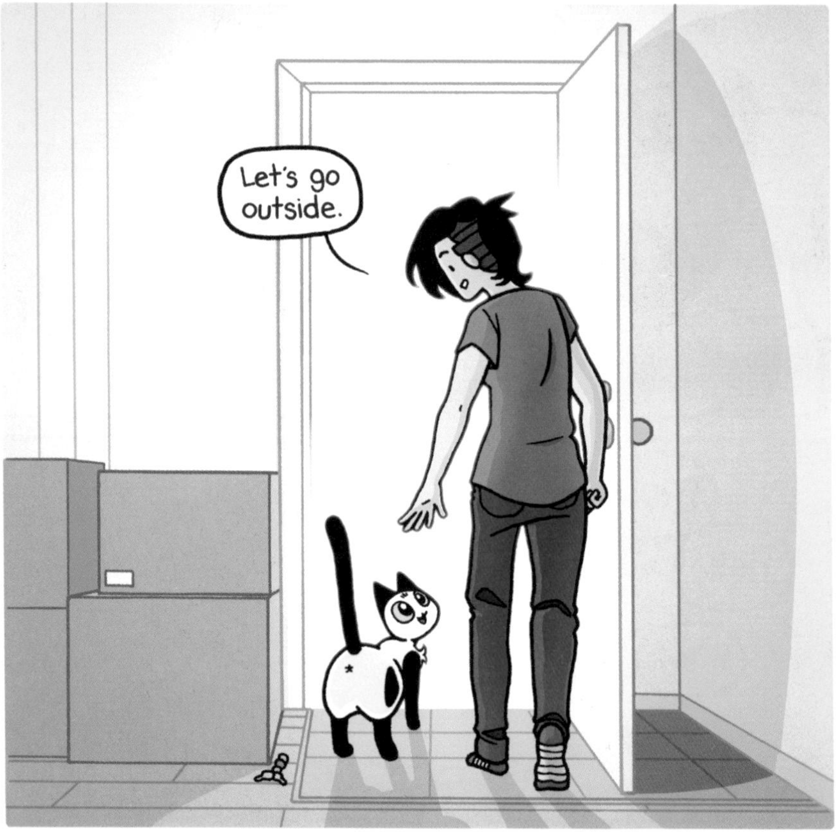
Let's go outside.

Rachel Dukes

hails from San Diego, California. A 2013 graduate of The Center for Cartoon Studies, they work as a cartoonist and illustrator in Los Angeles, California with their spouse and two cats. Rachel is thankful for coffee, gingham, and readers like you.

You can read more of Rachel's comics online at: www.mixtapecomics.com

Quick Tips for Aspiring Cat Parents:

If you want to get a feel for cats before you bring one home, I'd recommend visiting a cat café. A cat café is a coffee shop where you can watch and play with cats, some of whom are adoptable.

Cat Café Lounge (Los Angeles) | catcafelounge.com
The Cat Café (San Diego) | catcafesd.com
The Catcade (Chicago) | thecatcade.org
Java Cats Café (Atlanta) | javacatscafe.com

Prior to finding Frankie, we had planned to adopt and researched local shelters and breeders to ensure they treated their cats humanely. Whether you choose to adopt or shop for your cat, consider searching charitynavigator.org to see what your adoption fees are financing.

Once you've found your perfect cat, have them vaccinated and spayed or neutered. We used FixNation for Frankie's initial vaccinations and they charged us on a sliding scale.

FixNation | fixnation.org

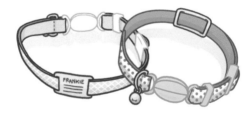

Make sure your cat has a snag-proof breakaway collar to protect them from being caught on trees or fences if they go outside; and that they wear an ID tag with their rabies license. (Even if your cat is indoor-only — just in case they go out by accident.) Include your name and phone number along with your cat's name.

In addition to ID tags, have your cat microchipped. If your cat loses their collar, a microchip ensures a shelter or vet can identify your cat and contact you if you and your cat are separated.

It's a myth that cats are aloof and don't want attention. Cats love routine and need at least 10 minutes of undivided attention a day. Schedule cat play time and affection time into your daily routine.

Cats need their own spaces and furniture to feel comfortable in their home, just like we do. Make a space for your cat in each room of your home with cat furniture and a cat scratcher. (This will also keep energetic cats from scratching on couches or chairs.)

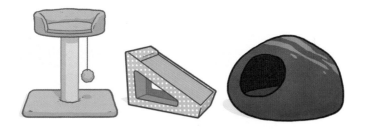

Other Ways to Help Cats:

Donate to or volunteer at a cat advocacy organization or your local cat shelter.

Alley Cat Allies | alleycat.org
Santé D'Or (Los Angeles) | santedor.org

Donate to or volunteer for a Trap-Neuter-Return (TNR) program. TNR is when feral cats are humanely trapped, spayed or neutered, vaccinated, eartipped, and then returned to their neighborhood of origin. Socialized cats are adopted into loving homes like yours.

Feral Change (Oakland) | feralchange.org
TrapKing Humane Cat Solutions (Tucker) | trapkinghumane.org
Flatbush Cats (Flatbush) | flatbushcats.org

Thanks

to Mike Lopez and Michael Sweater
for their early support of this project.

To Marc Calvary, whose Art Exchange Program Grant helped keep the *Frankie Comics* #1 mini-comic in print when I first started the series. To Matt Bors who paid to run the strip 'Life with/out a Cat' on The Nib after it had been shared on Reddit and gone viral without credits. To Sheena Wolf for supporting Frankie's webcomic run on GoComics.

And to Amanda Meadows for her ongoing support of the *Frankie* mini-comic series: who first invited *Frankie* to be a part of The *Devastator*'s Funny Book Fest back in 2015, and later became my wonderful, supportive, patient, and enthusiastic editor on this collected edition of the series. I'm so glad to have created this book with you.

Additional thanks to Nicole Griffee-Zuniga, Kathy Griffee, Leslie Masland, Avi Ehrlich, Benji Nate, Andrew Greenstone, Jourdan Enriquez, Guy Dalbey-Thomas, Rachel Ann Millar, and Mars Gearhart.Thanks to all the readers who have been so patient and supportive over the years. To those who sent me letters and emails, fan art, and pictures and videos of loved ones enjoying the mini-comic series.And to Kickstarter backers of *Frankie Comics* #4 mini-comic and my patrons on Patreon for their support throughout the creation of this collection.

Thanks to my family for their ongoing support of all my creative work, for their particular enthusiasm for this series, and for their acceptance of and love for our feline girls as their grand-kitties.

And, of course, all my thanks and love to Frankie, my good girl. You are the very best. I love you.

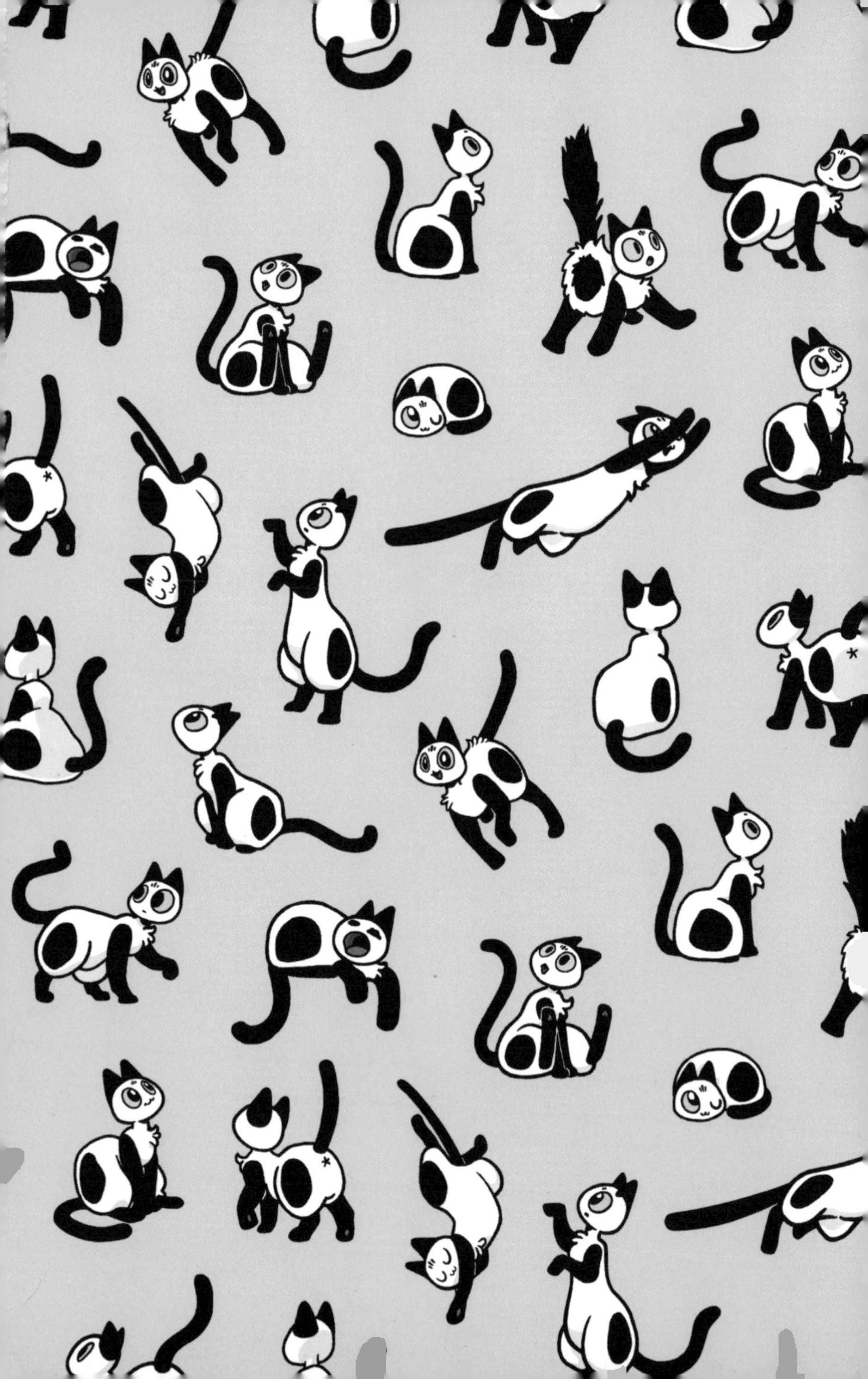

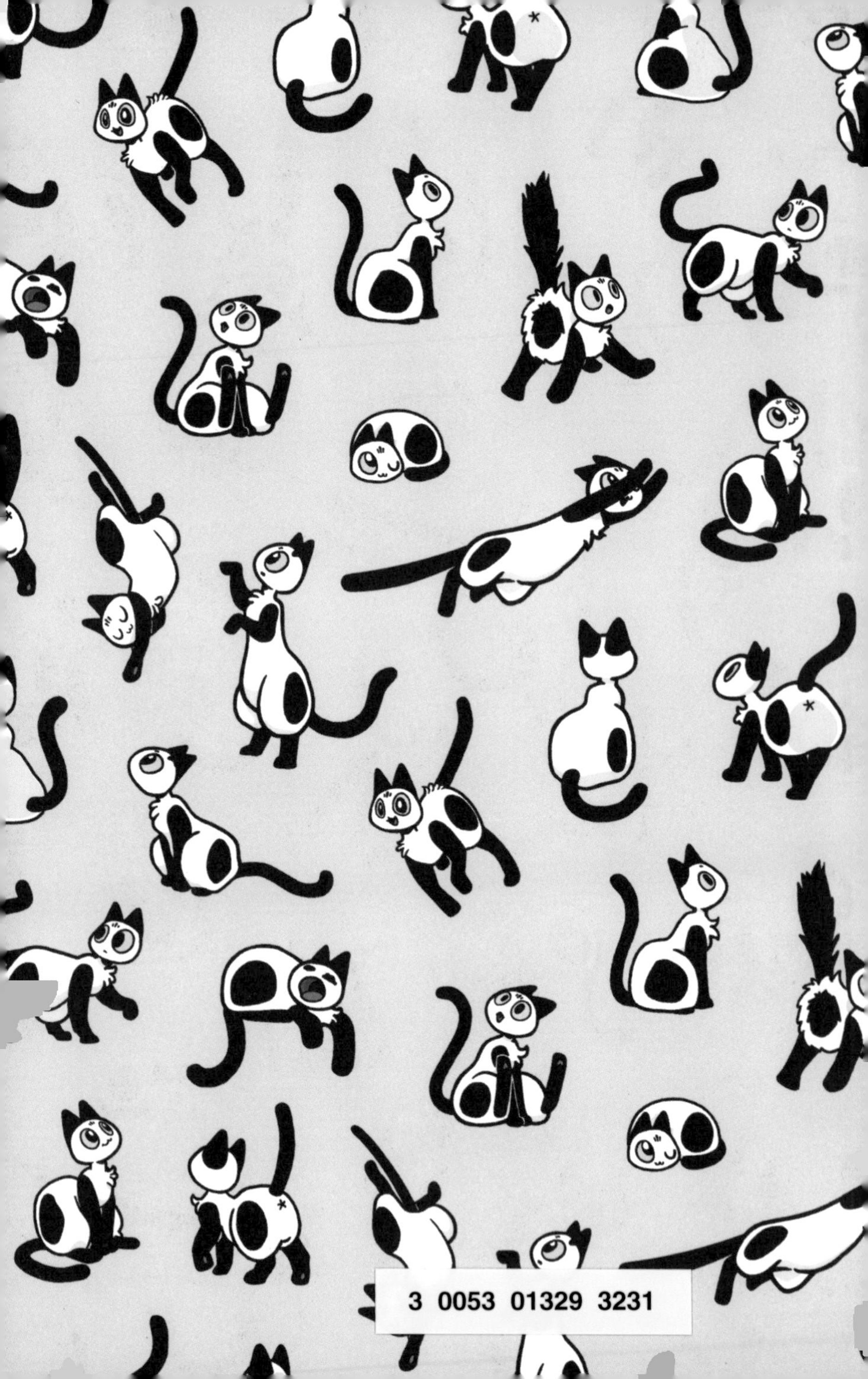